THE SIMON & SCHUSTER

ILLUSTRATED DICTIONARY OF SCIENCE

By Jeanne Stone

WANDERER BOOKS

PUBLISHED BY SIMON & SCHUSTER, INC.,.NEW YORK

First American Edition 1985
Text Copyright © 1985 by BLA Publishing Ltd.
Illustrations Copyright © 1985 by BLA Publishing Ltd.

All rights reserved
including the right of reproduction
in whole or in part in any form
Published by WANDERER BOOKS
A Division of Simon & Schuster, Inc.
Simon & Schuster Building
1230 Avenue of the Americas
New York, New York 10020
WANDERER and colophon are registered trademarks of
Simon & Schuster, Inc.
First published in Great Britain in 1985 by Cambridge University Press
under the title
CAMBRIDGE ILLUSTRATED DICTIONARY FOR YOUNG SCIENTISTS

Also available in Julian Messner Library Edition
10 9 8 7 6 5 4 3 2 1

ISBN: 0–671–54547–7
ISBN: 0–671–54548–5 (Lib. Ed.)

This book was designed and produced by
BLA Publishing Limited, Swan Court,
London Road, East Grinstead, Sussex, England.

A member of the **Ling Kee Group**
LONDON · HONG KONG · TAIPEI · SINGAPORE · NEW YORK

Illustrations by BLA Publishing, Elgin Press, Linden Artists
Phototypeset in Britain by BLA Publishing/Composing Operations
Color origination by Premier Graphics
Made and printed in Italy

About your science dictionary

What is a science dictionary?

A dictionary is a book which explains the meaning and use of words. We call the **meaning** of a word its **definition**.

Some words have several different meanings. In this science dictionary only the scientific or technical meaning of the word is given. Many of these scientific words do not appear in general dictionaries and so you will find your science dictionary very useful at home and at school.

Where it helps to clarify the meaning, the word is used in a sentence or phrase. Many of the entries are illustrated in full color.

How to use this book

The words to be looked up are printed in **bold** type and arranged in alphabetical order. This means that all the words beginning with **a** come first, then those beginning with **b** and **c** and so on, ending with **z**.

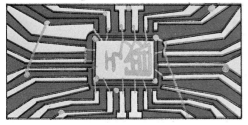

At the side of each right hand page you will find a blue disc. This shows the letter that the words on that page begin with. If you want to look up **fish** you would use this guide to find the section of the book that contains words beginning with **f**.

Where words begin with the same letter, the alphabetical order of the second letter is used: **fish** appears after **fabric** (because **i** appears after **a** in the alphabet). If the first two letters are the same, look at the alphabetical order of the third letter, and so on.

Guide words

At the top of each page there are two words separated by a vertical line, e.g. **abacus** | **adapt**. They are the first and last words to be found on that page. These guide words will help you to find the word you need quickly.

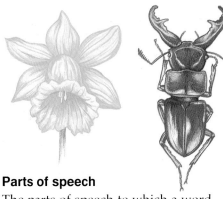

Parts of speech

The parts of speech to which a word belongs may vary, depending on how it is used in a sentence. A *noun* (marked *n.* or *n.pl.* if the plural form is given) is a word that is used to name something. A *verb* (marked *v.*) is a word that shows action. An *adjective* (marked *adj.*) is a word, like brittle, which describes or tells us something about a noun, e.g. the glass was **brittle**.

Look-up words

In some definitions you will see the symbol Ⓛ after a word, e.g. rhizomeⓁ; Ⓛ means look up this word if you are not sure what it means. It will help you to understand the definition, and tell you more about that word.

Beginnings and endings of words

As you learn more about words and science, you will discover that the beginning or ending of a word can help you to understand the word. Here are some of the most useful beginnings; they are called prefixes:

aer	to do with air (*aer*onautical)
bi	two (*bi*ped)
bio	to do with life (*bio*logy)
di	to do with two (*di*cotyledon)
geo	to do with the Earth (*geo*logy)
hemi	half (*hemi*sphere)
hydro	to do with water (*hydro*foil)
iso	the same (*iso*sceles)
micro	a millionth part of, or very small (*micro*scopic)
mono	single (*mono*cotyledon)
photo	to do with light (*photo*graphs)
poly	many (*poly*gon)
tele	at or over a distance (*tele*vision)
thermo	to do with heat (*thermo*meter)
tri	to do with three (*tri*angle)
zoo	to do with animals (*zoo*logy)

Here are some of the most useful endings; they are called suffixes:

metry	to do with measuring or shape (geo*metry*)
ology	the study of (bi*ology*)

A a

abacus *n.* (*pl. abacuses*) a simple kind of calculator used for addition and subtraction. Colored balls are moved along wires or grooves. First used about 5000 years ago in the Middle East. The Greeks and Romans brought it to the West. Merchants took it eastwards to China and Asia along the trade routes. It is still used in the East today.

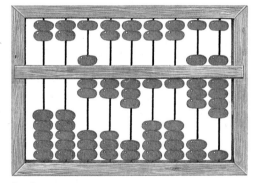

An abacus.

abdomen (1) *n.* in human beings and other mammals, the part of the body below the chest as far as the hips. The stomach, intestines, liver, kidneys and other important organs are in the abdomen. (2) in insects, the rear part of the body. The third division of an insect's body.

an insect abdomen

absorb *v.* to take in or soak up. *Green plants* **absorb** *sunlight to make their food.*

absorption *n.* the ability to absorb liquid, gases, sound or light.

accelerate (1) *v.* to increase speed in movement. *The driver* **accelerated** *out of the bend.* (2) to increase the speed of a chemical action. *The catalyst* **accelerated** *the chemical action.* (say *ack-selerate*)

acceleration *n.* the rate at which velocity⬚ is increased.

accumulator *n.* a group of battery cells, used for storing electrical energy. Used in car engines for starting the motor.

acid *n.* a sour tasting substance. The sour taste of lemons is due to citric acid. The sour taste of vinegar is due to acetic acid. These are weak acids. Strong acids burn and are poisons. Acids turn blue litmus paper red. Acids react with metals to form salts.

acid rain pollution⬚ caused by waste sulfur compounds in the atmosphere forming weak acids in rain water. Acid rain causes many water plants and animals to die and trees to lose their leaves.

acoustics (1) *n.* the study of sound and hearing. (2) the qualities of a building that affect how well sounds are heard or deadened. *The concert hall has good* **acoustics.** (say *a-koo-stiks*)

action (1) *n.* the use of energy⬚, causing something to happen. *The* **action** *of heat on ice causes it to melt.* (2) the moving parts of a machine or instrument.

adapt (1) *v.* to change so as to suit changing surroundings and conditions. *Plants and animals living in deserts have* **adapted** *to the hot dry conditions.* (2) **adaptation** *n.* the process by which organisms⬚ change to increase their chances of survival.

A

adrenalin a hormone◱ produced by the adrenal gland in vertebrates at times of fear, pain or exercise. It increases the flow of blood to muscles, heart and brain, and makes the body react quickly to danger.

adult *n.* a plant or animal that is fully grown or mature. An adult human is a fully grown man or woman.

aerial (1) *adj.* of the air. In the air: birds and bats are aerial animals. (2) aerial roots – plant roots which grow from nodes◱ on stems. They do not grow down into the soil. They take in moisture from the air. Tropical plants like orchids have aerial roots. (3) *n.* a radio or television antenna used for sending and receiving signals.

aerobic *adj.* describes organisms that need oxygen to live and grow.

aerodynamics (1) *n.* the study of the effect of moving gases, and the forces that act on objects moving in air. Aerodynamics is very important in aircraft design. (2) **aerodynamic** *adj.* describes the forces acting on an object when flying. (3) the design of a flying machine. (say *air-o-dye-nam-iks*)

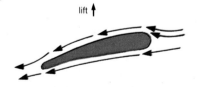

lift ↑

The air flowing over the upper surface of this aerofoil travels faster than the air beneath it. This reduces the air pressure above and causes lift.

aerofoil *n.* any surface, like an aircraft wing, aileron◱ or tailplane, which is shaped to produce lift when air flows over and under it.

aeronautics *n.* the science that has to do with the design, making, working and testing of aircraft.

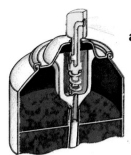

A section of an aerosol spray showing the pressure nozzle.

aerosol *n.* a system in which particles◱ can be sprayed out in a gas, producing a fine mist.

afterbirth *n.* the placenta◱ and membranes that are pushed out of the uterus◱ after the birth of a young mammal.

agar *n.* a jelly-like substance that is made from seaweed. It is used for growing bacteria◱.

agent *n.* something that is used to produce a result: bleach is a cleansing agent. *Wind is the* **agent** *that drives the windmill.*

agriculture *n.* the science of farming. Working the soil, growing plants and raising animals for food.

aileron *n.* a movable, hinged flap on the rear edge of an aircraft wing near the tip which controls the rolling movements of the aircraft. It allows banking to take place. (say *ayl-er-on*)

air *n.* the mixture of gases that makes up the Earth's atmosphere◱, which we breathe. We cannot see, smell or taste it. Air is made up of nitrogen, oxygen, carbon dioxide, and tiny amounts of other gases. Air always contains some water vapor.

The different gases in air.

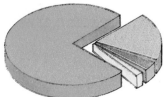

oxygen 21%

other gases 0.97%

nitrogen 78%   carbon dioxide 0.03%

A

aircraft *n.* any flying machine, with or without an engine. Balloons, gliders, and helicopters are aircraft.

This light aircraft has only one engine.

air pollution the presence of harmful substances in the air – car exhaust fumes, chemical waste from factory chimneys, radioactive fallout, crop-spraying chemicals. All these can damage and kill plant and animal life.

air pressure the pressure that air in the atmosphere exerts on everything it touches. Air pressure is greatest at sea level. This is because it is created by the weight of all the upper air above the Earth's surface.

An albino rat.

albino *n.* any animal or plant that lacks normal color. Albino animals have white skin, whitish hair and pink eyes; e.g. white rabbits or white blackbirds are albinos.

albumen *n.* the clear, colorless protein found in the white of an egg. It becomes white and solid when boiled.

alchemist (1) *n.* an early chemist who lived in the Middle Ages. Alchemists tried to turn iron and lead into gold. They also tried to find a substance which would stop people from growing old. They did not succeed.

alchemy *n.* an early form of chemistry.

alcohol *n.* a clear liquid without color which burns easily and evaporates□ very quickly. There are many different kinds. One is made from fruits, grains or sugar and is found in drinks like wine, beer and spirits. Others are made from wood or chemicals. Alcohols are very useful substances. For example, they are used in medicine, paints and dry-cleaning solvents□.

algae *n.pl.* simple plants, without proper roots, stems or leaves. They live in damp places, stagnant water or in the sea. Some are tiny single cells. The fine, green threads found on ponds, the slime on damp paths, and seaweeds are kinds of algae. (say *al-jee*)

This seaweed is a type of algae.

algebra *n.* a kind of mathematics used for solving problems. Letters and symbols are used with numbers. The letters are used in place of unknown numbers. By using the known facts in the sum, the value of the unknown number can be worked out.

alimentary canal the long tube from mouth to anus through which food passes, is digested, and leaves the body as waste.

alkali *n.* a chemical substance that neutralizes acids. Strong alkalis, like strong acids, burn. Alkalis turn red litmus paper blue.

allergy *n.* an abnormal reaction that some people have to certain foods, pollen, dust, animal furs and drugs. They may develop skin rashes, sneezing attacks, watery eyes or other problems when exposed to them.

alloy *n.* a special metal that is made when two or more different metals are melted together. *Brass, bronze and steel are* **alloys**.

alpha particle a tiny piece of matter that is given off when an atom breaks up. It has a positive electric charge.

alternating current an electric current that flows in one direction and then in the opposite direction. It changes direction regularly many times a second. A direct current flows only in one direction.

alternative energy another way of producing power that does not use precious fossil fuels like oil and coal, e.g. solar power from sunlight; wave power from tides; wind power from moving air; hydroelectric power from rivers.

alternator *n.* a machine that produces alternating electric current. A kind of generator.

altimeter *n.* an instrument that records height above sea level. Altimeters are used in aircraft to show the height at which they are flying.

altitude *n.* the height that something is above sea level. *At its peak Mount Everest has an* **altitude** *of 29,028 ft.*

aluminum *n.* a silvery-white metal that is lighter and softer than heavy metals such as iron. It is the most common metallic element found in the Earth's crust. It is used in aircraft and engines because it is light and strong, and does not corrode. Aluminum is used for making cooking utensils.

alveoli *n.pl. (sing. alveolus)* tiny thin-walled sacs that are filled with air and surrounded by capillary blood vessels. They are found at the end of the smallest air passages (bronchioles) in the lungs of mammals.

capillaries

An enlargement of an alveolus.

amber *n.* a hard, yellowish-brown, translucent substance. Amber is the fossil resin of pine trees.

amino acid amino acids are the building bricks of body cells. The body gets them by breaking down the proteins in food. They are needed for growth, and for replacing damaged or dead cells. (say *a-mee-no*)

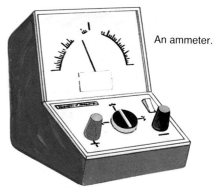

An ammeter.

ammeter *n.* an instrument that measures the strength of electrical current. It is measured in units called amperes.

A

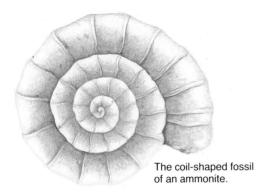

The coil-shaped fossil of an ammonite.

ammonite *n.* a type of extinct prehistoric animal found in fossil form. Its shell is shaped like a coiled spring.

amoeba *n.* (*pl. amoebas* or *amoebae*) a microscopic organism with only one cell. Its clear jelly-like body is always changing shape. (say *a-mee-ba*)

An amoeba is one of the simplest living organisms; every few days it reproduces by dividing into two.

ampere *n.* the unit used in measuring the strength of an electric current. It is named after the French scientist André Ampère (1775–1836).

amphibian (1) *n.* a cold-blooded animal with a backbone and a moist, smooth skin, which spends part of its life cycle

Amphibians, such as this newt, spend part of their life in water and part on land.

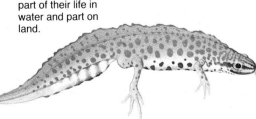

in water and part on land. Frogs, toads and newts are amphibians. The young have gills and live in water. Adult amphibians have lungs and breathe air and live mainly in damp places on land. (2) a vehicle that can move on land and water, or an aircraft that can take off and come down on water, as well as on land, are both amphibians. (3) **amphibious** *adj.*

amplify *v.* to make sound louder or an electrical signal stronger.

amplitude *n.* the distance between the top or bottom and middle of a wave.

Amplitude.

anaemia *n.* an unhealthy condition of the blood. It occurs when there are not enough red cells, or when the cells are short of the red coloring substance, hemoglobin. *People with* **anaemia** *feel tired and weak and look pale.*

anaerobic *adj.* describes an organism or process that can function without oxygen being present. Many microorganisms are anaerobic. Fermentation by yeasts in the brewing of beers is an example of an anaerobic process.

anaesthetic *n.* a drug or substance that causes a loss of feeling in the body. Surgeons use anaesthetics in operations to keep the patient from feeling pain. When a general anaesthetic is used, the patient goes into a deep sleep and becomes unconscious.

analyze (1) *v.* to discover what something is made of, by separating all its parts and identifying (naming) them. (2) *n.* **analysis** is the act of analyzing something.

anemometer *n.* an instrument used for measuring the speed of wind.

The cups of the anemometer spin in the wind and the wind speed is shown on a dial.

aneroid barometer a barometer in which air pressure is measured by the amount it squashes the thin metal sides of a circular box containing a vacuum⬜, and so moves a pointer.

angle *n.* the space between two surfaces or lines that meet each other. Angles are measured in degrees.

animal *n.* a living organism that is not a plant. Most animals can move about. They eat other animals or plants for food.

annual *adj.* describes something that happens every year. Some birds migrate annually. An annual plant is one that grows from a seed, flowers, makes new seeds and dies all in one year or season.

anode *n.* the positive electrode⬜ of an electrical instrument. The point to which electrons⬜ flow.

antenna (1) *n. (pl. antennae)* one of a pair of long feelers found on the heads of insects and some animals that live in shells, such as lobsters. (2) **antennas** *n.pl.* aerials⬜ for sending and receiving radio or television signals.

anther *n.* the tip of a flower's stamen⬜ that contains the pollen⬜.

antibiotic *n.* one of a group of substances made by molds⬜ and microorganisms⬜. Antibiotics are used by doctors to kill or stop the growth of other microorganisms that cause diseases. Penicillin⬜ is an antibiotic.

antibody *n.* a substance produced by the blood of an animal as a result of an infection. Antibodies protect the body against diseases.

anticline *n.* a fold like an arch in a layer of rock.

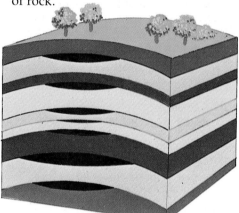

A section through an anticline showing the arching layers of rock.

anticyclone *n.* a large area of high atmospheric pressure⬜, from which all winds blow outward. It results in settled weather in the area it covers.

antidote *n.* a medicine that acts against the harmful effects of a poison. *The poisonous snake bite would have killed the explorer if he had not been given the* **antidote** *quickly.*

antiseptic *n.* a substance that kills or stops the growth of disease-carrying organisms⬜. A wound is cleaned with antiseptic to keep it from becoming infected.

A

antitoxin *n.* an antibody☐ made by the blood to protect it from a poison or disease.

anus *n.* the opening at the end of the alimentary canal☐ through which solid waste and undigested food leaves the body. (say *ay-nus*)

anvil (1) *n.* one of the three tiny bones found in the middle part of a human ear. (2) an iron or steel block on which horseshoes and other red-hot metal bars are hammered into shape.

aorta *n.* the largest artery☐ in the body. It leaves the left side of the heart, divides into several smaller arteries and carries blood to all parts of the body except the lungs. (say *ay-or-ta*)

ape *n.* a large type of monkey without a tail. Chimpanzees, orang-utans, gorillas and gibbons are all types of apes.

A gibbon is a type of ape; it has very long arms.

aperture *n.* an opening. The hole in a camera through which light enters and makes an image on the film inside.

The aperture on this camera can be made larger or smaller.

apex (1) *n.* (*pl. apexes* or *apices*) the highest point, the peak. (2) the pointed corner of a triangle.

apparatus *n.* any piece of equipment that is used for a special purpose, such as a chemical balance in a chemistry laboratory.

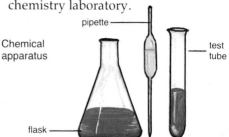

Chemical apparatus

pipette

test tube

flask

appendix *n.* (*pl. appendixes*) in humans, a short tubular growth (the width of a pencil) found at the beginning of the large intestine☐. It has no function. Inflammation of the appendix is called **appendicitis**. In plant-eating animals (herbivores) the appendix is much bigger and is an important part of the digestive system☐.

aquatic *adj.* living and growing on or in the water. Seaweeds are aquatic plants. Shrimps are aquatic animals.

aqueous *adj.* watery. An aqueous solution is one in which a substance is dissolved in water. (say *ack-kwee-us*)

aqueous humor a watery liquid which fills the space in the eye between the cornea and the lens.

arable *adj.* describes land suitable for growing crops.

arc (1) *n.* any part of the curved line of a circle. *A rainbow makes an* **arc** *in the sky.* (2) an electrical arc – a continuous band of luminous sparks which is made when an electric current jumps across a small gap between two electrodes. Lightning is a natural form of electric arc.

area (1) *n.* the amount of surface space inside a given boundary. (2) a region of land or part of the world: a rural area; a coastal area.

arithmetic (1) *n.* the study of numbers and their use in addition, subtraction, multiplication and division. (2) the act of adding, subtracting, multiplying and dividing numbers.

artery *n.* one of the tubes through which blood flows from the heart to all parts of the body.

arthropod *n.* one of a group of animals having a jointed, hard outer covering to support the body instead of a bony skeleton. Some arthropods, like crabs, live in water. Others, like insects and spiders, live on land.

This crab is an aquatic arthropod.

articulation *n.* the means by which different parts of a machine or an animal's body are able to move against each other. Articulation takes place at a joint.

artificial (1) *adj.* describes objects which are man-made, rather than natural. (2) artificial respiration⬛ is a way of forcing air into the lungs of a living person who has stopped breathing. It is used in life-saving to help people breathe again when they have nearly drowned. (say *are-ti-fishel*)

asbestos *n.* a greyish-white, fibrous mineral. It does not burn. Asbestos fibers are woven into fireproof cloth for firefighters' and astronauts' suits.

asphalt *n.* a sticky, black, tarry substance. It occurs naturally underground in certain parts of the world, and in surface lakes in Trinidad. It can be made by refining⬛ petroleum. Asphalt forms a waterproof covering for roofs. It is mixed with grit to make a hard surface for roads.

asteroid *n.* one of many thousands of small, rocky planets that revolve in orbits⬛ around the Sun. Most of them have orbits between those of Mars and Jupiter.

asthma *n.* a disease of the lungs. It makes people wheeze and they have difficulty in breathing.

astronaut *n.* a person who is specially trained to fly in a spacecraft and to carry out experiments in space.

An astronaut walking on the Moon.

astronomy *n.* the science that deals with the behavior and movements of the Sun, Moon, planets, stars, galaxies⬛ and other heavenly bodies.

atmosphere (1) *n.* the mass of air that surrounds the Earth. (2) the mixture of gases that surrounds other heavenly bodies such as Mars and Venus.

atom *n*. the smallest particle⬜ of any chemical element⬜ that can exist having all the properties of that element. All the matter in the universe is made up of different atoms. Each atom has a central nucleus with one or more electrons revolving around it.

atomic energy energy that is stored in the nucleus⬜ of an atom. It can be released by nuclear fission⬜, as in a nuclear reactor, or by nuclear fusion⬜, as in the Sun.

attraction *n*. the force that draws two things together. In magnetism⬜, the opposite poles⬜ of two magnets will attract each other.

audible *adj*. able to be heard. *Some very high notes are* **audible** *only to certain animals.*

auricle *n*. also called atrium. One of the muscular chambers of the heart in animals with backbones (vertebrates). Fish have one auricle; birds and mammals⬜ have two. The auricle receives blood from the big veins in the body and pumps it into the ventricle⬜. Birds and mammals have two ventricles; fish and amphibians have one.

automatic (1) *adj*. describes something that works, moves or acts by itself when started. An automatic washing machine will carry out a whole washing, rinsing and spinning cycle when switched on. (2) describes something done without human thought or control. *We breathe* **automatically** *during sleep. A heartbeat is an* **automatic** *action.*

automation *n*. the use of machines to do jobs that at one time were done by people. A combine harvester and an automobile assembly plant are examples of automation.

autotroph *n*. a living green plant that can make food from simple substances by using the energy from sunlight. (say *aw-toe-trofe*)

axis *n*. an imaginary straight line around which a body, such as the Earth, spins or seems to spin. *The Earth's* **axis** *passes through both the North and South Poles.*

axle *n*. a shaft or rod around which one or more wheels revolve.

axon *n*. the long thin part of a nerve cell that carries messages away from the cell body.

B b

backbone *n*. the spine. The column of small jointed bones, called vertebrae, in the middle of the back. The vertebral column. It protects the spinal cord and supports the body. Humans and other mammals, birds, reptiles, amphibians⬜ and fish have backbones.

bacterium *n*. (*pl. bacteria*) a microorganism⬜. Some bacteria are harmful and cause disease. Others are useful and break down dead plants and animals. This makes the soil richer. Milk is turned sour by bacteria.

baffle *n*. a piece of equipment with a special surface which stops sound waves from bouncing back to form echoes. Some concert halls have baffles. They are also used in the silencers in automobile exhaust pipes to reduce noise.

balance (1) *n*. an instrument used for weighing. One type of balance has two similar scale pans. The object to be weighed is placed in one pan. Known weights are placed in the other pan. When the masses in the two pans are the same, the scale pans will be level. A top-pan balance has one pan only, and the weight of the object being weighed forces the pan down against a spring. The weight is recorded on a dial. (2) the ability to keep your body steady without falling. (3) *v.* to maintain balance. *I can* **balance** *on one foot.*

ballast *n.* heavy material, such as earth, rocks or sand, used to weigh an object down or maintain its balance. Ballast is used in empty cargo ships to keep them steady in the water. Airships and balloons sometimes carry sandbags as ballast. These can be off-loaded to give the aircraft lift.

ball bearing (1) a device for reducing friction⎕ in the moving parts of a machine. The moving part glides freely over a number of loose steel balls contained in a ball race⎕. (2) a single steel ball.

In a ball bearing the steel balls run around a small track called a ball race.

ball race a grooved track in which steel ball bearings roll to help a wheel turn freely.

balsa *n.* a tropical American tree with very lightweight wood that is strong but easy to cut. It is used to make models and life-rafts. (say *ball-sa*)

bar *n.* a unit of pressure, roughly equal to atmospheric pressure⎕ at sea level. This is the same as 1000 millibars.

barb (1) *n.* in birds, one of the fine, stiff structures on the shaft of a feather. Barbs form the web of the feather. (2) in plants, a stiff hooked hair on the stems of some plants; a prickle.

bark (1) *n.* the sound made by certain animals, such as dogs and foxes. (2) the outer covering of the roots, trunk and branches of a tree. It may be thick and rough or thin, smooth and papery. We get cork from the thick bark of a certain kind of oak tree. Plane trees can live in cities and industrial areas because when the bark is full of dirt and soot it peels off, leaving new bark underneath.

barometer *n.* an instrument that measures atmospheric pressure⎕. Falling pressure usually means there is stormy weather ahead. Rising pressure usually forecasts fine weather. See **aneroid barometer**.

barren (1) *adj.* describes animals that are unable to bear young. *The cow was* **barren** *and could not produce calves.* (2) describes land on which nothing will grow; *a* **barren** *field.*

basalt *n.* a very hard, dark, igneous⎕ rock, formed by the cooling and hardening of molten volcanic material.

Basalt is the commonest volcanic rock.

base (1) *n.* the lowest part; the side on which a solid shape rests. (2) a chemical substance that reacts with an acid to form a salt. (3) in arithmetic, the main counting unit of a number

B

system, e.g. 10 is the base of the decimal system; 2 is the base of the binary⌸ system. (4) in geometry, the horizontal line on which a triangle, rectangle or other figure stands.

basin (1) *n.* all the land that is drained by a river and its branches (tributaries). (2) a great hollow in the Earth's surface filled by an ocean. (3) a wide, hollowed out area of land where the layers of rock all slope toward the middle.

Bats have well developed ears which help them to find their prey in the dark.

bat *n.* a flying mammal. It has a furry body with thin leathery wings. It is active at night and sleeps by day. A bat uses a kind of radar⌸ to avoid objects and to catch insects. In flight it gives out high-pitched squeaks. These sounds bounce off objects in its path as echoes and are picked up by its large ears. If the echo comes back very quickly the bat knows it is close to something.

bathysphere *n.* a round watertight chamber with windows. It can be lowered by cable into the sea. From inside scientists can study marine life at great depths. (say *bath-i-sfere*)

battery *n.* a series of two or more electric cells which make and store electricity. *My transistor needs a new* **battery**.

A battery used in a car to start the engine.

beak *n.* the hard, usually pointed mouth parts of a bird; a bill. Birds of prey such as hawks and owls have curved, hooked beaks that tear the flesh of their prey. Ducks have flat beaks.

Beaks come in different sizes and shapes.

beaker *n.* a glass container, with straight sides and a lip, used for pouring liquids in a laboratory.

beam (1) *n.* a ray of light, or radiation such as X-rays; radio waves going out along a narrow path in one direction only. A laser⌸ beam. (2) a length of timber used as a support in a building. An oak beam. (3) a large iron or wooden beam used in the beam engine. The beam engine was used for pumping water out of coal mines. (4) the breadth of a ship at its widest point. *This ship has a very broad* **beam**.

bearing *n.* a part of a machine that allows a moving part to turn or slide more easily. Bearings need to be lubricated by a film of oil that reduces friction and wear. (say *bare-ing*)

beetle *n.* a land or freshwater insect that has hard, shiny front wings and delicate back wings. When the beetle is at rest, the hard front wings fold over the back wings and protect them. A beetle has strong biting mouth parts. Some beetles are harmful to plants and to wood in houses.

The front wings of this beetle are folded over the back wings.

behavior *n.* the way plants and animals act or react. Animals may be born with certain types of behavior, e.g. birds make nests. Other types of behavior are the result of learning or experience, e.g. automobile drivers slcw down on slippery roads.

belt (1) *n.* a narrow strip of land; a region or area of land. *It rains heavily along the coastal* **belt** *of West Africa.* (2) a strong band that connects two pulleys or wheels together and passes power from one to the other.

berry *n. (pl. berries)* a juicy, fleshy fruit containing one or several seeds, e.g. cranberry. Some berries are poisonous, e.g. deadly nightshade.

beta particle a minute particle given off by a radioactive substance. It has a negative charge⬜ and is a very fast-moving electron.

biceps *n.* the large muscle in the front of the upper arm. The biceps bend the arm at the elbow joint. (say *buy-seps*)

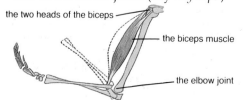

the two heads of the biceps

the biceps muscle

the elbow joint

biennial (1) *adj.* happening once every two years. (2) *n.* a plant that blooms and sets seed in its second year of growth. A foxglove is a biennial plant.

bilateral *adj.* of animals, plants and objects, having parts arranged symmetrically on both sides.

bile *n.* a bitter, yellowish-green liquid produced by the liver. It is stored in the gall bladder and passes into the intestine through the bile duct. Bile helps to digest fats.

bill (1) *n.* the hard, projecting mouth parts of a bird. (2) a narrow piece of coastland that juts out into the sea.

binary *adj.* in counting and calculating, it is a scale of numbering with a base⬜ of 2, instead of 10 as in the decimal system. The binary system is used for computers since it has only two different digits, 0 and 1. These can be represented by an electric current switched OFF or ON.

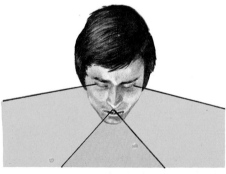

binocular vision seeing a single image when looking at an object with both eyes. The brain combines the image from each eye into a single image. The result is called stereoscopic vision.

biodegradable *adj.* describes things that can be broken down by bacteria⬜. Things made from plants and animals are biodegradable; plastic is not.

B

biology *n.* the science of living organisms. Biology deals with the structure, functions and development of plants and animals, their behavior and environment, and where they are found on the Earth.

biomass *n.* the total amount of animal and plant life on the Earth.

biosphere *n.* the part of the Earth and the air around it where living organisms⬚ can be found. (say *bye-oh-sfere*)

Humans and birds are bipeds.

biped *n.* any two-footed animal. Humans are bipeds. (say *bye-ped*)

bird *n.* any one of a class of warm-blooded animals that has a backbone, wings and a body covered with feathers. It lays eggs protected by shells. Most birds are able to fly.

birth *n.* the moment, at the end of a pregnancy⬚, when an animal enters the world and separates from its mother. The act or time of being born. *The bitch gave* **birth** *to four puppies.*

bit (1) *n.* in computing, a bit is a binary digit⬚. It is the smallest unit of information in a computer. A bit represents a choice between two alternatives, ON and OFF, 1 and 0. (2) the hard, sharp, cutting part of a tool or machine that drills holes in wood, stone or metal.

This mussel is a bi-valve; it can open its shell to help it move.

bivalve *n.* an animal having a shell made of two halves. They are hinged together so that the shell can open and close. Mussels and clams are bivalves.

black hole in astronomy it is the region left behind after a very large star explodes. Its force of gravity⬚ pulls everything into the center. The force is so great that even rays of light cannot escape. That is why it is called a black hole.

bladder (1) *n.* the hollow bag in the body of many animals where urine is stored. (2) a small sac filled with air, found in fish. It helps with balance. (3) some water plants have air bladders, e.g. bladderwrack, a kind of seaweed.

blade (1) *n.* a thin, narrow leaf of grass. (2) the broad, flat part of a leaf that grows out from the stem. (3) the sharp, flat part of a cutting tool. *These scissors have very sharp* **blades**.

bleach (1) *v.* to cause something to lose color, fade or become white. Colored fabrics become bleached by the Sun. (2) *n.* a chemical substance that bleaches. Most bleaches are made of chlorine and lime.

bleed (1) *v.* to lose blood from damaged blood vessels, caused by a cut, for example. (2) to lose fluid. Sap will bleed from the trunk of a tree if it is cut. Rubber tappers use this fact in getting the liquid latex from rubber trees.

blind spot a small area at the back of the eye, where there are no nerve cells sensitive to light. It is where the optic□ nerve leaves the eye.

block mountain a mountain formed when the land on one side of a fault□ rises steeply above the level of land on the other side.

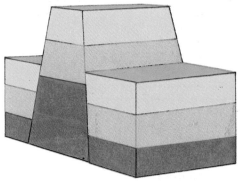

Block mountains, like the Sierra Nevada, are formed where a mass of rock is raised with faults on either side of it.

blood (1) *n.* the fluid, usually red, that flows around the body through the heart, arteries and veins of animals with backbones. It carries oxygen, food and other important substances to all the body cells. It carries away all the waste from the cells.(2) a similar fluid is found in animals without backbones.

blood group any one of several groups (A, AB, B and O) into which human blood is classified. It is important to know a person's blood group before giving a blood transfusion□. This is because when blood from some groups is mixed, it causes a clumping together of the red blood cells. In the body this would cause death.

boil (1) *v.* to reach the temperature where a liquid becomes a vapor□. (2) to make a liquid boil by heating it. (3) *n.* a painful swelling beneath the skin caused by an infection.

bond (1) *n.* something that binds things together, e.g. glue, solder. (2) in chemistry it is the force which holds atoms together to form molecules□.

A section of the thigh bone or femur—one of the strongest bones in the body.

bone *n.* one of the very hard pieces of stiff, strong tissue which makes up the skeleton of an animal with a backbone. There are large, long bones in arms and legs but many small bones in hands and feet. Bones protect and support the body.

boom (1) *n.* a sonic boom; a loud, explosive sound heard when an aircraft reaches and passes the speed of sound. (2) a long beam attached to a crane or derrick□, used for lifting and moving heavy loads.

bore (1) *v.* to tunnel into the earth, wood, stone or metal by drilling or

The bore of a gun barrel.

B

digging out. (2) *n.* a hollow part of a tube or gun barrel or its width across the center (diameter). (3) a wall of water that rushes up a river when a large wave builds up in the estuary🔲.

botany *n.* the scientific study of plants. Botany describes the many different kinds of plants, their form, how and where they grow, and how they adapt to changing conditions.

bowel *n.* the intestine; part of the long tube in the abdomen🔲, from the stomach to the anus🔲. Food passes through it and is digested.

brain *n.* the mass of nerve cells and fibers contained inside the skull of animals with backbones. The brain lets us think, feel and remember. It also controls all the processes necessary for life, such as breathing, the pumping of blood around the body, digestion, and excretion of waste products. Different parts of the brain do different things.

brake *n.* a device that slows or stops the motion of a vehicle or machine. A bicycle brake presses against the rim of the wheel and stops it from turning.

branch *n.* one of the parts that grows out from the main trunk of a tree or shrub. Smaller branches grow from it, and bear the leaves.

brass *n.* a hard, yellowish metal made from copper and zinc.

breath *n.* the air that is taken into the lungs and forced out again during breathing.

breathing *v.* the act of taking air into the lungs and giving it out again.

breed (1) *v.* to produce young. (2) to rear animals or plants. *The farmer* **breeds** *cattle. The gardener* **breeds** *roses.*

brittle *adj.* hard and easy to break. Glass is brittle.

bronchus (1) *n.* (*pl. bronchi*) one of two tubes into which the trachea🔲 divides at its lower end. The bronchus divides into smaller bronchi, which in turn divide into tiny bronchioles in the lungs. The bronchus has a lining that makes mucus🔲, which traps the dust in the air. Tiny hairs (cilia) in the lining sweep the dust and mucus up into the throat. It is coughed out as phlegm. (2) **bronchitis** *n.* inflammation of the bronchi, a disease mainly of humans. It causes coughing and shortness of breath.

bronze *n.* a hard, brownish metal made from copper and tin. Used to make ornaments and statues.

bud (1) *n.* part of a plant; a small swelling on the side of a twig or stem that will grow into a new leaf, stem or flower. (2) a swelling on the side of some simple animals like corals🔲 that grows into a new animal.

An aphid is a bug that sucks plant juices

bug (1) *n.* a general term for a type of insect that may or may not have wings. They feed by sucking into a sharp, tubelike mouth. Some bugs cause disease. (2) a mistake in a computer program. (3) a fault in a machine. (4) a device used for listening in to another person's conversation from a distance. *His telephone has been* **bugged** *by the police.*

bulb (1) *n.* a small plant stem covered with fleshy leaves. It stores food and lives underground. New stems, leaves and flowers grow from it each year and then die down. Daffodils and tulips grow from bulbs. (2) an electric light bulb. It gives light when an electric current passes through it.

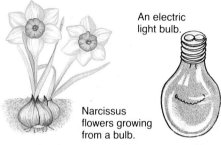

An electric light bulb.

Narcissus flowers growing from a bulb.

burette *n.* a piece of chemical apparatus; a long, narrow glass vessel with a tap. It is used for measuring the amount of liquid passed through the tap.

burn (1) *v.* to be on fire, to give out light or heat, to set on fire. (2) to hurt by heat, fire or chemicals. *John* **burned** *his hand when he touched the cooker. The splash of acid* **burned** *her skin.*

An orange-tip butterfly.

butterfly *n.* an insect with a long body, two long feelers on its head and four large wings, which are often brightly colored. In butterflies, there is a small swelling at the tip of each feeler. Moths, on the other hand, never have this swelling, or clubbing, as it is called.

byte *n.* a number, made up of 8 bits⬜. A byte is used in binary⬜ calculations. (say *bite*)

C c

cable (1) *n.* a thick, strong rope made of twisted wires. (2) a bundle of wires protected by a thick plastic tube for carrying an electric current. (3) a message sent through a cable, underground or under the ocean. (4) cable television: a system of television that allows many different channels⬜ to be transmitted and received.

cactus *n. (pl. cacti)* a desert plant which has spines in place of leaves to reduce water loss. The thick, fleshy stems store water.

calculator (1) *n.* a person who calculates. (2) a machine that does rapid calculations. *Jane often uses her pocket* **calculator** *to check her arithmetic.*

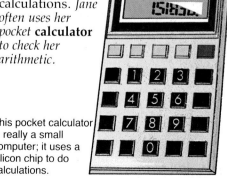

This pocket calculator is really a small computer; it uses a silicon chip to do calculations.

C

caliper, calliper (1) *n.* a kind of splint used to support a weak joint or fractured bone, especially in the legs. (2) **calipers, callipers** *n.pl.* a pair of movable legs, fastened at one end, used to measure the thickness or diameter◻ of something. It is hinged at the top.

This pair of calipers can be used for making small accurate measurements.

calorie (1) *n.* a unit of measurement of heat. (2) the unit used to measure the amount of heat energy in food.
A boiled egg has about 77 calories.
A medium-sized raw carrot has about 16 calories. (say *kal-or-ee*)

cambium *n.* a layer of cells◻ found in the stem of many plants. The cambium forms layer after layer of new cells on either side of it (xylem and phloem). As a result the stem grows thicker.

camouflage *n.* the means by which some animals protect themselves from predators◻. Their bodies have colors and patterns, which blend into their surroundings, and make them difficult to see. (say *kam-a-flaj*)

The yellow crab spider is almost invisible against this flower.

canal (1) *n.* a man-made waterway used for joining river systems or two different seas. Barges carry cargo along canals. (2) a tube in the body that carries food, liquid or air. The alimentary◻ canal carries food through the body. The semicircular canals in the inner ear help us to keep our balance.

cancer *n.* a malignant condition of the body where some cells◻ multiply more rapidly than normal and form lumps (tumors) of cancer cells. These destroy healthy tissue◻, and can spread through the body. Doctors are beginning to find cures for some forms of cancer.

canine (1) *adj.* dog-like; of the family of animals that includes dogs, wolves, foxes and jackals. (2) a canine tooth; a sharp, pointed tooth, used for tearing flesh. Mammals, including humans, have four, one on each side of the incisors◻ in the upper and lower jaws.

cantilever (1) *n.* a solid beam of stone, metal or concrete that stands out from a wall. It supports a balcony or an upper floor of a building. (2) a bridge formed by two cantilevers that join together to form an arch or span.

canyon *n.* a deep gorge, or valley, with steep sides. Canyons are formed by river action which slowly cuts through rock.

capacitor *n.* a device for storing electricity. The simplest type is made from two parallel metal plates seperated by an insulator◻, such as air. (say *ka-pass-i-tor*)

capacity (1) *n.* the amount of space within something that can be filled. *The bottle has a* **capacity** *of one liter.* (2) vital capacity: the largest amount of air that can be forced out of the lungs after taking a deep breath.

capillary (1) *n.* (*pl. capillaries*) a very narrow tube often used in chemical experiments. (2) one of many tiny blood vessels which join small arteries to veins. They can be seen only through a microscope.

capsule (1) *n.* a kind of dry fruit. It contains many seeds. A capsule opens to let out the seeds, e.g. a poppy fruit head has many tiny holes or pores to let out the seeds. (2) a small gelatin⬛ case that contains medicine. (3) the part of a spacecraft where the crew works. It can be separated from the rest of the spacecraft.

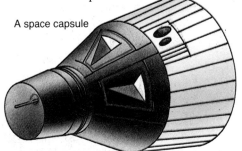

A space capsule

carbohydrate *n.* any substance made up of carbon, oxygen and hydrogen. Carbohydrates are made by green plants. Starches, cellulose and sugars are carbohydrates. Animals get the carbohydrate necessary for metabolism⬛ by eating plants or other animals. (say *car-bo-high-drate*)

carbon *n.* a widespread chemical element⬛ found in animals and plants. It is also found in coal and all other fossil⬛ fuels. Diamonds and graphite are crystalline⬛ forms of carbon.

Three different forms of carbon.

graphite

coal

diamond

carbon cycle the circulation of carbon atoms in nature. Plants take carbon dioxide from air to make food. Animals eat plants and change them into animal tissues. Plants and animals both give out carbon dioxide during respiration. Animals and plants die. Bacteria⬛ and fungi⬛ use the dead tissues as food, and carbon is put back into the air as carbon dioxide.

carbon dioxide one of the gases in air. It has no color or smell. It is made up of carbon and oxygen. It is released into the air when animals breathe out and when any substance containing carbon burns. Plants use carbon dioxide to make carbohydrates⬛. Carbon dioxide forms the bubbles in fizzy drinks.

carboniferous (1) *adj.* it describes the rocks in the Earth's crust that contain layers of carbon and coal. (2) the **Carboniferous Era** a warm damp period in the Earth's history when coal beds were gradually formed from great forests. (say *car-ba-nif-er-us*)

carbon monoxide a very poisonous gas. It has no smell or color. It is formed when any substance containing carbon does not burn completely; e.g. automobile exhaust fumes contain carbon monoxide.

cardiac *adj.* to do with the heart. Cardiac muscle: the special kind of muscle that forms the walls of the heart. It beats automatically at a steady rate.

caries *n.* decay of teeth caused by bacteria⬛. The commonest disease of the mouth. Sugar and soft drinks worsen the caries. Fluoride⬛ helps to prevent caries.

carnivore *n.* a flesh-eating animal. Eagles and lions are carnivores. Their bodies are specially suited for catching

C

prey and tearing the flesh. They move very swiftly. Some plants, such as the Venus flytrap, catch insects; they are also sometimes called carnivores. (say *carn-i-vore*)

carpals *n.pl.* the small bones of the wrist joining the forearm to the hand.

carpel *n.* the part of the flower that makes the seeds. It is made up of a stigma⬚, a style⬚ and an ovary⬚. There may be one or more carpels in each flower.

carrier wave a constant radio wave that carries the varying sound and picture signals from a transmitter to a receiver.

cartilage *n.* a tough, flexible material fixed to the joints of all animals with backbones. It helps to keep the joints stable. It helps the bones to move smoothly within the joint. The flexible part of the nose is made of cartilage.

cartography (1) *n.* the making of maps or charts. (2) **cartographer** *n.* a person who makes maps or charts.

cartridge *n.* a small container that holds material for a larger device; e.g. a film cartridge is used in a camera; an ink cartridge is used in a pen.

cassette *n.* a small case that holds magnetic recording tape. It is used in a tape recorder. Video cassettes are used in video recorders. They carry recordings of pictures and sound.

catalyst *n.* a substance that speeds up a chemical change. The catalyst itself is not changed. Enzymes⬚ are catalysts. (say *cat-a-list*)

cataract (1) *n.* a large waterfall. (2) a large flood or rush of water. (3) a disease that affects the lens⬚ of the eye. The lens becomes cloudy; light cannot pass through it and the person becomes blind. A cataract can often be cured by an operation.

caterpillar *n.* the larval stage in the life of a butterfly or moth. The caterpillar hatches out of the egg. It has a soft body divided into sections. It may be furry or smooth and is often brightly colored. It eats the leaves of plants.

cathode *n.* the part of an electrical instrument from which electrons⬚ flow. A negative electrode⬚.

cathode-ray tube (CRT) a type of vacuum tube⬚ in which streams of electrons⬚ can be beamed on to a screen. Light is produced when the electrons hit the screen.

A cathode-ray tube.

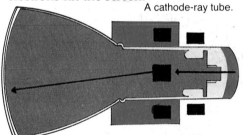

cell *n.* a very small part of living matter. It is made of protoplasm⬚ surrounded by a thin membrane⬚. Plant cells also have a cell wall. Most cells have a nucleus⬚. There are many different kinds of cells; each has a special job to do in the body of a plant or animal, e.g. liver cells, muscle cells.

This microorganism is made of one cell.

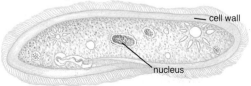

— cell wall

nucleus

celluloid *n*. the trade name for the earliest form of plastic. It was made in the United States. A clear, brittle plastic that burns easily. It is made mainly from cellulose⬜. It was used for making household goods, combs, cups, plates, boxes, dolls. Early photographic film was made from celluloid.

cellulose *n*. the material that forms the walls of plant cells. Cellulose is used to make paper, textiles, plastic and many other materials.

Celsius scale a temperature scale with 0° as the melting point of ice and 100° as the boiling point of water. The official name for the centigrade scale. It is named after Anders Celsius (1701–44). (say *Cell-see-us*)

cement (1) *n*. a grey powder made from a mixture of limestone⬜ and clay. It is mixed with water to make a paste. When dried out it becomes as hard as stone. It is used in buildings to bind bricks, stone and concrete blocks together. *We built the wall with bricks and* **cement**. (2) a hard substance in the root part of the teeth of mammals. (3) a kind of cement used by dentists when filling teeth.

center of gravity the point in a body or system around which its weight is evenly balanced or distributed. *The racing car can corner well because it has a low* **center of gravity**.

centigrade *n*. a temperature scale, in which ice melts at 0°C and water boils at 100°C.

centimeter *n*. a unit of length in the metric scale; one-hundredth part (1/100) of a meter.

central nervous system the controlling part of the nervous system. It coordinates all the activities of an animal. In animals with backbones, it is made up of the brain and spinal cord. In simple animals like worms, the central nervous system is made up of a few long nerve fibers joined to small swellings full of nerve cells.

central processing unit (CPU) the part of a computer that controls the circuits that carry out orders. It holds the arithmetic unit and the memory⬜.

centrifugal force the force that appears to make something move outward and away from the center when it is rotated. The true force is the centripetal force. (say *sen-trif-igal*)

Centripetal force keeps this ball rotating around and around.

centripetal force the inwards force that keeps a body, such as a satellite, moving in a curved path around a center. It depends on the mass of the body, its distance from the center and its speed. (say *sen-trip-ital*)

cephalopod *n*. one of a group of animals without a backbone; a type of mollusc⬜. It has a soft, muscular body. Its head has strong, armlike growths around the mouth with suckers on them. Octopus and squid are cephalopods. (say *sef-alepod*)

cereal (1) *n*. any grain used for food, such as rice, oats, wheat, and barley. (2) any food made from these grains.

cerebellum *n*. the part of the brain that makes the muscles in the body work together so that we can use our arms and legs to sit, stand, run, bend over or pick things up without falling over. It controls balance and coordination⬜. (say *sere-bell-um*)

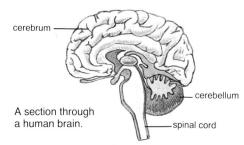

cerebrum

cerebellum

A section through a human brain.

spinal cord

cerebrum *n.* the largest part of the brain. It is divided into two halves (hemispheres). The cerebrum takes messages from all the sense organs◻ in our skin, tongue, nose, ears and eyes. It sends out messages to all parts of the body, telling them what to do. It controls our thinking and stores our memory. The right side of the cerebrum controls the left side of the body and vice versa. (say *se-ree-brum*)

cervix *n.* (*pl. cervices*) the neck, or lower end, of the uterus◻. It opens into the vagina◻. Tiny glands in the cervix produce mucus◻. The mucus keeps the vagina moist.

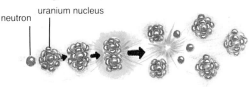

uranium nucleus

neutron

A chain reaction builds up when a uranium nucleus is bombarded with neutrons.

chain reaction a chemical reaction that produces a substance. This substance causes another reaction to take place. This second reaction produces another substance, which causes a third reaction to occur, and so on. The energy released by nuclear reactors is the result of a controlled chain reaction in the element uranium◻.

chalk *n.* a soft, porous, greyish-white limestone rock, made of tiny fossil◻ seashells.

channel (1) *n.* the part of a waterway that is deep enough for ships to use. (2) a narrow passage of water that joins two larger areas of water; a strait. (3) a band of frequencies◻ used for sending radio and television signals. (4) *v.* to make a channel; to pass information. *In my place of work, instructions are always* **channelled** *through one person.*

characteristic (1) *n.* a feature or quality special to a species of animal or plant. The square stem is a characteristic of plants belonging to the stinging-nettle family. (2) *adj.* a hollow stem is a characteristic feature of many water plants. (say *care-ac-ter-is-tic*)

charcoal *n.* a black, woody material made of carbon. It is the result of wood being partly burned in the absence of air. Used as a fuel since early times.

charge (1) *v.* to fill with electrical energy◻. (2) *n.* an amount of electricity held within something.

chassis *n.* the basic framework upon which the body and working parts of a machine or vehicle are supported. *It was such a bad accident that it even bent the* **chassis.** (say *chass-y*)

chemical bond the force with which one atom is linked to another atom in a chemical compound◻.

chemical energy the form of energy that is stored in a substance. It can be changed by a chemical reaction◻ into another form of energy.

chemistry *n.* the scientific study of substances to find out what they are made of, how they react with other substances and what special properties they have.

C

chew v. to bite and grind food into tiny pieces in the mouth, using teeth and tongue. *It is best to* **chew** *food thoroughly before swallowing.*

chicken pox a disease found mainly in children. A rash of small blistery spots breaks out over the body. These burst and scabs form. A raised temperature is present in the early stages.

china clay also called kaolin. A fine, white clay. It is used to make porcelain.

chip (1) n. a small piece that has broken off, e.g. a chip of wood or rock. (2) in computers, a tiny piece of silicon⬚, with a complete electronic circuit etched into it. A chip is just an integrated circuit⬚ with all the electronic parts made from silicon.

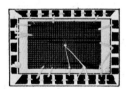

Computers and washing machines use silicon chips like this.

chitin n. the strong, hard material which forms the outer coverings of insects and the shells of their eggs, and the cell walls of many fungi⬚. It contains nitrogen.

chlorine n. a poisonous gas, greenish-yellow in color. It has a strong, unpleasant smell. Chlorine is a chemical element. It is used to kill bacteria⬚ and as a bleach⬚.

chlorophyll n. the green substance in plants. Chlorophyll uses the energy in sunlight to turn water and carbon dioxide into sugar and oxygen; this is photosynthesis⬚. (say *klor-a-fill*)

cholesterol n. a chemical substance found in animal blood cells, in bile and in egg yolk. An excessive amount of this substance in the blood can cause disease of the arteries⬚.

chromatography n. a method of separating a mixture of soluble substances (solutes). The solutes are dissolved in a solvent. Chromatography uses the fact that different substances travel different distances through a column of inactive⬚ substance. Different substances produce different colored bands in ultraviolet light. This fact is used to find out what substances the mixture contains.

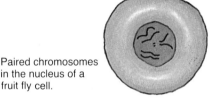

Paired chromosomes in the nucleus of a fruit fly cell.

chromosome n. one of a number of paired, microscopic⬚, threadlike structures found in the nucleus⬚ of a cell. They are easier to see when a cell is dividing. Chromosomes carry the characteristics⬚ of a plant or animal, for example, the color of skin and hair; the shape and color of a flower; the type of tree. (say *krome-azome*)

chrysalis n. the pupa⬚ stage in the development of a butterfly or moth from a caterpillar. The caterpillar fixes itself to a stem or wall. While it is inside the chrysalis, the caterpillar changes into a butterfly or moth. (say *chris-alis*)

C

cilia *n. pl.* microscopic hairs that grow out from the surface of some animal cells. The cilia beat together in a wavelike motion. Some tiny aquatic animals use cilia to waft food into their mouths. They also use them to paddle themselves along. In mammals, cilia push the egg cell along a narrow tube into the womb▢. (say *seel-eea*)

ciliary muscle a muscle in the eye. It changes the shape of the lens▢ so that it can focus on both near and distant objects. (say *sill-ee-airy*)

circuit *n.* the complete path of an electric current around a series▢ of wires and connections. If there is a break in the circuit, the current will not flow.

circulation (1) *n.* the act of going around and around the same space. *The* **circulation** *of air in the room was helped by the fan.* (2) the blood circulates through the blood vessels of the body because it is pumped by the heart.

circumference (1) *n.* a curved line forming the outer limit of a circle or spherical object. (2) the distance measured by such a line. The circumference of a wheel.

cirrus *n.* a type of white, wispy, curly cloud that appears high in the sky. It is made up of tiny ice crystals▢. (say *seer-us*)

classify *v.* to group together plants, animals or objects that have similar characteristics▢. A class is a group of animals or plants that have similar characteristics.

clavicle *n.* the collar bone. It joins the shoulder blade (scapula) to the breast bone (sternum).

claw (1) *n.* a curved nail with a sharp point on the toes of birds, mammals and certain other animals. (2) the grasping limb of a lobster or crab.

The sharp, curved claw of a bird of prey, such as an eagle.

clay *n.* a kind of fine-grained earth. Water drains through it very slowly. Clays are used in making bricks and pottery.

climate *n.* the usual weather conditions of a region of the Earth throughout the year. The climate is affected by many factors, including rainfall, temperature and moisture in the air. A temperate climate has four seasons, spring, summer, autumn and winter. Many tropical parts of the world have separate rainy and dry seasons.

clone *n.* an animal or plant that has developed from a single cell of another plant or animal. A clone is identical to the plant or animal it was taken from.

clot *n.* a clot is formed when the solids floating in a liquid clump together. A blood clot forms when a blood vessel is damaged. A chemical substance is produced which causes the blood cells to clump together. This seals the break and prevents further bleeding.

cloud *n.* clouds are made of tiny droplets of water, or ice crystals▢. These group together in the sky to form clouds.

coal *n.* a hard, black mineral found naturally in layers beneath the earth. It is mostly made of carbon. Coal was formed millions of years ago from decaying vegetation. It is mined and used as a fuel.

cochlea *n.* a coiled tube in the inner ear, where vibrations from sound waves are changed into nerve messages (impulses). These are sent to the brain. The brain interprets them as sounds. (say *coke-leea*)

The cochlea of a human ear.

cocoon *n.* a case of spun threads that a caterpillar or insect larva⬜ spins around itself. It turns into an adult insect, such as a moth, inside the case. We get silk from the cocoon of the silkworm moth.

code *n.* a set of symbols, words or signals, used for sending messages. One example is the Morse code, made up of short and long sounds (dots and dashes). Semaphore is a kind of code that uses flags.

coil (1) *v.* to wind around and around a center. (2) *n.* a device used in electromagnetism⬜. When an electric current is passed through a coil of wire, a magnetic force is produced.

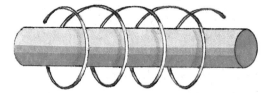

coke *n.* a solid black material used as a fuel. It burns hotly with little smoke. Coke is made by heating coal with little or no air present.

cold-blooded *adj.* describes animals that cannot control the temperature of their bodies. The body temperature changes with that of the surrounding air or water. Except for mammals and birds, all animals are cold-blooded.

cold front when cold air meets warm air, a cold front is formed. This line of cold air makes the warm air rise, and clouds are formed.

colon *n.* in mammals, the large intestine⬜. Part of the long tube (alimentary canal) through which food passes.

colony *n.* a group of animals or plants of the same kind that live together in the same area. Corals⬜ live and grow in colonies. *We have a* **colony** *of ants near the house.*

color-blind *adj.* being unable to tell the difference between some colors. Red and green are the colors that are most often confused. It is due to a fault in the retina⬜ of the eye. More males are color-blind than females.

combine (1) *v.* to join together. Chemical substances combine to form another chemical substance called a compound. (2) *n.* a combine harvester is a machine that carries out different jobs connected with harvesting and threshing crops.

combustion *n.* the process of catching fire and burning when a substance reacts with the oxygen in the air. Heat is always given out and flames may occur.

comet *n.* a small body in the solar system⬜ made of dust and gases. It goes around the Sun on a very stretched-out path. It has a tail that

A comet with a bright, streaming tail.

C

always points away from the Sun. Halley's Comet is a bright body that can be seen every 76 years.

command (1) *n.* an order that tells someone to do something. (2) a command is an instruction that tells a computer what to do next. A computer program is made up of a set of such commands. (3) **command module** the part of a spacecraft where the operations are controlled by the commander. Instructions are received from ground control.

community *n.* a group of different animals or plants that live together in special surroundings. They depend on each other for food or survival, e.g. a forest is a large community.

compass (1) *n.* an instrument used to show directions. It has a magnetic needle that pivots☐ freely and always points to the magnetic North Pole. A

compass is used for navigating ships and aircraft. (2) **pair of compasses** an instrument used for drawing circles, made of two arms, hinged at the top. One arm holds a pencil; the other ends in a point.

competition *n.* in nature, the struggle among living organisms☐ for a limited supply of such things as food, water, oxygen or space in which to live.

component *n.* a part of something, especially of a machine or engine. Automobiles are made up of hundreds of different components, such as pistons, cylinders and wheels.

composition *n.* the parts of something; the way they are put together, e.g. the notes in a piece of music; the chemicals in a substance.

compound *n.* a substance that contains two or more chemical elements☐ in fixed amounts. The elements are held together by chemical bonds☐. Water is a compound of hydrogen and oxygen. .

compress (1) *v.* to squeeze together so that the gas or solid takes up less space. (2) *n.* a compress is a pad of gauze or wool used to reduce swelling and heat in a fever or on a sprained wrist or ankle. A cold compress is usually filled with crushed ice. A hot compress is soaked in hot water.

compression *n.* the squeezing together of things under great pressure. A pushing force. The opposite of tension☐, which is a pulling force.

compressor *n.* part of a gas turbine☐ or jet engine in which air is put under great pressure. Compressors are used in refrigerators to compress a gas. When the pressure is taken away, the gas expands quickly and cools down. This cools the air inside the refrigerator.

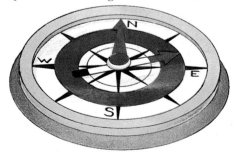

compute *v.* to calculate; to work out by using addition, subtraction, division or multiplication.

computer *n.* an electronic device used for solving complicated mathematical problems at very high speeds. Computers use information fed into them. They store information in a memory and can use this information over and over again.

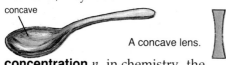

computer program a set of instructions fed into a computer that makes it do a certain job or solve a problem.

concave *adj.* curved inward. The inside of a spoon is concave. Some lenses are concave; they are thinner at the center.

concave

A concave lens.

concentration *n.* in chemistry, the amount of a substance that is dissolved in a volume of liquid. The smaller the amount of liquid used, the stronger the solution. We say it is more concentrated. (say *con-sen-tray-shun*)

conception *n.* in humans, the joining of a sperm⬜ with an egg cell or ovum to form an embryo⬜. This will grow into a baby inside the mother's body.

concrete *n.* a building material. It is made from cement, sand, pebbles and water. Concrete hardens when it dries.

condensation (1) *n.* the process of changing a gas into a liquid by cooling it. (2) the liquid formed by such a process. *The* **condensation** *of steam on the cold windows made it difficult to see out.*

condense *v.* to squeeze something into a smaller space. To change a vapor or gas into a liquid by cooling it. A liquid takes up less space than a gas.

condenser (1) *n.* a piece of chemical apparatus used to change a gas into a liquid by cooling it. A condenser is used to purify (distil) some liquids. (2) part of a steam engine that uses the condensation of steam to make a partial vacuum⬜. (3) a system of lenses in a microscope or photographic enlarger. It makes the image⬜ bigger.

conduct *v.* to direct or transmit⬜ forms of energy. A copper wire conducts electricity. Metals conduct heat well. The tiny ossicles (bones) in the middle ear conduct sound waves to the inner ear.

conduction *n.* the movement of heat, electricity and other kinds of energy through a solid object.

cone (1) *n.* a solid shape that has a flat, circular base and a point at the top. (2) a seed cone of a tree such as pine, fir and spruce. (3) the nose cone of a rocket. (4) one of the special cells in the retina⬜ of the eye, which is sensitive to colors (color vision).

congenital *adj.* relating to something that is present in an animal or baby at the time of birth. A congenital defect is something that is wrong with part of a baby. The baby is born with it.

conifer (1) *n.* a tree, usually evergreen, that produces cones as fruit, e.g. pine, fir, spruce. (2) *adj.* **coniferous** describes a tree that produces cones. A coniferous forest largely consists of such trees.

connection (1) *n.* a place where two things join together. (2) a device used

C

to join parts of an electrical circuit.
(3) a relationship. The connection
between the Moon and tides.

conservation *n.* the protection and
careful use of forests, rivers, country-
side and seas. The protection of
animals and plants and their natural
surroundings. The careful use of
natural products such as coal and oil.

constellation *n.* a group of stars that
forms a pattern or shape in the sky
which we can recognise, e.g. the
constellation of Cancer, the crab.

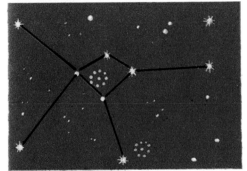

The constellation of Cancer.

contagious *adj.* describes a disease or
illness spread by direct contact
(touching) with a patient or the
patient's belongings.

continent *n.* one of the large land
masses on Earth. There are six
continents: North America, South
America, Africa, Asia, Europe and
Australia. Antarctica is sometimes
regarded as a seventh continent.

continental drift the gradual
movement apart of the large
continental land masses. It is caused
by the constant movement of the
large floating plates□ forming the
Earth's crust. The continental land
masses and oceans float over these
plates and move with them.

continental shelf a shelf of land
beneath the ocean. The shelf slopes
gently away from the coast until it
meets the steep continental slope.

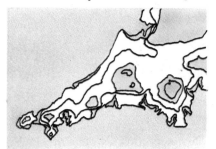

Contour lines on the map of a headland.

contour *n.* a continuous line on a map.
The line joins all the points that are of
the same height above sea level.
(say *con-toor*)

contract *v.* to become shorter or
smaller in size. Most gases, liquids
and solids contract when they are
cooled or put under pressure. *Muscles*
contract *to cause body movements.*

control (1) *v.* to direct, guide or
command something or someone.
The brain controls the actions of the
body. (2) *n.* the power to guide or
direct something or someone. *The car*
went out of **control** *when the driver fell*
asleep. (3) *adj.* to do with control or
guidance. *The airport* **control** *tower*
gives the airliner permission to land.

control unit part of the central
processing unit (CPU) in a computer.
It controls the arithmetic logic unit,
(ALU), where all the calculations are
carried out.

convection *n.* the movement of heat in
a liquid or gas. The hot liquid or gas
rises to the top; the cold sinks to the
bottom. The process is continuous,
and a convection current is set up.

converge *v.* to come closer together; to come together at a point. Rays of light converge when they pass through a convex lens. The lens bends the rays toward each other.

convex *adj.* curved outward. The outside of a spoon is convex. A convex lens is curved outward. It is the reverse of concave.

coordination *n.* the smooth working together of all parts of the body in animals. The brain and special chemical messengers in the blood coordinate the body's actions. **Coordination** *between the left hand and the right hand is important when playing the piano.*

copper *n.* a reddish-brown metallic element. It is easily shaped. Copper is a very good conductor of heat and electricity. Copper-bottomed pans heat up more quickly than others.

copulation (1) *n.* the mating of a male and female animal. During copulation the male deposits sperm cells inside the body of the female. (2) **copulate** *v.* to deposit sperm inside the body of a female animal.

coral (1) *n.* a hard, stone-like substance found in warm (tropical) seas. It has many different shapes and colors. Coral is formed by the skeletons of microscopic sea animals. (2) the tiny marine animal that forms coral. Coral reefs are found near the coasts of tropical islands.

core (1) *n.* the hard part in the center of fleshy fruits, such as apples, containing the seeds. (2) the center of the Earth. The inner core is solid metal and very dense. The outer core is made up of hot liquid rock. (3) the center of a nuclear reactor.

cork *n.* the soft, light bark of the cork oak tree. It is formed by a layer of cells called the cork cambium. Cork floats on water. Cork has many uses: stoppers for bottles, floats for fishing nets, and life rafts.

cornea *n.* the transparent covering in the front of the eyeball. The cornea covers the iris and lens.

corolla *n.* all the petals of a flower. They have many different shapes and colors. (say *ko-roll-a*)

Corolla of a lily.

Corona of a narcissus.

corona (1) *n.* the central cup-shaped part of some flower petals, e.g. the daffodil. (2) the outer edge of the Sun's atmosphere, seen during a total eclipse of the Sun. (3) a ring of colored light that can sometimes be seen around the Sun and Moon in misty weather.

coronary heart disease a disease that partly or completely blocks the artery□ to the heart (coronary artery). Blood cannot reach the heart muscle cells. They become short of oxygen, and the heart stops beating. The person with coronary heart disease may suffer a 'heart attack' or 'coronary'.

corpuscle *n*. any of the red and white cells in the blood. (say *core-pussel*)

corrosion *n*. the slow wearing away of metals by chemicals in the air. The corrosion of iron by moist air produces rust. *Parts of my old automobile have been damaged by* **corrosion**. (say *core-roshun*)

cosmic ray streams of tiny, charged particles from outer space. They are bombarding the Earth all the time, but cannot be seen with the naked eye.

cosmonaut *n*. a Soviet astronaut□.

cotton *n*. a natural fiber. It comes from the fluffy white or grey fibers that grow in the seed pod of the cotton plant. It grows mainly in India, parts of Africa and the southern states of the United States. Cotton is woven into threads and used to make textiles.

cotyledon *n*. a leaf found within a seed. Some seeds have only one (monocotyledons). Other seeds have two (dicotyledons). When a seed starts to grow (germinates), the cotyledon is the first leaf to grow.

countdown (1) *n*. counting backwards in seconds to zero. (2) The system of control checks that is carried out before 'blast-off' in a rocket launch.

courtship *n*. a special kind of display□ behavior seen in male and female animals before mating takes place. *The peacock spreads its beautiful tail during* **courtship** *to attract the peahen.*

cracking *n*. the breaking down of chemicals by heat under pressure to form simpler ones. The cracking of mineral oil produces petroleum.

crane (1) *n*. a large wading bird. It has a long neck and bill, and long, slender legs. (2) a large machine, used for lifting and moving heavy loads, especially on building sites.

cranium *n*. the hollow dome of the skull. It is made of several thin, flat bones that are joined together. It holds and protects the brain.

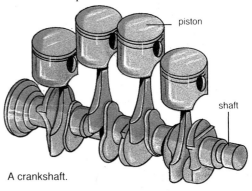

A crankshaft.

crankshaft *n*. the main driving rod in an engine. It is turned by an arm called a crank, which is connected to a piston.

The crater of a volcano.

crater *n*. a deep hollow in the ground, shaped like a bowl. The mouth of a volcano is a crater. Many craters are visible on the surface of the Moon.

crescent (1) *n.* the curved shape of the Moon in its first and last quarter. (2) anything so shaped.

crevasse *n.* a deep crack in thick ice or in a glacier⬚. *The mountaineer slipped and fell into a* **crevasse**. (say *kre-vas*)

crop (1) *n.* the growth and yield of a particular plant used for food or other purposes. In order to keep the land fertile⬚, farmers sometimes grow different crops on the land each year. This is called crop rotation. (2) a pouch in the neck of a bird, where it stores food. (3) *v.* to cut or bite off the top of something, especially plants. *The sheep* **cropped** *the grass in the valley.*

crust *n.* the rocky, outer layer of the Earth. The crust is divided into several enormous sections called tectonic plates⬚. These plates float and move on top of the hot liquid rock (the mantle).

crustacean *n.* an animal with a hard outer shell to the body. Most crustaceans, such as crabs, lobsters and shrimps, live in water. (say *cre-sta-tion*)

crystal (1) *n.* a clear, solid substance with flat surfaces that always meet at the same angles. They are regular in shape. Different substances have crystals of different shapes and colors, e.g. red rubies and green emeralds. (2) the solid form of some chemical substances, e.g. salt, sugar.

cube *n.* a solid figure with six flat, square faces of equal size. All the angles are right angles, 90°. Sugar and salt crystals are in the form of cubes.

cultivate (1) *v.* to make the soil suitable for growing plants. (2) to grow plants.

culture *n.* a group of microscopic organisms⬚ grown in a special liquid or jelly.

cumulonimbus *n.* a large, billowy type of cloud that soars up into the sky. It is made of several cumulus⬚ clouds. They cause thunderstorms and showers. (say *kume-ya-low-nimbus*)

cumulus *n.* (*pl. cumuli*) a heavy, fluffy-looking cloud with a rounded top. Cumuli are present in fine weather, but they can build up into cumulonimbus⬚ clouds which may bring rain.

current (1) *n.* a flow of electricity along a conductor. (2) the movement of liquid or gas in a particular direction. *There are dangerous* **currents** *in the river. A* **current** *of air cooled their faces.*

The cuticle of a finger.

cuticle (1) *n.* a thin layer, without cells⬚, found on the outside of plant leaves and stems. It keeps the plants from losing too much water. (2) the strong, hard outer covering of insects. (3) the strip of skin at the base of a toenail or fingernail. (say *cue-tical*)

cycle (1) *n.* a continuous chain of events that occur in the same order, over and over again. The cycle of the seasons, spring, summer, autumn, winter. (2) the life-cycle of an organism consists of all the different stages of its growth, from egg to adult. Some animals, like the frog, have complicated life-cycles. The eggs (frog spawn) hatch into tadpoles; the tadpoles change gradually into frogs. (3) the circulation⬜ of certain chemicals in nature, e.g. the water cycle. The water falls as rain. It passes into the soil and rivers. The surface water turns back into water vapor (evaporates) and rises to form clouds. It falls back to the Earth again as rain. Nitrogen and carbon have similar cycles in nature.

cyclic (1) *adj.* to do with moving or happening in cycles. (2) a type of chemical compound⬜, which has its atoms held in a ring.

cyclone (1) *n.* an area of low pressure covering a large part of the Earth. The pressure is always lowest in the center of a cyclone. This is usually called a depression⬜. (2) an extremely violent tropical storm which occurs in the tropics, with winds circling at speeds above 75 mph (120 kph). Tropical cyclones in the Atlantic Ocean are called hurricanes⬜. If they occur in the west Pacific Ocean, they are called typhoons⬜.

cylinder (1) *n.* a hollow or solid tube, with circular ends of the same size. *He rolled the sheet of paper into a* **cylinder**. (2) part of an engine in which a piston moves up and down.

The cylinder of a piston engine.

cyst *n.* a swelling found in some animal and plant tissues. It is enclosed by a tough layer (capsule). It may be filled with liquid or a disease organism. (say *sist*)

cytoplasm *n.* a thin, clear, jelly-like substance found inside the cell membrane⬜. The nucleus⬜ and other cell bodies are found in the cytoplasm.

D d

dam (1) *n.* a barrier built across a large river. It controls the flow of water. The weight of water held behind a dam can be used as a source of energy. Hydroelectric power plants change this energy into electricity. *When the* **dam** *burst the whole valley was flooded.* (2) a breeding female horse or other four-legged animal.

data *n.pl.* facts given, from which other facts may be worked out. Information fed into a computer. Data can be alphabetical, numerical or both.

data base a large body of information. It is kept in a computer's memory⬜, on disk or tape.

data processing the grouping, sorting and storing of data⬜ in a computer, so that the data can be issued on demand.

decay (1) *n.* the rotting of dead animals and plants. It is caused by bacteria and fungi in the soil. (2) the breaking up of radioactive⬜ substances.

decibel (dB) *n.* a measure for comparing the loudness of sounds. A soft whisper has 0 decibels (dB). A jet aircraft taking off has 110–140 dB. Sounds louder than 140 dB can cause pain in the ear. They may harm the hearing. (say *des-ibel*)

deciduous *adj.* describes plants that lose their leaves in winter. Oak and ash are deciduous trees. (say *desid-uous*)

Deciduous oak trees shed their leaves in winter.

decimal *adj.* to do with the number 10. The decimal system of numbers is based on a scale of ten symbols from 0 to 9. Decimal places are the number of figures written to the right of the decimal point. The point separates whole numbers on the left from decimal fractions on the right.

decompose (1) *v.* to decay; to rot. Animal and plant remains decompose in the soil. (2) in chemistry, to break down a chemical substance into simpler substances.

defecate *v.* to pass solid waste matter (feces) from the body through the anus□.

degree (1) *n.* one of the equal units of measurement on a temperature scale. At sea level water boils at 100° Celsius (100°C). Water freezes at 0° Celsius (0°C). (2) a unit for measuring the arcs of a circle or angles. Each angle in a rectangle is 90° (a right angle).

degree of freedom the amount of movement that can be made by each joint of a robot□.

dehydration (1) *n.* a lack of water in animal or plant cells. Animals and plants lose water all the time as part of their natural functions. This is replaced by drinking or taking in water from the atmosphere or soil. Dehydration occurs when the animal or plant loses water faster than it can take it in. Plants become dehydrated in very hot, dry weather. (2) a process that removes water from some substances, e.g. dehydrated milk becomes dried milk powder.

delta *n.* a triangular area of sand and rocks at the mouth of a large river. These are deposited as the river slows down as in the Nile delta and the Amazon delta. In a delta the river flows into the sea through several channels with sandbanks or islands between them. A delta is so named because it is shaped like the Greek letter delta (Δ).

A delta

dendrite *n.* part of a nerve cell□. The branching end of a dendron□. It carries messages toward the cell body.

dendron *n.* one of several fine threads of cell matter, growing out from the cell body of a nerve cell☐. Its end divides into branches called dendrites☐.

density *n.* the mass of a substance compared with its volume. The density of water is 1 gram per cubic centimeter, or 62 lb per cubic foot. Density is equal to mass divided by volume. **dense** *adj.* describes any material or substance with a high density. Lead is a dense metal.

dental *adj.* to do with the teeth, e.g. dental caries; dental treatment.

dentine *n.* the hard tissue of a tooth. It lies under the enamel. Dentine is like bone but has no cells. (say *den-teen*)

deposit (1) *v.* to set down; to leave lying. Rivers deposit sand and silt in estuaries or deltas as they slow down. (2) *n.* something that is laid down or left behind by water or wind.

depression (1) *n.* an area of low atmospheric pressure☐. (2) a dent or hollow in the surface of something. A depression fracture of the skull. (3) a medical condition that affects humans, particularly after an illness. People who suffer from depression feel miserable and without hope.

derrick (1) *n.* the framework of girders built over an oil well. It supports the heavy drilling machinery. (2) a large machine with cables, pulleys and beams; used for lifting and moving heavy objects, especially on building sites and in cargo docks.

desert *n.* a dry, barren area of land. It has little or no rainfall. Daytime temperatures are very high. At night the temperature may drop below the freezing point. Desert animals and plants are well-suited (adapted) to these conditions. A camel stores fat in its hump as a food reserve on long journeys across the desert.

detergent *n.* a chemical substance used to remove dirt, oil or grease from surfaces or materials. Most soap powders are detergents. (say *de-ter-gent*)

develop (1) *v.* to grow or cause to grow; to become mature or adult. Athletes develop their muscles with exercise. Tadpoles develop into frogs. (2) in photography, films are treated with chemicals to bring out (develop) the picture.

dew *n.* small drops of water that are formed on surfaces when warm air cools. Dew is formed on grass and plants at night.

dew point the temperature at which dew forms when the atmosphere☐ is full of (saturated) water vapor (moisture).

diabetes (mellitus) *n.* a disease in which there is too much sugar (glucose) in the blood. The body tries to get rid of it by excreting it in large amounts in the urine☐. Insulin☐ controls the amount of sugar in the blood. Lack of insulin causes diabetes. If no insulin is present, the person dies. Insulin can be manufactured. Daily injections of insulin can control diabetes.

diagnosis *n.* discovering, by means of examination, what disease a human patient, plant or animal may be suffering from. *The doctor has not yet made his* **diagnosis**, *but he thinks it is a case of food poisoning.* (say *die-ag-no-sis*)

diagonal (1) *adj.* describes a line that has a slanting direction. Going from one corner to the opposite corner. (2) *n.* a line drawn from one corner of a rectangle⊡ to the opposite corner.

diagram *n.* a figure, or plan, that shows how something is made or how it works.

dial *n.* the front, or face, of an instrument that is divided into units by numbers or figures. A pointer moves across the face and indicates measurements. *The* **dial** *of an ammeter shows the strength of an electric current.*

diameter *n.* a straight line that passes from one point on the circumference⊡ of a circle, through the center, to a point on the opposite side; the distance across such a line.

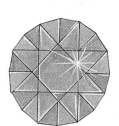 

These diamonds have been cut and polished.

diamond *n.* a very hard gemstone. The pure crystalline⊡ form of carbon. Diamond was formed millions of years ago from the carbon in volcanic eruptions. The crystals formed as the carbon cooled under great pressure. It is used in cutting tools and as a precious stone.

diaphragm (1) *n.* a layer of muscle that separates the chest from the abdomen in mammals. It is used in breathing. (2) a thin, vibrating disk that changes sound waves into electrical signals. Telephones and microphones⊡ have diaphragms. (3) a device on a camera that controls the size of the aperture (opening). It controls the amount of light that enters the camera. A similar device is also found on a light microscope. (say *die-a-fram*)

dicotyledon *n.* a flowering plant that has two leaves (cotyledons⊡) inside the seed. The leaves of a dicotyledon have a network of veins.

diesel *n.* a type of internal combustion engine that burns heavy diesel oil in its cylinders. Many ships, locomotives and automobiles have diesel engines. It was named after a German scientist, R. Diesel, (1858-1913). (say *deezel*)

diet *n.* what humans and other animals usually eat and drink. The kinds of food and quantities of each that are eaten. A balanced diet contains all the foods, vitamins and minerals needed for health. *She is having to control her* **diet** *as she is overweight.*

differential *n.* in a car, the set of gears that changes the drive of the propeller shaft into the drive of the back wheels. It allows each wheel to turn separately when the car is cornering. (say *differ-en-shal*)

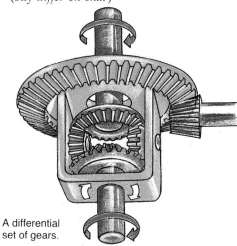

A differential set of gears.

D

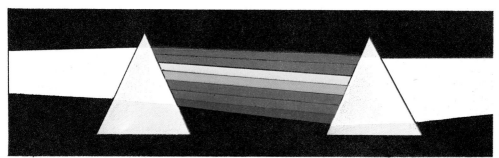

diffraction (1) *n.* the splitting up of a ray of light into dark and light bands. (2) the splitting up of a ray of white light into all the colors of a spectrum⬜. This is done by passing the ray of white light through a prism⬜. The glass in the prism bends different colored light by different amounts and so produces the seven bands of the spectrum. If the spectrum is passed through another prism, the opposite way up, it is changed back to white light again.

diffusion (1) *n.* the process by which molecules⬜ of a substance spread through a liquid or a gas. Diffusion stops when the molecules are spread evenly throughout. This action can be seen when a colored crystal is dropped into a beaker of water. The color gradually spreads out until all the water is evenly colored. (2) carbon dioxide, oxygen and soluble substances diffuse across the cell membranes⬜ of plants and animals.

digestion (1) *n.* a process that living organisms carry out. It breaks down food into simple substances. The organism uses them for growth and energy. (2) **digest** *v.* to break down food into simple substances which an organism can use for growth and energy. *When I am tired, I have difficulty in* **digesting** *food.*

digestive system the parts of a body connected with the digestion of food. In most animals it consists of the gut or alimentary canal⬜ and organs such as the liver and pancreas⬜.

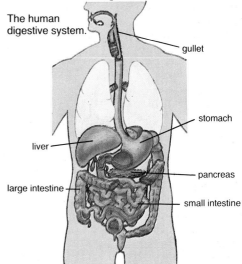

The human digestive system.

gullet

stomach

liver

pancreas

large intestine

small intestine

digit (1) *n.* any one of the numerals 0, 1, 2, 3, 4, 5, 6, 7, 8, 9. (2) a finger or a toe. (say *dijit*)

dilution (1) *n.* the quantity of a substance that is dissolved in a given amount of liquid. The smaller the quantity of substance in the liquid, the weaker the solution. We say it is more dilute. (2) **dilute** *v.* to make weaker or thinner by adding more liquid.

dimension *n.* the size of something. The measurement of the length, width and sometimes depth or thickness of something. A box, which has length, width and depth, is a three-dimensional figure.

dinosaur *n.* any of several types of extinct reptiles that lived on Earth millions of years ago. Their bodies had a covering of hard, bony plates, or scales. Dinosaurs were the most successful animals on Earth for more than 200 million years. They became extinct about 65 million years ago. No one really knows why, but scientists think the Earth became too cold for them.

Tyrannosaurus was a large flesh-eating dinosaur.

diode *n.* a valve with two electrodes⬜. It conducts electricity in one direction only.

direct current an electric current flowing in one direction only.

dirigible (1) *adj.* able to be directed or steered. (2) *n.* a large, cigar-shaped airship. It is driven by a motor and, unlike a balloon, can be steered. (say *diri-jible*)

discharge (1) *v.* to give up an electric charge⬜. (2) to give out a gas or liquid. *The car exhaust was **discharging** fumes.* (3) *n.* the process by which something is discharged.

disconnect (1) *v.* to separate a connection or pull apart. (2) to remove a source of power from a machine. To unplug an electric machine. *Please **disconnect** the vacuum cleaner when it is not being used.*

A rose leaf affected by the fungus disease black spot.

disease *n.* sickness, illness. A condition that does not let the body or mind, or a plant, function normally. Diseases in living organisms can be caused by (a) bacteria⬜ and viruses⬜; (b) pests, mainly in plants; (c) lack of one or more foods, vitamins or minerals that are necessary for health.

disinfectant *n.* a powerful chemical substance that is used to kill the microorganisms⬜ that cause disease.

disk, disc (1) *n.* a thin, flat, round object. (2) a phonograph record. (3) a ring-shaped piece of elastic cartilage⬜ found between the bones of the spine (vertebrae). (4) in computers: (a) a floppy disk is a thin, circular, flexible plastic disk, coated with magnetic material; (b) a hard disk is similar to a phonograph record and is also coated with magnetic material. Floppy disks and hard disks record and store information.

dislocate *v.* to put, or force, a bone out of place. *Mary **dislocated** her shoulder when she fell downstairs.*

solid object

object totally submerged

liquid displaced

liquid

liquid

displacement (1) *n.* the weight or volume of a liquid that is displaced by a solid object when the object is submerged in the liquid. (2) the weight of water displaced by a ship.

display *n.* a pattern of showy behavior in animals. They use it to attract or warn off other animals. Courtship is a form of display that animals use before mating.

dissect *v.* to cut into, or separate, parts of an organism in order to study an animal or plant. *The student* **dissected** *an earthworm to examine its nervous system.*

dissolve *v.* to make a solid substance or a gas break up and disappear into a liquid. Together they make a solution. Salt dissolves in water and makes a salt solution.

A soluble solid is added to a liquid. It slowly dissolves and spreads evenly through the liquid.

distil *v.* to change a liquid into a vapor (gas) by heating it, and then to change all or some part of the vapor back into a pure liquid by cooling it (condensing).

distillation *n.* the process of distilling. Distillation is used to separate a mixture of liquids with different boiling points. It is also used to make a pure liquid. This is possible because the impurities⊡ are left behind in the flask when the liquid becomes a vapor. The pure vapor cools and condenses as a pure liquid.

The balloon is distorted when squeezed between the hands.

distortion (1) *n.* the bending or twisting of something out of its usual shape. (2) **distort** *v.* sound and radio waves can be distorted. Red blood cells are distorted as they pass through the tiny capillary⊡ blood vessels.

diurnal (1) *adj.* describes an animal that is active during daylight. (2) describes an event that happens every day (every 24 hours). Diurnal rhythm: the regular changes in plants and animals that are linked to the light and dark cycle.

DNA (DeoxyriboNucleic Acid) *n.* a substance in the nucleus⊡ of each living cell that holds all the inherited characteristics of the plant or animal. A molecule of DNA is made up of two spiral chains of atoms, called a double helix.

domain *n.* a small area in a piece of metal which behaves like a tiny magnet. (say *doe-mane*)

dominant (1) *adj.* in nature, dominant describes the major (most important) plant species in a community⊡, e.g. beech trees in a beech wood, pine trees in a pine forest. (2) in some species of animals there is a dominant male who controls the herd or pack. (3) in inheritance, some factors are dominant over others, e.g. in humans, the factor for brown eyes is dominant over that for blue eyes.

dormant *adj.* describes a living organism that is at rest and not actively growing. Plant seeds remain dormant in the soil until rain and warmth start their growth. Animals that become dormant during the winter are said to hibernate⬜.

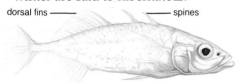

dorsal fins ——— ——— spines

The dorsal fin and spines on a fish.

dorsal *adj.* back; posterior; describes the upper surface of four-legged animals. In two-legged animals (humans) that stand upright, the dorsal surface is the back of the animal along the backbone. The dorsal fin of a fish.

dose *n.* the correct amount of medicine that is taken at one time.

down *n.* small, soft feathers of a bird. In adult birds, down feathers are found under the stiff feathers that give a bird its shape. They are the only feathers present on a young chick.

Down feathers on a young chicken. Air trapped between the down feathers keeps the bird warm.

drag (1) *n.* the resistance a moving object meets as it moves through a gas or liquid. *The swimmer struggled against the* **drag** *of the tide.* (2) *v.* to pull along with force.

drain (1) *v.* to draw off or lose liquid. *The ditches* **drained** *the flood water from the land.* (2) *n.* a pipe, or similar device, that draws water away. The passage of water through soil.

drill (1) *n.* a cutting tool for making holes; a large boring machine for drilling oil wells. (2) *v.* to make holes by using a drill.

drive (1) *v.* to control the movement of a machine or vehicle. (2) *n.* part of the transmission⬜ in a motor vehicle.

drone (1) *n.* a male honeybee. (2) a low, continuous sound. *We could hear the* **drone** *of the aircraft in the distance.*

droplet *n.* a very small drop of liquid.

drought *n.* a long, dry period of weather, with little or no rainfall. *The* **drought** *caused the crops to fail.*

drug (1) *n.* any substance used as a medicine. (2) *v.* to give a drug, in order to make someone sleepy.

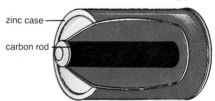

zinc case ———

carbon rod ———

A dry cell.

dry cell consists of an outer zinc case containing a white paste. A carbon rod is placed in the middle of the container. The carbon rod forms the positive side of the dry cell and the zinc case forms the negative. A voltage of 1.5 volts is supplied by the dry cell. It can only be used for short periods at a time, as in a flashlight.

duct *n.* a tube or pipe that carries a liquid or air in living organisms or buildings. Bile travels down the bile duct from the liver to the duodenum☐ (intestine). Tears are carried from the tear glands to the eyes along very fine ducts.

dune *n.* a sandhill or ridge that has been built up by the wind on the seashore or in a desert.

The sand in dunes is often held in place by grasses.

duodenum *n.* part of the digestive system (alimentary canal☐); in mammals the part between the stomach and the small intestine☐. Bile and the digestive juices from the pancreas☐ pass into the duodenum. (say *duo-denum*)

dwarf star a small, dense star that has used up most of its nuclear energy☐.

dye *n.* a substance used to give color to cloth, leather, paper, plastics and some foods. Some dyes are made from plants and animals. Most dyes are made from chemicals.

dynamite *n.* an explosive containing nitroglycerine.

dynamo *n.* a machine that changes movement (kinetic energy☐) into electric energy, e.g. the dynamo on a bicycle uses the movement of the wheel to make electricity.

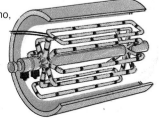

In a simple dynamo, electricity is generated by the rotation of coils of wire between opposite poles of a magnet.

E e

ear (1) *n.* the part of the body with which animals hear sound. The external (outside) ear; the parts that can be seen on each side of the head. (2) the part of a grain-producing plant that holds the seed (grain); an ear of wheat; an ear of corn.

eardrum *n.* the thin, tough layer of tissue (membrane) that separates the outer and middle parts of the ear. It vibrates when sound waves strike it, and transmits the vibrations to the tiny ossicles☐ in the middle ear.

The inside of the ear showing the position of the eardrum and tiny ossicles.

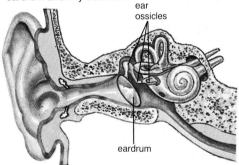

ear ossicles

eardrum

Earth *n.* the planet on which we live. Part of the solar system. Earth contains all the materials needed to support life, including an atmosphere of air. No living organisms have been found on any other planet.

earthquake *n.* a sudden shaking or trembling of the Earth's crust. In a severe earthquake cracks may appear. The ground and buildings collapse. An earthquake is caused by movement along a fault☐ beneath the Earth's surface or by volcanic activity.

earthworm *n.* a type of worm (annelid) found in the soil in large numbers. Its body is divided into parts (segments) and is covered by a thin layer, the cuticle. Most of the segments have four pairs of tiny hairs. These help the earthworm to grip the surface as it moves. Each worm has male and female parts.

ebb tide the outgoing tide, when the sea flows away from the shore. Seaweed, rocks and shells are exposed on the shore at ebb tide. *The ships left harbor on an* **ebb tide**.

echo (1) *n.pl. echoes* the sending back of a sound. Echoes are formed when sound waves are reflected, or bounced, off a hard surface. (2) *v.* to echo. *Voices* **echo** *in tunnels and among mountains.* (say *ecko*)

echolocation *n.* a method of locating objects and working out their direction by means of echoes. A way of finding or avoiding objects by sending out very high pitched sounds (ultrasounds) and listening for the echoes of the sounds. *Bats and some sea animals use* **echolocation** *to avoid obstacles and to find food.*

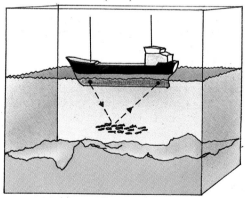

A ship using an echo sounder to detect a shoal of fish

echo sounder an instrument used on boats for testing the depth of water, using sound. A sound pulse⌷ is sent down to the sea bed; it is reflected (bounced back) and is received by the instrument. The time taken is measured. The speed at which sound travels through water is known, so the depth of the water can be calculated. *Fishing boats use* **echo sounders** *to find shoals of fish.*

eclipse *n.* the dark shadow that is cast when one body in space blocks the view of another body in space. A partial eclipse blocks part of a body. A total eclipse blocks the whole of a body. A lunar (Moon) eclipse happens when the Moon passes into the Earth's shadow. A solar (Sun) eclipse happens when the dark disk of the new Moon passes between the Earth and the Sun.

A total solar eclipse.

ecology *n.* the science that deals with the relationship of animals and plants to their natural surroundings (environment) and to each other. An ecologist is a scientist who studies the relationship between animals and plants in their natural environment.

ecosystem *n.* a balanced community of living organisms and microorganisms that exist together without interference by humans. An ecosystem includes the nonliving environment, e.g. buildings, industries, soil and rocks in which the community exists.

effector *n.* a part of the body, such as a muscle, that does something in response to a received message.

effort *n.* the force needed to do work. Lever systems, such as a wheelbarrow, are used to make work easier. There are three important parts of such systems: the load, which has to be moved; the fulcrum, or turning point, about which the lever moves; and the effort needed to use the lever.

egg *n.* a female reproductive cell (ovum) in an animal or plant.

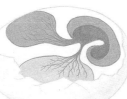

A fertilized hen's egg.

elasticity *n.* the ability (property) of a material to return to its former shape after it has been stretched out of shape. *A rubber band has* **elasticity**.

electric charge the amount of electricity held within something.

electric circuit a connected series of conducting wires and apparatus

A simple electric circuit.

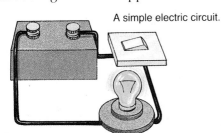

through which an electric current flows. If a switch in the current is 'off' (or open), the circuit is broken and current cannot flow.

electric current the flow of free electrons⬜ through a conductor such as a copper wire.

electricity *n.* electrical energy.

Vacuum cleaners and washing machines use electric motors.

electric motor a machine that changes electrical energy into mechanical energy.

electrode *n.* a terminal that conducts (leads) an electric current into, or out of, an electric device. A positive electrode is called an anode. A negative electrode is called a cathode.

electrolysis *n.* the breaking down of a substance in a solution into ions⬜ by passing an electric current through it. The process is used in industry for placing a thin layer of one metal over another metal, e.g. chromium-plating, silver-plating.

electromagnet *n.* an iron bar, surrounded by a coil of wire. It acts as a magnet when an electric current flows through the wire. When the current stops, the magnetic effect disappears.

electromagnetic waves waves combining electric and magnetic forces that are radiated⬜ through space. Radio waves, ultraviolet rays, infrared rays and X-rays are all forms of electromagnetic waves.

E

electron *n.* a tiny particle of matter in orbit around the nucleus⬜ of an atom. It has a negative electric charge. A free electron is one that has become separated from its atomic orbit.

electronics *n.* the study of the behavior of free electrons and their uses in science and industry.

electron microscope a very powerful microscope which uses a beam of free electrons⬜ instead of light to make objects look larger (magnify). It magnifies objects many hundreds of thousands of times.

element *n.* a simple substance made of one type of atom. It cannot be broken down any further by a chemical change.

ellipse *n.* an oval shape. The orbits of the planets are ellipses. An ellipse has two 'centers', known as foci. (say *ee-lips*)

An ellipse.

elver *n.* a young eel.

embryo (1) *n.* the tiny plant inside a seed, before it has started to grow. (2) in animals, the earliest stages of growth of the fertilized egg cell, e.g. a baby in the womb; a chick forming inside its shell. (say *em-bree-o*)

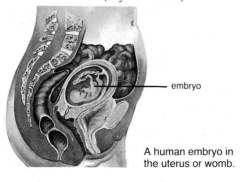

— embryo

A human embryo in the uterus or womb.

emit *v.* to send out. *A radio **emits** sound.*

emission *n.* the giving out of radiant heat, light, sound, radio waves, ultraviolet rays, electrons and other kinds of radiation.

emulsion *n.* it is formed from two liquids that do not mix (a colloidal solution). One liquid is suspended (held) in the other when the two are shaken, e.g. olive oil in water. If the emulsion is not fixed by a special substance (emulsifying agent), the two liquids will separate into two layers. The oil rises to the top. Soap and detergents are two emulsifying agents. There are many others.

enamel (1) *n.* the hard, white layer covering the dentine, on the top of a tooth outside the gum. (2) a kind of oil paint which contains a resin.

endocrine system a system of glands in animals that produce hormones⬜. The hormones are the chemical messengers that work with the nervous system to control body functions.

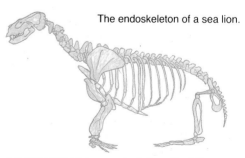

The endoskeleton of a sea lion.

endoskeleton *n.* a skeleton that lies completely inside the body of an animal, e.g. the bony skeleton of all vertebrates (animals with backbones). The muscles are attached to the skeleton. It supports the body and protects the organs inside; it gives the body shape and helps in movement.

E

energy *n.* the power and ability something has to do work. There are many forms of energy, e.g. chemical energy, as in fuels. This energy can be used in machines to produce mechanical energy. Energy can be changed from one form to another.

engine *n.* a machine that uses one type of energy to produce another type of energy.

environment *n.* the surroundings in which animal and plant organisms live. It includes all the conditions affecting the way of life of an organism. The human environment includes buildings, plant life, climate and the land itself. People are affected by the whole environment in which they live.

enzyme *n.* a catalyst□ produced in living things. Each enzyme controls a particular chemical reaction, e.g. different enzymes control the different stages of the digestion of food. (say *en-zime*)

epicenter *n.* the point on the Earth's crust that lies immediately above the center of an earthquake. (say *epi-senter*)

epidemic *n.* a disease that suddenly attacks many people in a community. *An* **epidemic** *of influenza spread through the town.*

epidermis *n.* the outer layer of tissue that protects plants and animals from injury and from loss of water.

lower epidermis

epiglottis *n.* a flap of tissue behind the tongue which closes over the glottis during swallowing. It stops the food or liquid going into the windpipe (trachea).

equation (1) *n.* in mathemathics, a written statement that two quantities are equal or balance each other. (2) in chemistry, equations are used to state the kinds of material used and produced in a chemical reaction.

equator *n.* an imaginary circle around the Earth, halfway between the North and South Poles. It divides the Earth into a northern and southern hemisphere. *When the ship crossed the* **equator** *at midday, the Sun was directly overhead.*

equatorial *adj.* to do with the region and climate at, or near, the equator. *The Amazon basin has an* **equatorial** *climate.*

the equator

equilibrium (1) *n.* a state of balance. Forces which balance are in equilibrium with each other. Unequal forces will disturb the balance or equilibrium. (2) a state of balance (coordination) between muscles, which allows an animal to stay in a certain position. (say *eequi-lib-reeum*)

equinox *n.* one of the two times in the year when day and night are of the same length in all places in the world. It happens at the time when the Sun crosses the equator. The spring or vernal equinox is about March 21st, and the autumnal equinox is about September 22nd.

era *n.* a division of geological time, in which each era spans millions of years. There are several eras, e.g. the Paleozoic Era; the Mesozoic Era.

erode *v.* to wear away rock and soil by the action of wind, rain, rivers and sea.

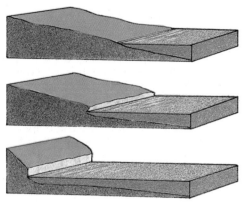

These three diagrams show how the coastline is eroded by the sea.

erosion *n.* the gradual wearing away of weathered rocks by the action of wind, rain, rivers and sea. Desert sands are caused by the erosion of rocks. Soil erosion is a serious problem to farmers in some parts of the world, especially where the tropical rain forest has been cleared to provide farmland. As a result, the heavy rains fall directly on to the soil and wash it away.

Showers of lava (liquid rock) from a volcanic eruption can be hurled over a wide area.

eruption (1) *n.* a volcanic eruption occurs when the hot molten lava⬜ and gases burst through the Earth's crust. The place where this occurs is called a volcano. Between eruptions a volcano is said to be dormant (inactive). The volcano Helgafell in Iceland surprised scientists by erupting in 1973 after being dormant for 5000 years. (2) a rash that appears on the skin. It is due to an infection, allergy⬜ or nervous condition.

escape velocity the minimum speed which an object has to reach in order to escape the pull of the Earth's gravity⬜. The escape velocity of the Earth is about 40,000 kph. The escape velocity of the Moon is about 8500 kph.

esophagus *n.* the tube down which food passes from the throat to the stomach.

estuary *n.* the wide mouth of a river where river currents meet the sea tides.

ether (1) *n.* one of a group of colorless, highly flammable liquids called ethers. One of the ethers is used as an anaesthetic⬜. (2) an imaginary substance that was once thought to fill all space, through which light and other radiation⬜ could pass.

Eustachian tube the tube that joins the middle ear to the back of the throat. It contains air and equalizes the air pressure on the eardrum, so that the drum can vibrate (move to and fro) when sound impulses strike it. (say *Yoo-stashun*)

The Eustachian tube.

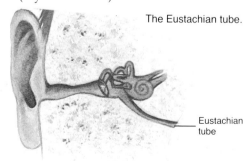

Eustachian tube

evaporate (1) *v.* to change a liquid into a vapor by using heat or moving air. (2) **evaporation** *n.* the changing of a liquid into a vapor by heat or moving air. Evaporation of water from rivers, ponds and oceans is caused by the heat of the Sun and wind.

evergreen *adj.* having green leaves all year around, e.g. holly and pine trees are evergreens. Some evergreen leaves like pine and spruce are specially formed to cut down water loss, and to let snow slide off them during winter.

evolve (1) *v.* to change slowly. New forms of plants and animals evolve over millions of years. (2) **evolution** *n.* the way in which plants and animals have changed gradually over millions of years from simple to more complex forms. *The human brain has gradually increased in size as a result of* **evolution**.

excretion *n.* the means by which living organisms get rid of their soluble waste matter. In microscopic organisms the waste substances pass out through the cell membrane⬜. More complex animals get rid of their waste substances through the skin, lungs or gills, and kidneys. Some plants excrete waste materials in their leaves and bark.

exhale *v.* to breathe out. It is the opposite of inhale, to breathe in.

exhaust (1) *v.* to use up a supply of something completely, e.g. coal in a mine. To make very tired by using up the body's energy. (2) *n.* the gas or steam given off as waste by a working engine.

exhaustion (1) *n.* the act of exhausting or being exhausted. (2) heat exhaustion: a mild form of heat stroke caused by the loss of too much water and salt from the body.

exoskeleton *n.* the hard outer covering of some animals which gives the body shape, and protects the organs inside, e.g. the shells of snails and other molluscs; the cuticle of animals such as insects and lobsters and the bony plates in the skin of tortoises. (say *exso-skeleton*)

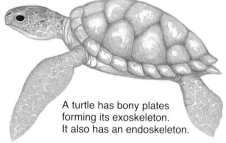

A turtle has bony plates forming its exoskeleton. It also has an endoskeleton.

expand (1) *v.* to get larger, to swell, to spread out into space. Gases and metals expand when heated. The wings of a butterfly or moth expand as they come out of the chrysalis or pupa. (2) **expansion** *n.* tending to expand. Expansion of the universe: the theory that the universe is expanding.

expel *v.* to push out with effort. Air is expelled from the lungs. Feces are expelled from the body. A baby mammal is expelled from the uterus during birth. Waste gases are expelled from engines through the exhaust pipes.

experiment (1) *n.* a test carried out in order to discover something unknown, or to demonstrate something that is already known. (2) *v.* to carry out or perform such a test. *In a chemical* **experiment** *we discovered that oxygen is a gas.*

E

expire (1) *v.* to breathe out air from the lungs; to exhale. (2) to die.

explode (1) *v.* to blow up or burst with great force and noise. *The boiler* **exploded** *when the pressure of steam became too high.* (2) to cause a violent explosion by a chemical or nuclear reaction□. (3) **explosion** *n.* a sudden expansion of gases, exerting a strong force; the breaking apart of something with great force. (4) **explosive** *adj.* tending to explode. *Dynamite is a highly* **explosive** *substance.*

exposure (1) *n.* being open or exposed to the effects of some force or element such as extreme heat or cold or wind. *The shipwrecked sailors suffered from* **exposure**. (2) in photography, the act of letting light fall on a photographic film or plate in a camera.

exterior (1) *n.* the outside surface of a living organism or object. (2) *adj.* to do with anything on the outside of an organism or object, e.g. exterior wall.

external *adj.* describes something on the outside of an organism or object, e.g. the external ear, the outer part of the ear which is found on each side of the head.

extinct (1) *adj.* no longer existing. Dinosaurs are extinct reptiles. (2) no longer active. *The volcano is* **extinct**.

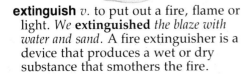

A pterodactyl, an extinct type of reptile.

extinguish *v.* to put out a fire, flame or light. *We* **extinguished** *the blaze with water and sand.* A fire extinguisher is a device that produces a wet or dry substance that smothers the fire.

extract (1) *v.* to take out or remove. To extract a tooth. To extract a mineral from the Earth, either as an element□ or as an ore□. The element is then extracted from the ore by a chemical reaction, or smelting. (2) **extraction** *n.* the taking out of one substance from a mixture of substances. (3) the process of taking out an element from an ore.

eye *n.* the sense organ for sight in humans and other animals. Many different forms of eye are found in the animal kingdom.

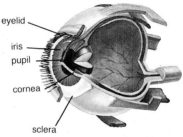

eyelid
iris
pupil
cornea
sclera

eyeball *n.* in animals with backbones (vertebrates) it is the ball-shaped part of the eye which contains a focusing lens and light-sensitive nervous tissue.

eyelash *n.* one of many short hairs found along the outer edges of the eyelids in mammals. They protect the eye from dust and other foreign bodies.

eyelid *n.* one of two muscular folds of skin in front of the eye. One eyelid lies above the eye and one below. They have eyelashes along the outer edges. Eyelids can close to protect the eye. In humans the tear gland lies under the upper lid. It makes tears which wash away any dust or grit that could damage the eye.

eyepiece *n.* the lens, or lenses, at the viewing end of a telescope, microscope or other optical instrument.

F f

fabric (1) *n.* any material made from natural or synthetic☐ fibers, e.g. wool, cotton, nylon. (2) the basic structure of something. *The fabric of a machine.*

Shops usually store fabric in rolls.

facet (1) *n.* any of the faces or surfaces on a solid object such as a crystal. A cubic crystal like sugar or salt has six facets. (2) the polished surfaces on a gemstone, such as a diamond. (3) the cornea☐ covering one ommatidium☐ of an insect's eye. (say *fa-sit*)

factor (1) *n.* a condition in the environment. The climate, the soil condition, and the presence of water are all factors that determine an environment. *The sudden cooling of the Earth millions of years ago is thought to have been a* **factor** *in the disappearance of giant reptiles from the Earth.* (2) any number that can be divided exactly into another number; thus the numbers 1, 2, 3, 4, 6, 8, 12 and 24 are all factors of 24.

fade (1) *v.* to lose color. *The paintwork had* **faded** *badly over the years.* (2) *n.* the weakening of a radio or television signal. Fading in is produced by increasing the strength of the signal.

Fahrenheit *n.* a temperature scale on which water boils at 212°F and freezes at 32°F. Named after a German scientist, G.D.Fahrenheit (1686–1736). (say *Fa-ren-hite*)

Fallopian tube in female mammals a slender tube leading from each ovary☐ to the uterus☐. The egg cell (ovum) leaves the ovary and is wafted along the Fallopian tube to the uterus by tiny hairlike cilia☐.

fallout *n.* the dangerous radioactive☐ material in the air which falls slowly down to the Earth after a nuclear explosion.

family (1) *n.* in biology, one of the units of classification☐ of animals and plants, e.g. lions, tigers and pumas are members of the cat family. A family is divided further into genera *(sing. genus)*, and the genera are divided into species. (2) a family unit consists of a male and female animal and their offspring.

famine *n.* a serious shortage of food. It causes starvation among the people. It is usually caused by a lack of rain over a long period of time, so that the crops do not grow.

fat (1) *n.* a yellowish-white, soft, greasy substance. It is usually solid at room temperature (20°C). Fats that are liquid below 20°C are called oils. Fat is found in animal tissue and plant seeds, e.g. fish liver, olives, peanuts, butter. Fat is an important animal food, with a high energy content. Some fats are naturally rich in vitamins A and D, e.g. cod liver oil. (2) the blubber under the skin of whales is nearly all fat. Fat keeps an animal warm. It is also a good energy store. Hibernating☐ animals live off their fat during the winter.

fatigue (1) *n.* in healthy animals, a feeling of extreme tiredness. They recover after a period of rest. (2) muscle fatigue due to a build-up of soluble waste products in the muscle cells during exercise. (3) a symptom of

F

some diseases, especially anemia. (4) metal fatigue, the tendency for metals and other substances to crack under repeated stress.

fatty acid an organic chemical substance made of carbon, hydrogen and oxygen. Fatty acids are found in plant and animal tissues. One of the components of fats. Fatty acids are produced when fat is digested.

fault (1) *n.* a break in the Earth's crust. A fault occurs where a mass of rock has moved up or down or sideways. A block mountain is formed where an area is raised, with faults on either side of it. (2) something that prevents a machine from working correctly. A mistake in the design of something, e.g. in an aircraft or building, which makes it unsafe or unworkable.

A fault in the Earth's crust.

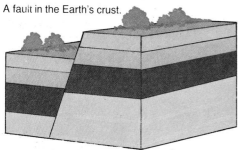

fauna *n.pl.* the animals that live in a particular region or during a period of time, e.g. the desert fauna of the Sahara region; the fauna of the Mesozoic Era in evolution.

A contour feather.

feather *n.* one of the growths that cover the skin of birds. Feathers are made of the same material as hair and fur on mammals and can be moved by muscles. Outer contour feathers give the adult bird its shape and characteristic markings. Soft down feathers lie under the contour feathers and act as an insulating layer. A feather is made up of a central shaft and barbs. The barbs bear barbules which link together.

feces *n.pl.* the solid remains of undigested food which are held in the rectum⬚. They are passed out through the anus⬚ from time to time. (say *fee-ces*)

feeler (1) *n.* an antenna⬚; one of a pair of fine, long-jointed growths found on the heads of arthropods⬚, e.g. butterflies and crabs. They are sense organs for touch and smell. (2) the tentacles of animals, such as octopus or squid. They are muscular and not jointed. They are used for feeling, gripping prey, or swimming.

feldspar (or **felspar**) *n.* any of several types of light-colored crystalline minerals found in igneous⬚ rocks such as granite. The most common feldspars contain silicon, sodium, potassium, aluminum and calcium.

female (1) *adj.* of, to do with, the sex that lays eggs or gives birth to young. (2) in plants, the female part of the flower produces the tiny ovules, which grow into seeds after they have been fertilized by the male pollen grains. (3) *n.* any female animal or plant.

femur *n.* in animals with backbones (vertebrates) it is the long bone found in the upper part of the hind leg. The top of the femur forms a joint (articulates) with the hip girdle, and the lower end articulates with the tibia bone at the knee. In humans it is the upper leg bone, sometimes called the thigh bone.

ferment (1) *v.* to break down organic substances (mainly carbohydrates) by the action of yeasts, producing alcohol and carbon dioxide. (2) **fermentation** *n.* used in the making of beer, wine and spirits. (3) the yeast or enzyme⬜ that causes fermentation.

fern *n.* a green plant having roots, stems and feathery leaves (fronds). It does not bear flowers or seeds. It reproduces from spores⬜ on the underside of the leaf. Ferns were one of the earliest plants to grow on the Earth. Giant ferns 25 m. tall grew during the Carboniferous Period. The warm, damp conditions suited them.

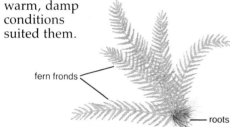

fern fronds

roots

fertile (1) *adj.* able to produce young, seeds or fruit. (2) capable of developing into a new organism, such as a fertile egg. (3) soil that is rich in nutrients and suitable for growing plants.

fertilization *n.* the joining together of male and female reproductive cells to start the growth of a new organism. The ova (egg cells) in flowers are fertilized by male pollen cells. The egg cells in animals are fertilized by the male sperm cells. (say *furtil-li-zashun*)

fertilize (1) *v.* to make the soil rich and fertile by adding plant nutrients (fertilizers). (2) to join a male to a female reproductive cell to produce a new organism.

fertilizer *n.* any material added to the land to make it fertile, e.g. manure, compost, chemical fertilizers.

fetus *n.* a young mammal in the later stages of development in the uterus⬜, when it begins to look like the adult mammal. (say *feetus*)

fever (1) *n.* a condition in which the body temperature is higher than normal (about 37°C or 98.6°F). (2) **feverish** *adj.* having a fever. *Jane was* **feverish** *when she had measles.*

fiber (1) *n.* a thin strand or thread of a material: (a) linen, cotton and hemp are natural plant fibers made of cellulose⬜. Wool and silk are natural animal fibers. (b) manmade fibers, e.g. nylon. (2) dietary fiber; plant fiber (cellulose) found in fruit and vegetables. A very important part of our diet. It helps to keep the digestive system healthy.

fiberglass *n.* very fine glass fibers that can be woven into a cloth. After being soaked in a resin, fiberglass is molded into shapes. Because it is light and strong it is used in making such things as canoes and yachts. Fiberglass wool is used to insulate⬜ buildings.

fiber optics (1) a branch of science that deals with the passage of light along strong, fine, bendable glass fibers. Each fiber is about the thickness of a human hair. Signals are changed into a series of light impulses which travel along a cable. They are changed back into signals by the receiver at the end

A fiber-optic cable contains many fine glass fibers.

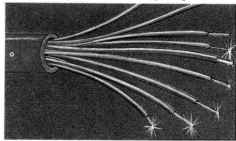

F

of the cable. The signals travel at the speed of light. (2) the fine glass fibers used in fiber-optic instruments and cables. A fibroscope is a fiber-optic instrument which can be used to see into dark and difficult places. A clear, bright image is reflected back along the inside of special viewing fibers. Surgeons use them to see inside the human body. Engineers use them to examine engines without taking them apart.

fibrinogen *n.* a soluble protein in blood. It changes to an insoluble network of fibers (fibrin) when a blood vessel is broken. The blood cells are trapped in the network, and a clot is formed. This plugs the hole in the blood vessel and stops bleeding.

fibula *n.* in humans, one of the two long bones in the lower leg, between the knee and the ankle. A similar bone in the lower part of the hind leg of animals. (say *fib-yala*)

field (1) *n.* a piece of land used for growing crops or grazing farm animals. (2) in physics, a field of force: the region inside which either magnetic, electrical or gravitational forces are active. (3) in computers, a field is one of the parts into which an 8-bit byte⬜ is divided: 2 bits, 3 bits, 3 bits⬜.

filament (1) *n.* a very fine thread. A very thin wire with a high melting point in an electric light bulb, which glows white hot when an electric current is passed through it. (2) in plants, the fine stem of a stamen, which supports the pollen head (anther).

filament

file (1) *n.* a steel tool with a ridged surface. It is used for grinding down a hard surface, cutting or smoothing. (2) in computers, a file is a collection of data, which is stored in a file directory. (3) *v.* to shape or smooth with a file.

filings *n.pl.* the small particles produced when a metal is filed, e.g. iron filings.

film (1) *n.* a thin, flexible strip of material, with a light-sensitive coating, used in cameras. An image (picture) is formed on the film when light falls on it. (2) a very thin layer of liquid, vapor or solid which forms, or is deposited, on another surface. (3) *v.* to take pictures with a camera. (4) to coat with a thin layer of something. *The windows were* **filmed** *with dirt.*

filter (1) *v.* to separate an insoluble solid from a liquid by passing it through a filter. The filter may be paper or glass fiber. The filter holds back the solid and the liquid passes through. The liquid that has passed through the filter is called the filtrate. (2) to separate dust from air by passing the air through a carbon filter. (3) *n.* the material used to filter: filter paper, sand, charcoal, glass fiber. (4) transparent material (usually colored) which changes the nature of the light that passes through the lens of a camera or telescope.

funnel with filter

filtrate

filtration *n.* the removal of solid particles from a liquid, or air, by passing it through a filter. *The* **filtration** *of drinking water removes solid impurities.*

fin (1) *n*. a movable, flat, winglike structure which protrudes (sticks out) from the body of a fish. It is made of small bones joined by a band of skin. Fish use fins for swimming and balancing in the water. (2) a fixed blade on an aircraft which keeps it steady in flight; a tail fin.

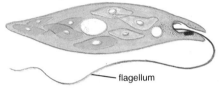

The tail fin of an aircraft.

fish *n*. a cold-blooded animal with a backbone (vertebrate), and fins instead of legs. Fish live in the sea or fresh water (rivers, lakes and ponds) and breathe through gills. Cartilaginous fish have a skeleton made of cartilage, e.g. rayfish and sharks. Bony fish have a skeleton made of bone, e.g. all fish except rays and sharks. The bodies of most fish are covered with scales of different types.

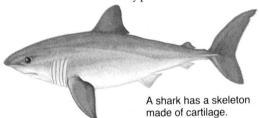

A shark has a skeleton made of cartilage.

fission (1) *n*. the splitting up of the nucleus☐ of an atom. Fission releases an enormous amount of energy. Nuclear fission is brought about by bombarding the nucleus with

A cell dividing to form two new organisms.

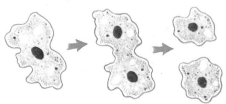

neutrons☐. (2) in biology, a form of reproduction in simple organisms in which the parent body divides into parts and each part becomes a new individual, e.g. as in the budding of yeast cells. (say *fishun*)

flagellum *n*. (*pl. flagella*) a long, whiplike structure found on some microorganisms. It works like a propeller and drives the organism through the water. Human sperm cells and some single-celled algae☐ have flagella. (say *fla-jellum*)

flagellum

flammable *adj*. able to burn easily. Alcohol is a flammable liquid.

flange *n*. a raised edge, or rim, on a pipe or wheel. It gives extra strength, holds something in place or attaches it to something else, e.g. the rim of a railway wheel. (say *flanj*)

flap (1) *n*. a surface attached to the rear edge of an aircraft's wing (aerofoil). It can be lowered to increase lift. *The pilot lowered the **flaps** as he came in to land*. (2) *v*. to flap, to move up and down, as in the flight of a bird.

flare (1) *n*. a very bright light used as a distress signal. (2) a violent explosion on the surface of the Sun, sending out large amounts of energy. (3) *v*. to burn brightly for a short time.

flask (1) *n*. a glass container with a narrow neck, used in laboratory experiments, e.g. a conical flask, round-bottomed flask, flat-bottomed flask. (2) vacuum flask. A container for keeping hot liquids hot and cold liquids cold.

F

flax *n.* a strong, natural fiber obtained from the stems of the flax plant. It is spun into thread which is used to make linen fabric. Linseed oil is obtained from the crushed seeds of the flax plant.

flea *n.* an insect without wings, that moves by jumping. It has piercing mouthparts. Fleas are parasites⃞ that live by sucking the blood of mammals and birds. Flea bites itch and can spread disease such as typhus fever.

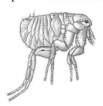

A flea uses its strong hind legs to jump great distances.

fledgling *n.* a young bird that has just hatched. It has few feathers and cannot fly.

flex (1) *v.* to bend a joint or contract a flexor muscle; to bend an arm or leg. (2) *n.* a bendable cable used to carry electric current. *The electrician fitted a new* **flex** *to the iron.*

flexible *adj.* able to be bent without breaking. Some plastics and rubber are flexible materials.

flight *n.* the act of flying; moving through air or space.

flint *n.* a very hard mineral; a type of quartz⃞ rock. It makes sparks when struck against steel or another flint. Flintstone splits easily along flat, sharp planes. Because of this, Stone Age people were able to use flints for spears and cutting tools.

flip-flop *n.* in electronics, a single computer circuit, with two stable states representing 1 and 0. It switches from one to the other (ON and OFF) in binary⃞ counting.

flipper *n.* a broad, flat forelimb in aquatic mammals and some birds, e.g. seals and penguins. Flippers are well-adapted for swimming.

flipper

float (1) *v.* to be supported on the surface or at the surface of a liquid. (2) to drift slowly downwards through air. *The parachute* **floated** *to the ground.* (3) *n.* an object that floats or keeps something afloat, e.g. a cork which keeps a fishing line afloat; a raft; a buoyancy tank on a seaplane. An object will float if it is less dense than the liquid in which it is suspended.

floppy disk a small, thin, plastic disk with a magnetic coating on which information can be recorded and stored by a computer.

flora *n.* the plants that grow in a particular region, e.g. alpine flora; or at a particular time in the evolution of the Earth, e.g. the flora of the Carboniferous Period consisted mainly of giant ferns and cone-bearing trees.

Cone-bearing trees form the main part of the flora of cold, northern forests.

flow (1) *n.* the continuous movement of a liquid, e.g. stream, river, water from a tap. (2) the movement of an electric current along a conductor⃞. (3) *v.* to move like a liquid.

F

flowchart *n.* a diagram that shows a continuous chain of operations in the order in which they must be carried out. Flowcharts are used in computer programs.

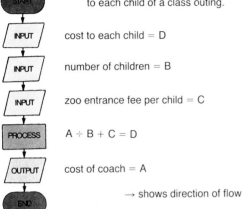

A simple flowchart to find the cost to each child of a class outing.

START

INPUT — cost to each child = D

INPUT — number of children = B

INPUT — zoo entrance fee per child = C

PROCESS — A ÷ B + C = D

OUTPUT — cost of coach = A

END

→ shows direction of flow

flower *n.* the reproductive part of seed-bearing plants. It may contain male and female organs, e.g. buttercup; or the male and female organs may be found on different flowers on the same plant, e.g. marrow and hazel tree; or the male and female organs may be borne on separate plants, e.g. primrose and holly. The female organ consists of the ovary, style and stigma. The male organ consists of the stamens, which produce the male pollen cells.

fluid (1) *n.* a nonsolid substance that flows. Any liquid or gas is a fluid, e.g. air, oil, water and petrol. All fluids, whether liquids or gases, take on the shape of the vessels in which they are placed. (2) *adj.* capable of flowing.

fluorescence *n.* a glow of light produced by certain substances that are capable of absorbing light of one wavelength and in its place emitting (giving out) light of a longer wavelength. Ultraviolet⊡ light is invisible, but fluorescent substances absorb it and can emit light of a longer wavelength, which is visible. The coloring of the fluorescence depends on the substance. Blue and green are quite common. The fluorescence disappears when the rays of ultraviolet light are cut off. (say *flur-essence*)

fluoride *n.* a chemical compound of fluorine and another element. Very small amounts of fluoride are put into main drinking water supplies because it reduces tooth decay. Too much fluoride can be harmful.

fly (1) *n.* a two-winged insect such as a housefly or gnat. (2) a hooked lure that looks like a fly, used in fishing. (3) *v.* to move through the air by using wings like a bird or butterfly. (4) to travel through the air in an aircraft. (5) to be propelled through the air, e.g. a missile, an arrow. (6) to pilot an aircraft or spacecraft; to fly a kite, balloon, etc.

flywheel *n.* a large heavy wheel attached to the rotating part or crankshaft⊡ of an engine. It helps to keep the speed steady and the rotation⊡ smooth.

flywheel

focus (1) *n.* (*pl. foci* or *focuses*) the point at which light rays meet to form a clear, sharp image after passing through a lens, or being reflected from a mirror. (2) the distance of this point from the center of the lens (focal length). (3) in mathematics, in an ellipse⊡ the foci are the two fixed points or 'centers'. The sum of the

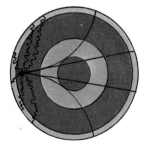

A section through the Earth showing shock waves radiating from the focus of an earthquake.

distance from each focus to any point on the curve remains the same. (4) in geology, the point in the Earth's crust from which an earthquake shock comes. Shockwaves radiate from the focus of the earthquake. Those closest to the focus cause the greatest damage. (5) *v.* to produce a sharp, clear image by using a lens or optical instrument, such as a camera, microscope or telescope.

fog *n.* an atmospheric condition; a ground mist, in which the cooling water vapor condenses on dust particles in the air. It is very difficult to see in a fog. In some parts of the world fog can cause pollution⬜.

fold (1) *v.* to bend over so that one part lies on top of another, or to press close to the body. *Birds* **fold** *their wings at rest.* In geology, layers of rock under great pressure become folded, forming mountain ranges such as the Rocky and Andes Mountains. (2) *n.* an enclosed area for keeping sheep and other animals; a pen.

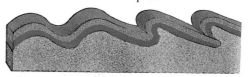

Mountains formed by the folding of layers of rock.

foliage *n.* a mass of leaves; the leaves on a plant. (say *fole-eeij*)

follicle (1) *n.* in plants, a dry seed capsule⬜, formed from one carpel⬜ that splits down one side to release the seeds. (2) in animals, any small sac⬜ or cavity. A hair follicle is a small cavity in the skin from which a hair grows. A sac forms part of certain glands.

food *n.* any substance taken in by a plant or animal which it can use for energy and growth; nourishment.

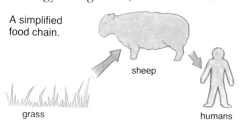

A simplified food chain.

grass   sheep   humans

food chain a series of living things that depend on each other for food energy. The chain starts with a plant which is eaten by an animal. That animal is eaten by another animal, and so on. Each organism gets energy by eating the organism that comes before it in the chain, and gives energy when it is eaten by the organism that comes after it.

food web a linked series of food chains⬜. Organisms may feed on more than one organism. They in turn

These food chains are linked through the badger to form a food web.

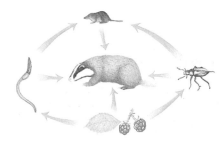

may be eaten by many other organisms. All these food chains are linked to form a complex food web.

foot (1) *n.* a unit of linear measurement, equal to 12 inches or 0.305 meters. (2) the part of the body on which an animal stands or walks. (3) the part of the muscular body of a mollusc☐ that is used for movement.

force *n.* energy, power, strength. A force cannot be seen; only its effect can be seen and measured. A force is anything that can start or stop the movement of an object, change its direction when already moving, or change the shape of an object. Gravity, wind, flowing water, magnetism, are all common forces. When the forces acting on an object are balanced, the object is in a state of equilibrium (at rest). *The wind had such* **force** *that it blew a huge tree down.*

forecast *v.* to predict what events will happen in the future, after having studied past events. To forecast the weather, based on present temperature, humidity and wind changes. Weather forecasting is not always exactly right, but, with modern techniques using satellites, predictions can be very accurate.

foreleg *n.* one of the two front legs of an animal.

forest *n.* a large area of land where trees and undergrowth are dominant. A mixed forest contains deciduous☐ as well as coniferous, trees, e.g. oak and pine. A coniferous forest contains cone-bearing trees, e.g. pine, spruce.

forge (1) *n.* a workshop, with a furnace, anvil and tools, where metal is heated and hammered into shape. (2) *v.* to work or shape metal by heating and hammering it. *The farrier* **forged** *new shoes for the horse.*

form (1) *n.* the shape and structure of an organism or object. (2) the bed of a hare, a shallow hollow, shaped to the hare's body. It is above ground. (3) *v.* to make or shape an object; to make a substance by means of a chemical change.

formation (1) *n.* the process of making a substance by a chemical change. (2) causing an effect by a physical change, e.g. the formation of mist by condensation. (3) rock formation, the pattern of rock strata (layers). (4) a pattern of flight shown by some birds. *Migrating geese fly in a V* **formation**, *with the leading bird at the point of the V.*

formula (1) *n.* (pl. formulae, formulas) chemical symbols written together which show the atoms of each element☐ in a molecule☐ of a compound. The formula gives the composition of a substance, e.g. a molecule of water is written as H_2O. This is because two H (hydrogen) atoms combine with one O (oxygen) atom. (2) a set of symbols that expresses a mathematical fact, e.g. $c = 2\pi r$, the circumference of a circle is equal to 2 times the constant π times the radius. (3) a prescription for a medicine.

A fossil of a sea animal similar to a sow bug.

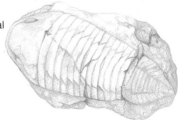

fossil *n.* the hardened remains, or shape, of an organism preserved in rock. We learn about organisms that lived millions of years ago by studying their fossils.

fossil fuel fuels such as coal, oil or natural gas, formed from the remains of living organisms millions of years ago.

fovea *n.* the 'yellow spot'; a small dip in the center of the retina⬜ in the eye of some vertebrates, including humans. It contains many cones⬜ but no rods⬜. It is the area where daylight vision is sharpest. (say *foe-veeah*)

fraction *n.* a part of something. (a) in chemistry, a part that has been separated from a mixture by a process such as distillation⬜. (b) in mathematics, part of a whole number expressed in terms of a numerator and denominator, 1/2, 3/4, 1/16, etc. A decimal fraction, e.g. 0.5, which is equal to 5/10; 0.05 is equal to 5/100, etc.

fractionating column a tall tube used in distillation⬜. The mixture of liquids is heated and the vapors cool as they rise in the tube; each vapor condenses at a different level and is

In this fractionating column crude oil is distilled.

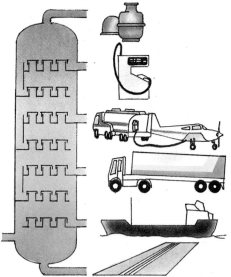

collected. The different substances produced from crude oil are collected in this way.

fracture (1) *n.* a break, split or crack in a hard material. A break in a bone. (2) the texture of the broken surface of a mineral, such as a metal or rock. (3) *v.* to break, crack or split a hard material or object.

freeze *v.* to change a liquid to a solid by cooling it to a low temperature. Different substances freeze at different temperatures. Pure water freezes to form ice at 0°C or 32°F. A pure substance always freezes at the same temperature, called its freezing point. Freezing is the opposite of melting.

←a frequency of 2 waves per second→

frequency (1) *n.* (*pl. frequencies*) in physics, the number of complete vibrations⬜ (usually per second) in a wave motion. The greater the frequency in sound waves, the higher the pitch of the sound. There is a wide range of radio waves, all with different frequencies. (2) the number of times something happens within a given time. *Trains run with greater* **frequency** *during the rush hour.*

freshwater *adj.* of, or living in, water found in lakes, and in rivers containing water that is not salty. *The minnow is a* **freshwater** *fish.*

friction *n.* the force that slows down movement and produces heat; the drag effect when two surfaces are rubbed together. Rough surfaces produce greater friction. Oil is used to reduce friction between the moving parts of a machine.

A poison arrow frog. Frogs spend much of their time on land but lay their eggs in ponds.

F

e.g. coal, oil, wood, petroleum. (2) in living organisms, the food that is taken in, absorbed and broken down to release energy.

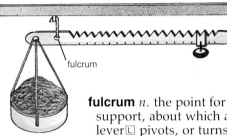

fulcrum

frog *n.* a cold-blooded, amphibian⬛ vertebrate (animal with a backbone). It has a smooth, moist skin with no scales; long, powerful hind legs; webbed feet and no tail. It moves by leaping. It swims in water.

front (1) *n.* the part of an animal or object that faces forward. (2) in meteorology (weather science), a boundary or line along which a mass of air meets and moves into another mass of air, which is either colder or warmer. *See* **cold front; warm front**.

frost *n.* frozen dew or water vapor, in the form of crystals, deposited on or near the ground, when the temperature is below freezing point.

frostbite *n.* injury to the tissues on exposed parts of the body, face, ears, hands and feet, due to intense cold. Frostbite damages the blood supply. In severe cases of frostbite the injured tissue dies and drops off.

fruit *n.* in biology, the ripe ovary of a plant containing the seeds. There are many different types of fruit: berries, capsules, pods (legumes), etc. Tomatoes, apples, cucumbers, nuts and peas are all types of fruit.

fry *n.* a young fish, e.g. salmon fry.

fuel (1) *n.* a material that is used to produce heat or power by burning. Most fuels are carbon compounds,

fulcrum *n.* the point for support, about which a lever⬛ pivots, or turns.

function (1) *n.* the work carried out by any part of a living organism. The function of the blood is to carry oxygen and nutrients⬛ to the body tissues and to carry away the soluble waste. *The* **function** *of plant rootlets is to take in water and salts from the soil.* (2) the work done by any machine or the purpose of that work. (3) *v.* to work as intended. *The* **function** *of robots is to perform tasks automatically.*

fungus *n. (pl. fungi)* any one of a large group of simple plants, that includes yeasts, molds, rusts, mushrooms and puff balls. Fungi contain no chlorophyll⬛. A fungus may consist of a single cell or a mass of cellular, tubelike threads (hyphae). They usually feed off dead or decaying organisms. Fungi usually reproduce by spores⬛. Spores are produced by special organs that grow up from the hyphae.

Two types of fungi.

funnel (1) *n.* a piece of chemical apparatus with a wide mouth and a narrow tube. It is used for pouring liquids into narrow-necked containers. It is also used to hold a filter, when liquids are filtered. (2) separating funnel: a special funnel fitted with a tap. It is used to separate two liquids that do not mix.

fur (1) *n.* the soft, thick hair covering the body of many mammals, e.g. rabbits, moles. It keeps the body warm. (2) *v.* to become coated with a furry deposit, e.g. the scale of calcium and magnesium carbonates in a kettle that has been used for boiling water.

furnace *n.* an enclosed construction with a controlled air supply, used for burning fuels to provide great heat. The heat may be used in heating and hot water systems or for smelting ores and refining metals.

fuse (1) *v.* to heat a powdered solid so that it melts and forms one solid mass. (2) *n.* a long, slow-burning cord used to fire explosives from a distance. It gives time for the people setting the charge to get clear of the explosion. (3) a device that contains a thin wire which heats up and melts if too strong an electric current is passed through it. This breaks the circuit and acts as a safety device. Without a fuse a whole circuit can overheat and cause a fire. *The electric iron has blown a* **fuse.** *There must be a fault in the wiring.*

fuselage *n.* the main body of an aircraft, not including the wings, tail and engines. (say *few-selaj*)

fuselage

fusion (1) *n.* a melting together of two or more solid substances, to form a new substance. (2) nuclear fusion: the joining together of a number of lighter nuclei to form a heavier one, e.g. when hydrogen atoms are joined together to form helium, great energy is released. This is the nuclear fusion process. (say *few-shun*)

G g

galaxy *n. (pl. galaxies)* a huge system of stars, planets, dust and gases, in outer space. There are millions of galaxies. The Sun, Earth and planets belong to the galaxy called the Milky Way; it is a spiral-shaped galaxy.

X marks the position of Earth—a tiny speck in the enormous Milky Way galaxy.

gale *n.* a very strong wind. In meteorology (weather science), a wind that blows at speeds between 32 and 63 mph (between 51 and 101 kph). Gales are winds of force 7–10 on the Beaufort scale.

gall bladder a small sac⊡, close to the liver, where bile⊡ is stored. The bile passes from the gall bladder, down the bile duct, to the duodenum, where it helps to digest fat.

gallon *n.* a unit of liquid measure, equal to 8 pints or 4.54 liters in the UK gallon; 231 cubic inches or 3.78 liters in the US gallon.

galvanize *v.* to cover an iron surface with a layer of zinc. The metal object is dipped in hot liquid (molten) zinc. The zinc keeps the iron from corroding (wearing away by chemical action).

gamete *n.* a male or female reproductive (sex) cell. It has half the normal number of inheritance bodies (chromosomes) in its nucleus⊡. A male gamete is very small and swims with a flagellum⊡. A female gamete is usually bigger and contains a lot of extra cell material. It does not move.

A male animal gamete swims using its tail.

A male plant gamete of a pollen cell is moved by insects and wind.

gamma ray a harmful radiation⊡ of very short wavelength. It is given out by radioactive atomic nuclei.

gas (1) *n.* a state of matter that has a mass but no shape. It fills and takes the shape of a container. Air is a mixture of gases. (2) **gaseous** *adj.* like a gas. (say *gaseeus*)

gasoline *n.* petrol; a highly inflammable liquid. It is used as a fuel for internal combustion engines, e.g. cars.

gastric (1) *adj.* to do with the stomach. The stomach produces gastric juices for digestion. (2) **gastric ulcer** a painful condition in which part of the lining of the stomach wears away. (3) **gastritis** *n.* inflammation of the stomach lining.

gate *n.* an arrangement of transistors⊡ that works on pulses⊡ traveling along the circuits of a computer. All the processing is done through the gates.

gauge (1) *n.* a measuring instrument. (2) a standard measurement, as in the width of railway tracks, the bore (inside width) of a gun barrel, and the thickness of a wire. (3) *v.* to measure accurately with an instrument. (4) to assess, or judge, by using facts already known. (rhymes with *rage*)

gauze (1) *n.* a fine, loosely woven cloth, usually made of cotton, used for surgical dressings and bandages. (2) a similar material made of fine wire. (say *gawze*)

gear (1) *n.* a system of cogs (toothed wheels) which transfer movement from one part of a machine to another part. In a car the gears in the gearbox change the spinning speed of the crankshaft⊡ to a lower speed, to drive the wheels. (2) a group of machine parts, as in the landing gear of an aircraft.

The teeth on the cogs in this gear link to transfer movement from one cog to another.

gearbox *n.* the container that holds the gear system.

gearwheel *n.* a wheel, with teeth or cogs, that connects with a similar wheel, or a chain, to transfer motion, e.g. as on a bicycle.

Geiger counter an instrument that detects and measures radioactivity (chiefly alpha, beta and gamma rays). Named after Hans Geiger (1882–1947). (say *Guy-gur*)

G

gelatin *n.* a soluble protein found in animal bones and cartilage; a yellowish, transparent solid. It is used in photography, in the making of glues, and in foodstuffs. (say *jell-etin*)

gem *n.* a precious stone; a very hard, transparent, crystalline mineral that splits along definite planes. When cut and polished, gemstones sparkle in light and are used as jewels. Diamonds, rubies, sapphires and emeralds are gemstones.

gene *n.* a small part of a chromosome⬜ which controls or causes the development of a characteristic of an organism, e.g. the genes for eyes or hair color. (say *jean*)

generate (1) *v.* to produce; to bring into being. *Heat is* **generated** *in some chemical reactions.* (2) to produce electricity by using a generator.

generation (1) *n.* a single stage in a family history. Parents and offspring belong to two different generations. Brothers, sisters and cousins belong to the same generation. (2) in technology (esp. robotics), the stage of invention, e.g. second-generation robots are the second range of models, more advanced than first-generation.

generator (1) *n.* a chemical apparatus that produces a supply of gas. (2) a machine for changing mechanical energy⬜ into electrical energy.

A bicycle dynamo is a generator that uses mechanical energy from the turning wheel.

genetic *adj.* to do with genes and inherited characteristics.

genus *n.* a unit of classification of living organisms, into which a family is divided. A genus is divided into species.

geography *n.* the study and description of the Earth's surface. Geography teaches about countries and people; about oceans, rivers and mountains; about crops and climate; and about the natural resources such as minerals, oil and coal.

geology *n.* the scientific study of the Earth's crust. Geologists examine the layers of soil, rocks, fossils, and the minerals in the Earth. They work out how mountains, continents and oceans were formed, and how the surface of the Earth, and the animals and plants, have changed during the millions of years of the Earth's history.

geometry *n.* the mathematical study of points, lines, angles, surfaces and solid shapes, e.g. squares and cubes, circles and spheres.

geostationary orbit one in which a satellite is orbiting around the Earth at a speed that exactly matches the speed of the Earth's rotation, so that it always stays above the same point on the Earth's surface. To an observer on Earth the satellite appears to be stationary in the sky.

geothermal energy energy that comes from the heat deep inside the Earth. Hot-water springs and geysers⊡ are examples of geothermal energy. Some countries use this energy for central heating and to generate electricity.

In the desert, gerbils rely mainly on seeds for their food.

gerbil *n.* a small, mouse-like mammal with a long tail and long hind legs. It moves by leaping. Gerbils are desert animals and live in parts of Africa and Asia. They are sometimes kept as pets.

germ (1) *n.* any microscopic organism, such as a bacterium⊡ or a virus⊡, that causes disease. (2) a seed or bud that can grow to form a new organism. (say *jerm*)

germinate *v.* to start to grow; in plants, seeds and spores germinate and grow into new plants called seedlings. Conditions of warmth and moisture must be suitable for **germination** *(n.)*.

gestation *n.* the period of development of an embryo mammal inside the uterus⊡; the time between fertilization of the egg cell and the birth of the fetus⊡. Small mammals have a shorter gestation than large mammals. Gestation in humans is 9 months. Gestation in elephants is 3 years.

geyser *n.* a natural, hot spring that shoots hot water and steam up into the air at intervals. Some geysers are fairly regular. 'Old Faithful', in Yellowstone National Park, shoots out steam for about 4 minutes every hour. (say *guy-zer*)

G

An active geyser.

gill (1) *n.* an organ of respiration⊡ (breathing) of many animals living in water. The gills, rich in tiny blood vessels, take in dissolved oxygen from the water and give out carbon dioxide into the water. (2) the radiating membranes⊡ on the underside of some cap fungi such as the mushroom. The gills bear the spores, which grow into new fungi.

girder *n.* a long, strong beam used to support the framework and floors of buildings, rocket launch pads, bridges, oil rigs, etc. It is usually made of steel, but may be made of concrete or wood.

gizzard *n.* a strong, muscular sac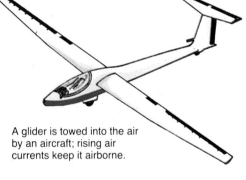
found in birds and some animals
without backbones (invertebrates),
such as molluscs 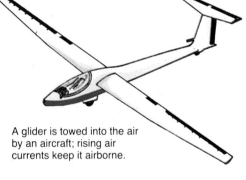. The gizzard is
part of the digestive system. It comes
after the crop and is used for grinding
the food. In birds, it often contains
small stones which help to break up
the food.

glacial *adj.* to do with ice and glaciers.
Glacial soil is soil deposited by
glaciers. (say *glay-shal*)

glacier *n.* a slow-moving river of ice.
Glaciers are formed from deep snow
on high mountains. The weight of
snow presses down so hard that the
snow beneath is turned into a solid
sheet of ice. The whole ice sheet flows
like a river, but very slowly,
sometimes only a few centimeters a
year. Other glaciers may move as
much as 100 meters a year.

gland (1) *n.* in plants, a small organ
that produces certain chemicals, e.g.
gum, resin, tannin and latex, on the
surface of some plants. (2) in animals,
an organ that takes certain chemicals
from the blood and turns them into
special chemicals. The body either
uses these for certain functions, such
as digestion, or excretes them through
the kidneys or skin as waste products.

Section of the skin showing a gland.

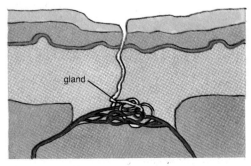

gland

Glands that pass their chemicals
straight into the blood are called
endocrine glands. Glands that pass
their chemicals into small tubes
(ducts) that open into the gut or onto
the skin are called exocrine glands.
Sweat glands are exocrine glands.

glass *n.* a hard, transparent, brittle
material. Most glass is made from
sand, lime and soda ash, which fuse
together to form a clear, very thick
(viscous) liquid. This can easily be
shaped into flat sheets for window
panes or into containers such as
glasses or bowls. The glass sets hard
as it cools. It is not easily attacked by
chemicals.

A glider is towed into the air
by an aircraft; rising air
currents keep it airborne.

glide *v.* to ascend or descend smoothly
and gradually at a normal angle in an
aircraft without an engine (glider). It
is possible to glide over long distances
by using air currents. Rising currents
of hot air (thermals) help gliders gain
height. Gliders have simple controls,
which pilots use to direct their flight.
Birds such as the albatross are also
excellent gliders.

glucose *n.* a soluble sugar; a type of
carbohydrate 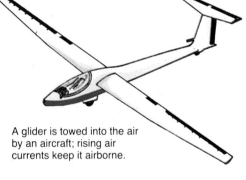 found in animals and
plants. It is produced in green plants
from carbon dioxide and water, using
the energy from sunlight

(photosynthesis). In animals, glucose is produced as the last stage in the digestion of carbohydrates.

glue *n.* a thick, sticky liquid used for sticking things together. It is called an adhesive. Glues are made from animal bones, hoofs and tree resins.

gold *n.* a heavy, yellow, metallic element; a precious metal used in coins, jewellry and ornaments. It is easily beaten into shape and can be drawn out into thin wire.

gonad *n.* in animals, the male or female organ, that produces the reproductive cells (gametes); the ovary□ or testes□. There are two gonads in each animal. In some animals, including humans, the gonads also produce chemicals (hormones) that affect growth and development.

gorge *n.* a deep, narrow pass with steep, rocky sides. A river may flow through it.

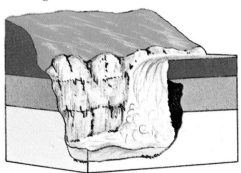

A waterfall tumbling into a deep gorge.

gourd (1) *n.* the fruit of a plant related to the melon, pumpkin and squash family. It has a tough skin, which is often striped in bright green, yellow and orange. It is not fit to eat. Gourds are often dried and varnished and used as ornaments. They can also be hollowed out and used as bowls or ladles. (2) a trailing or climbing plant belonging to this family.

gradient (1) *n.* an ascending or descending slope. (2) the steepness or degree of such a slope. (3) in physics, the rate of change of temperature or pressure.

graft (1) *v.* to join one thing to another: (a) in plants, to insert a shoot or bud into the stem of another plant. (b) in surgery, to take a piece of skin or bone from one part of the body and replace it in another part, where it will grow. (2) *n.* the bud, shoot or animal tissue that is grafted.

grain (1) *n.* the small, hard seed in the fruits of cereal crops such as wheat, barley, rice, maize and oats. (2) a tiny, solid particle of matter, e.g. a grain of sand or salt. (3) the smallest unit in the Troy system of weights. It is used by goldsmiths to weigh small amounts of precious metals. Grain weights are sometimes used in dispensing tiny doses of medicine.

gram *n.* a unit of weight in the metric system. 1 kilogram is equal to 1000 grams.

Granite is used in making roads.

granite *n.* a type of igneous rock; one that was formed from hot, liquid rock. Granite is very hard and contains different minerals: clear, glass-like quartz; pinkish feldspar; and shiny black mica. (say *gran-it*)

G

granule (1) *n.* a small piece of solid material, the size of several grains. (2) tiny particles of matter found inside plant and animal cells.

graph (1) *n.* a diagram in which a line is drawn to show the relationship between two changing quantities, e.g. the solubility of a chemical at different temperatures. (2) a bar graph, which shows quantities as thick lines or bars of different lengths, e.g. rainfall variation over 12 months, in one area.

graphite *n.* a soft, black, shiny form of carbon. It is used in pencil leads, and as a dry lubricant to ease locks and reduce friction (rubbing) in moving parts of some machines. (say *graf-ite*)

gravel *n.* a loose mixture of small pebbles and pieces of rock larger than grains of sand.

gravity *n.* the invisible force exerted by the Earth, Moon or other bodies in space, on all solids, liquids and gases. It attracts smaller objects, on or near the Earth's surface, toward its center. A stone thrown up in the air will fall to the ground. It is being pulled by gravity. Gravity gives people and objects weight. It draws plant roots down into the soil. The force of gravity decreases the further you are away from the center of the Earth.

grid (1) *n.* the system of linked electricity cables and pylons that allows electricity to be sent over great distances, even from one country to another when needed. (2) a network of crossing parallel lines forming squares, as on graph paper or a map. The grid lines on a map make it possible to find an exact position.

groove (1) *n.* a long, narrow cut hollowed out of a surface with a tool. (2) *v.* to make such a hollow in a surface.

group (1) *n.* a number of animals, plants or objects brought together (classified) because of similar characteristics. (2) in chemistry, a number of elements with similar properties, forming one vertical column in the periodic table of elements.

grow (1) *v.* to become larger in size because of a natural process; to develop. (2) to cause to grow by planting seeds and growing crops. *The farmers* **grew** *corn on their land.*

growth (1) *n.* an increase in size or development of a plant or animal. (2) a mass of cells (a tumor) in an animal or plant, which is not growing normally.

grub *n.* the short, fat, wormlike larva☐ of an insect, which hatches from the egg and develops later into the pupa☐ or chrysalis☐.

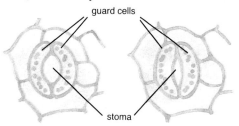

The guard cells on the left have allowed the stoma to become bigger. The guard cells on the right have almost closed up the stoma.

guard cell in plants, one of a pair of crescent-shaped cells. They control the size of the opening of the stoma☐, and so control the flow of gases and water vapor through the plant leaves and stems. As the plant loses water, the guard cells become floppy (flaccid) and close the stoma. This keeps more water vapor from leaving the plant.

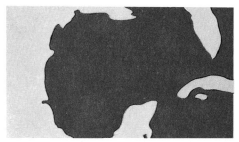

The Gulf of Mexico.

H h

gulf *n.* a large area of sea or ocean that is partly surrounded by land, e.g. the Gulf of Mexico.

gullet *n.* the tube that leads from the mouth to the stomach in animals. It is part of the alimentary canal⬜ and digestive system. It is also called the esophagus.

gum (1) *n.* the fleshy tissue around the roots of the teeth in mammals. (2) in plants, a sticky, liquid secretion which hardens as it dries. It is often produced where the stem or trunk is damaged. Some gums are only sticky when moist. They are used as adhesives to stick envelopes and other things together, e.g. gum arabic. (3) chewing gum, a sweetened, flavored gum.

gut (1) *n.* the alimentary canal⬜ in animals. The tube through which food passes and is broken down (digested) by digestive juices. The soluble food substances are absorbed from the gut and are used by the tissues. Undigested waste passes out from the body of the animal. (2) a tough cord made from animal intestines⬜. It is used to sew up surgical wounds and in stringed musical instruments such as the violin and cello. It was at one time used in tennis rackets, but nylon is now replacing it.

habit *n.* a special or usual way of doing something. Characteristic behavior in plants or animals, e.g. a twining habit of some plants such as honeysuckle. *A* **habit** *of leopards is to climb trees.*

habitat *n.* the place where a plant grows naturally, or the place where an animal usually lives in the wild. *The desert is the natural* **habitat** *of the giant cactus. The African savanna is the* **habitat** *of animals such as lions, zebra and giraffe.*

hail *n.* small pieces of ice that fall like rain during some thunderstorms. On rare occasions hailstones can be very large and cause damage to people and property.

hair (1) *n.* a fine, threadlike outgrowth on the bodies of mammals. The color depends on the amount of coloring pigment (melanin) in the hair, and the number of air bubbles. Air bubbles give the hair a silvery look. The color and distribution of body hair depend on the type of mammal. Whiskers are hairs that are very sensitive. Fur is very thick, soft, fine hair found on some mammals, e.g. cats. It protects against loss of heat. (2) in plants: (a) root hairs, special fine outgrowths

H

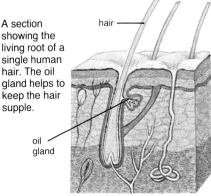

A section showing the living root of a single human hair. The oil gland helps to keep the hair supple.

hair

oil gland

from the outer cells of roots. Water and salts pass across them into the plant. (b) a stiff hooked hair (barb) found on stems, leaves and fruits of some plants.

half-shaft *n.* in a car, the shaft that carries one driving wheel so that it can turn independently of the wheel on the other side, when the car corners.

halo *n.* a ring of light that at times surrounds the Sun, Moon and other bodies. It is caused by the bending of light by ice crystals in the Earth's atmosphere.

hammer *n.* one of the three tiny bones (ossicles) in the middle ear of mammals. It lies next to the eardrum and the anvil. It is shaped rather like a hammer. The ossicles pass the sound vibrations from the eardrum to the inner ear.

hard *adj.* firm; solid to the touch; not easily dented. Metals and rocks are hard materials.

hard disk a rigid (firm), circular sheet of plastic, rather like a phonograph record. It is coated with a magnetic

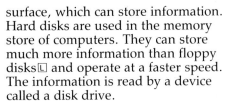

surface, which can store information. Hard disks are used in the memory store of computers. They can store much more information than floppy disks⬜ and operate at a faster speed. The information is read by a device called a disk drive.

hardware (1) *n.* the general name for the electronic parts of a typical computer. (2) articles made of metal, especially pans, tools and nails.

hard water water that does not easily form a lather (bubbles) with soap. The hardness is due to magnesium and calcium salts in the water. They combine with the soap to form scum (solid particles on the surface of the water). Temporary hardness is caused by soluble salts, but these can be removed by boiling the water. They are turned into insoluble salts, which form the furry deposit, or scale, in kettles.

hardwood *n.* strong, dense wood obtained from slow-growing trees such as the oak, teak and maple. Cone-bearing trees, such as pine, produce lighter softwood. Hardwood makes longer-lasting furniture, doors, window frames and floors than softwood. At one time it was widely used in building boats because it does not easily absorb water.

hatch (1) *v.* to break out of an egg, as a young animal. Some reptiles and birds hatch out of eggs by biting or pecking the shell. Many birds have a hard knob on their beaks which helps them break their shell. (2) to produce young from eggs after incubating them (keeping them warm and safe). Birds sit on eggs to incubate them. Some reptiles, such as turtles, bury their eggs in the warm sand to incubate them and protect them.

head (1) *n.* the part of the body in animals that contains the brain, mouth, eyes and ears. (2) an area of land that projects out to sea; a headland. (3) a flat, closely packed cluster of flowers as in a daisy or dandelion. (4) the top of an object such as a nail, screw or pin.

health (1) *n.* freedom from illness or disease in animals and plants. A condition of the body or plant in which all the factors necessary for life and growth are present, and all the natural processes are working normally. (2) **healthy** *adj.* having good health.

hear *v.* to receive and detect sounds through the ear.

hearing *n.* the ability to hear. Dogs have acute hearing. They can hear sounds that humans cannot.

heart *n.* the hollow, muscular organ in animals, which pumps blood around the body. In vertebrates (animals with backbones) the heart is divided into auricles□ and ventricles□. Mammals and birds have two auricles and two ventricles. Fish have only one auricle and one ventricle. Amphibians, such as frogs, have two auricles and one ventricle.

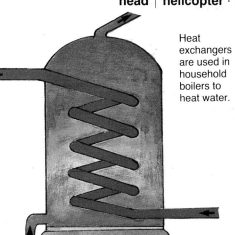

Heat exchangers are used in household boilers to heat water.

H

heat exchanger a device for transferring heat from one fluid to another, without the fluids actually mixing. An arrangement of pipes carries hot and cold liquids close together. Heat passes from the hot to the cold fluid and raises its temperature.

heavy (1) *adj.* having great mass. Lead is a very heavy metal. *Large concrete blocks are too* **heavy** *to move without machinery.* (2) in chemistry, (a) describing a precipitate, which sinks to the bottom of the liquid. (b) describing chemicals, such as sulfuric acid, lime, nitric acid and carbonates, which are used in large quantities in industrial processes. They are manufactured by the heavy chemical industry.

hectare *n.* a unit of surface measurement (area) of land in the metric system. 1 hectare = 10,000 square meters. (say *heck-tare*)

helicopter *n.* a kind of aircraft that can rise vertically from the ground, hover, or move in any direction. It does this by means of large, rotating blades (rotors), which are fixed to the top of the helicopter and turn horizontally.

The heart of an amphibian.

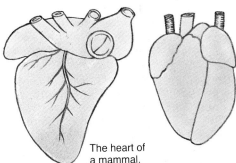

The heart of a mammal.

helium *n*. a simple chemical element; a very light gas, lighter than air. It has no color or smell. It does not react easily with other chemicals. It is used for filling balloons and airships, which are then able to float upward into the sky. (say *heel-eeum*)

helix (1) *n*. the rim of cartilage (gristle) that gives the outer ear its shape. (2) a spiral or coil shape, as found in some corkscrews. Certain protein molecules (such as DNA) have their atoms arranged in the form of a helix or double helix. Some snail shells are arranged in a helix shape.

hemisphere (1) *n*. half a sphere. In geography, the Earth is divided by the equator into a northern hemisphere and a southern hemisphere. It is also divided into a western hemisphere, which includes North and South America, and an eastern hemisphere to which Europe, Asia, Africa, India and Australia belong. (2) one of two halves into which the cerebrum⬜ of the brain is divided in mammals. (say *hem-is-fere*)

hemoglobin *n*. the red coloring matter in red blood cells⬜ of vertebrates (animals with backbones), and in the blood plasma of some invertebrates. It carries oxygen from the lungs to the body tissues. When it is carrying oxygen it is bright red in color, but when it gives up the oxygen it turns a deep bluish red. (say *he-mo-globin*)

hemp (1) *n*. a family of plants that grow in Asia. The stems provide a tough fiber which is used for making strong rope and coarse cloth. (2) the fiber itself. (3) a drug substance, also called cannabis, which is made from the dried leaves and flowers of the plant. It is smoked or eaten and is damaging to the health.

hen *n*. a female bird, especially the domestic fowl or chicken. A peahen is the female of the peacock. It is a drab-looking bird compared with the male.

heptagon *n*. a plane figure with seven angles and seven sides.

A regular heptagon.

herb (1) *n*. any seed plant that does not have a woody stem above ground. Some herbs die in the first year after forming seeds; others die down above ground but sprout again next year. (2) any plant whose leaves, stems, roots or flowers are used in medicines, e.g. the foxglove produces digitalis, a drug used to treat heart disease. (3) any plant used for flavoring food, e.g. rosemary, parsley.

Elephants are herbivores. They use their long trunks to reach high branches.

herbivore (1) *n*. any animal that feeds only on plants. (2) **herbivorous** *adj*. cows, sheep and giraffes are herbivorous animals. (say *her-bi-vore*)

herd (1) *n.* a group of cattle or other large animals which feed and live together in the wild, e.g. elephants, antelopes. (2) a group of cattle that can be driven (herded) across country. *The farmer has a dairy* **herd** *of sixty cows.*

hereditary *adj.* in animals and plants, to do with characteristics passed down from one generation to another. Eye color is hereditary. The color and shape of a flower is also a hereditary characteristic. Hemophilia is a hereditary disease of the blood that affects human males. The blood does not clot properly, and severe bleeding can occur from small injuries.

heredity *n.* the passing on of characteristics by plants or animals from one generation to another.

hermaphrodite (1) *n.* an animal with male and female sex organs, e.g. an earthworm. (2) a plant with stamens☐ and pistil☐ in the same flower. (say *her-maf-ri-dite*)

heroin *n.* a powerful habit-forming, narcotic drug, made from morphine.

hertz *n.* the international unit of frequency of radio waves. The symbol is Hz. 1 hertz is equal to 1 cycle per second. It is named after Heinrich Hertz, a German physicist, (1857–94).

heterotroph *n.* any living organism that cannot make food from simple substances. It gets food from plants, animals or decaying matter; all animals, fungi and most bacteria are heterotrophs. (say *hetero-trofe*)

hexagon *n.* a plane figure with six angles and six sides.

hibernate (1) *v.* in animals, to pass the winter in a dormant (not active) state. Dormice and frogs hibernate. (2) **hibernation** *n.* the state of being dormant during the winter.

hide (1) *n.* the natural skin of certain animals, e.g. elephant, rhinoceros. (2) the skin of a dead animal, e.g. cow, calf, goat, which is treated and dyed to produce leather. *My satchel is made of pure* **hide.** (3) a special tent or hut made to look like the surroundings (camouflaged). Scientists and people observe the behavior of animals, such as birds, from inside.

high pressure (1) having a high barometric pressure. (2) *n.* a mass of air near the Earth which presses down strongly because it is being cooled. The molecules of air gases move closer together and the gases become denser (heavier).

high tide the highest water level on the shore reached by the tide. There are normally two high tides and two low tides in every twenty-four hours. Tides vary with the phases of the Moon. Near the times of the new and full Moon, when the Sun, Moon and Earth are in line, the tides are higher. These are called spring tides, and happen twice a month. Very low, or neap, tides occur when the Moon is in its first or last quarter.

The hind legs of a kangaroo are very long and powerful.

hind leg one of the legs at the back or rear of an animal.

hinge (1) *n.* a type of joint on which doors and windows swing to and fro or up and down. (2) in humans, the knee and elbow joints are known as hinge joints, because of their action. *The cat flap was* **hinged** *to open both ways.* (3) *v.* to fix by means of hinges.

hip (1) *n.* in mammals and some other animals with backbones, the joint at which the thigh bone (femur) is attached to the pelvis⃞. It is a ball and socket joint. (2) rose hip: the fleshy fruit of the rose. It is rich in vitamin C.

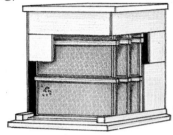

Trays of wax honeycombs are stored in this hive.

hive (1) *n.* a special case or box for keeping honeybees. (2) a colony of bees in a hive.

hoist (1) *n.* a device used to lift or raise something heavy, by means of a pulley or a lever. (2) *v.* to lift up or to pull up. *The cargo was* **hoisted** *aboard the ship.*

hollow (1) *adj.* not solid; having a space inside. Water passes through a hollow pipe. (2) *n.* a bowl-shaped dip in the ground. *We camped in a* **hollow** *in the woods.*

hologram *n.* a hologram is a picture that appears to have depth. It looks more realistic than an ordinary photograph. The image appears to be in three dimensions (3D). A hologram is made with the use of laser⃞ beams and photographic plates.

holography *n.* a type of photography that uses a laser⃞ beam and a photographic plate to produce a three-dimensional image. (say *holl-ow-gra-fee*)

hominid *n.* the scientific name for humans, and their ancestors.

Homo sapiens the scientific name for the only species of man alive today. From the Latin, meaning 'wise man'.

horizon *n.* the line where the sky appears to meet the ground or the sea. We cannot see beyond the horizon because the Earth's surface is curved. *The ship disappeared slowly over the* **horizon**.

horizontal *adj.* flat; level; lying parallel with the horizon. *The surface of still water is* **horizontal**.

hormone (1) *n.* a chemical messenger. One of many organic substances made in certain glands in the body. Hormones pass directly into the blood and have a rapid and important effect on other organs. They control growth and sexual development. Hormones, and the glands that make them, form the endocrine system⃞. (2) a substance in plants that controls the growth of the plant.

horn (1) *n.* a hard, pointed outgrowth found on the heads of some animals, usually paired, e.g. rhinoceros horn, deer antlers. (2) the substance of which horns are made.

horsepower *n.* a unit for measuring the power of an engine; one horsepower is equal to 746 watts. The unit was first used by James Watt, a famous Scottish mathematician and scientist (1736–1819).

horticulture *n.* the science of growing flowers, fruits and vegetables.

host *n.* any plant or animal that provides a parasite⃞ with food and protection.

hot spring a place where hot water and steam bubble up out of cracks in the ground. Hot springs are found in regions where Earth tremors, and sometimes volcanic activity, occur, e.g. New Zealand and parts of N. America. Hot gases from deep inside the Earth are forced up through cracks in the Earth's crust. Steam and sulfur gases may seep out through the cracks.

hour *n.* the unit of time equal to sixty minutes. There are twenty-four hours in one day.

hover *v.* to stay in the air over the same place. Humming birds hover as they suck nectar from flowers. Some birds of prey and dragonflies hover. They beat their wings very fast in a forward fanning movement. Helicopters are able to hover. Their rotating blades exert an upward pull. When this pull is balanced by the weight of the aircraft, it hovers.

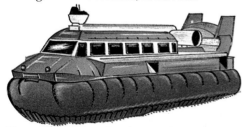

The cushion of air under a hovercraft keeps it above the ground or water, and allows it to move easily.

hovercraft *n.* a vehicle that moves over land and water. A hovercraft is held up by a cushion of air that is pumped underneath it. The air is held in place by a tough, flexible skirt. Hovercraft have many uses: as ferries, in search and rescue operations, in geographical surveying and in fire fighting.

hub *n.* the central part of a wheel that fits onto the axle.

The hub of a car wheel.

hull (1) *n.* the outer covering or husk of certain nuts, fruits, grains or other seeds, e.g. peas and beans. (2) the frame or main body of a ship or aircraft. *The* **hull** *of the Titanic was torn open by an iceberg.* (3) *v.* to remove the calyx or outer coverings of seeds.

human (1) *n.* a man, woman or child; a human being. (2) *adj.* to do with human beings or mankind in general. *The ability to read and write is a* **human** *talent.*

humidity (1) *n.* moisture; dampness. (2) the amount of water vapor in the air. It is measured on a hygrometer. When the air is full of water vapor, we say it is saturated. Warm air can hold more water vapor than cold air.

humus *n.* a dark brown organic material, produced by the decay of dead leaves and plants. It is rich in nutrients and helps to keep the soil moist. (say *hoo-mus*)

hurricane *n.* a violent tropical wind formed in the Atlantic Ocean near the West Indies. It blows at speeds of over 75 miles per hour (120 kilometers per hour).

husk *n.* the dry, outer covering of many seeds or fruits, such as of an ear of wheat and the shell of a nut. *The hairy part of the* **husk** *of coconuts is used to make coconut matting.*

hybrid (1) *n.* the offspring of two animals or plants of different species,

H

e.g. a mule is the hybrid offspring of a male donkey and a mare (female horse). (2) *adj.* having to do with being hybrid.

hydra *n.* a small, freshwater organism with a soft, tubelike body. Its mouth is at the top and is surrounded by tentacles⬜. The bottom of the tube is fixed to a rock or stone.

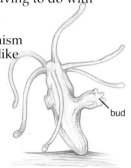
bud

The bud of this hydra will grow into a new organism.

hydrant *n.* a large water pipe connected to a water main. It is used to supply water for fire-fighting hoses.

hydraulic *adj.* describes something made to work by the pressure of liquids. Many vehicles have hydraulic brakes. (say *hi-drawlic*)

hydrocarbon *n.* a chemical compound that contains carbon and hydrogen atoms, e.g. petroleum, natural gas.

hydroelectric *adj.* producing electricity from the energy of moving water. The water drives huge turbines⬜, which in turn drive the generators⬜. The generators produce electricity.

hydrofoil

hydrofoil (1) *n.* a winglike structure fitted on each side beneath the hull of a boat. As the boat gathers speed, the hydrofoils lift the boat out of the water. Only the hydrofoils and propeller remain below the surface of the water. This reduces the drag of water on the hull, so that the boat can travel at very high speeds. (2) a vessel fitted with hydrofoils.

hydrogen *n.* a gas that has no color, taste or smell. It burns easily. It is lighter than air. Hydrogen is the simplest chemical element. It combines with oxygen to produce water.

hydroplane (1) *n.* a small, light motorboat fitted with hydrofoils⬜. (2) a small motorboat with a flat bottom that allows the boat to skim across the water at high speeds.

hygiene *n.* the simple rules of cleanliness which keep your body healthy and your food, home and surroundings clean. Hygiene helps to prevent disease by removing dirt and food particles in which disease organisms breed. *Brushing your teeth regularly and washing your hands before meals are two rules of* **hygiene**. (say *hi-jean*)

hygrometer *n.* an instrument used to measure the amount of moisture in the air (humidity).

hypotenuse *n.* the side of a right-angled (90°) triangle opposite to the right angle. (say *hi-pot-en-oos*)

hypotenuse

hypothermia *n.* a condition of warm-blooded animals, such as humans, in which the body temperature is below normal. It occurs mainly in old people and young babies in the winter. All the body processes slow down as the body gets colder and colder.

I i

ice *n.* water that has been frozen solid. It forms at 0°C, the freezing point of water.

Ice Age one of several long, cold periods in the history of the Earth, when glaciers covered large parts of the northern hemisphere.

iceberg *n.* a large mass of ice that has broken off from a glacier and floats in the sea. Icebergs are found in the Arctic and Antarctic Oceans. They are a danger to shipping. Two-thirds of an iceberg is underwater and cannot be seen.

ice cap a mass of ice covering part of the Earth's surface. It extends outward from a central point, as in the case of the north and south poles.

ice cap

ice floe a floating piece of sea ice found in the Arctic and Antarctic regions. A large group of ice floes forms an icefield.

icicle *n.* a pointed piece of ice that hangs down. An icicle is made from dripping water that freezes.

igneous *adj.* formed by great heat. Igneous rocks are formed by the cooling and hardening of the hot liquid magma⬜ forced out during volcanic eruptions. Granite is an igneous rock. (say *ig-neeus*)

ignition *n.* the act or process of setting fire to something. Particularly, the electrical system that ignites the explosive mixture in the cylinder of an internal combustion engine⬜.

The mirror image seems to come from a point behind the mirror.

image (1) *n.* the picture or appearance formed by light passing through lenses, as in a camera. (2) a picture formed by light reflected from a mirror.

immature *adj.* not fully grown or developed; not mature; not ripe. A green tomato is an immature fruit. A foal is an immature horse.

immunity *n.* the ability of living things to recognize and destroy foreign materials that enter the body. Natural immunity may be passed from parent to offspring. Artificial immunity, against particular diseases such as german measles and whooping cough, can be gained by vaccination⬜. Immunity can cause the rejection of kidney and heart transplants.

impermeable *adj.* not permeable; describes any material that does not let liquids or gases pass through it. Waterproof rubber and plastic are two impermeable materials. Clay particles are very small and form an impermeable soil. (say *im-per-me-able*)

impervious *adj.* not allowing a liquid to pass through or penetrate. *A rubber sheet is* **impervious** *to water.*

impulse (1) *n.* a force that acts for a short time and drives something forward, e.g. the force of a kick on a football. (2) a short burst of electrical current in one direction. (3) a stimulus passed along a nerve to a muscle.

impure *adj.* not pure. A chemical mixed with other substances is impure.

impurity *n.* (*pl. impurities*) a substance found in small quantities mixed with another substance. The color in some gemstones is due to impurities.

inactive (1) *adj.* describes a substance that has few chemical properties. It does not easily react. (2) not active; not moving; sluggish.

inaudible *adj.* describes a sound that cannot be heard.

inbreeding *n.* breeding from closely related organisms that have similar characteristics. Breeders use inbreeding to develop special desirable features in animals and plants, but it can also cause weakness.

inch *n.* a unit of length. Twelve inches are equal to one foot. One inch is equal to 2.54 centimeters.

incisor *n.* a sharp, chisel-shaped mammalian tooth with a single root. It is found at the front of the mouth. There are four incisors in each of the upper and lower jaws. They are used for biting, nibbling and gnawing. (say *in-sizer*)

The long incisor teeth of rodents grow continuously. They are worn down by gnawing.

incline (1) *n.* an upward or downward gradient or slope. (2) *v.* to lean, slant or slope. *The road* **inclined** *gently to the top of the hill. The builder* **inclined** *the ladder against the wall.*

incubation (1) *n.* hatching eggs by keeping them warm. The heat comes from the parent bird's body, the Sun, or a specially warmed box, called an incubator. (2) **incubation period** the time between infection of a person with a germ and the first signs of illness. The incubation period for mumps is 17 to 21 days.

incubator (1) *n.* a special heated box for hatching eggs. (2) a similar piece of equipment that provides the right temperature, moisture and oxygen for a baby that has been born earlier than is normal. (3) an apparatus for growing cultures of bacteria and animal tissues.

indigenous *adj.* describes animals and plants that live and grow naturally in a region of the Earth. It does not include those introduced to the area by humans. *Koala bears are* **indigenous** *to Australia.* (say *in-dij-inus*)

indigo (1) *n.* a blue dye obtained from a certain plant or made artificially. (2) a plant of the pea family from which we get the blue dye. (3) the color in the spectrum between blue and violet.

induce *v.* to make something happen; in physics, to cause an electric or magnetic effect in a body by placing it in a field of force.

industry *n.* any business or process connected with the production or manufacture of goods: the steel industry, the coal industry.

inert (1) *adj.* describes a substance that does not react with other substances. Krypton is an inert gas. (2) without the power to move; sluggish; inactive.

inertia *n.* the tendency for an object to stay in the same state, whether it is at rest or whether it continues moving in a straight line. A force is needed to overcome inertia. (say *in-ursha*)

infect *v.* to give or pass on a disease that is caused by germs⊔. *Many refugees were* **infected** *with typhoid through drinking polluted water.*

infectious (1) *adj.* describes a disease caused by germs⊔ that can spread to other organisms. Influenza is an infectious disease. (2) likely to cause an infection. *Children are most* **infectious** *in the first few days of measles.*

infertile (1) *adj.* unable to produce offspring; barren; not fertile. (2) poor soil in which plants will not grow.

infest *v.* to infect or swarm with parasites⊔; to live as parasites in large numbers on plants or animals, or on clothes and in buildings. *Fleas* **infest** *dogs and cats.*

inflame (1) *v.* to set on fire. (2) to cause a part of the body to become hot, red, swollen and painful, because of an injury or infection.

inflammable *adj.* able to be set on fire easily. Gasoline is highly inflammable. (say *in-flam-ible*)

inflammation *n.* the result of injury or infection in a part of the body. The part becomes hot, red and swollen, and may be painful. (say *in-flah-may-shun*)

inflate *v.* to cause something to swell and become firm, by filling with air or gas under pressure. *When the balloon was* **inflated** *with gas it rose into the sky.*

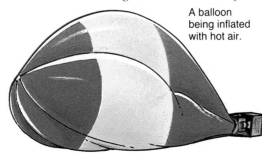

A balloon being inflated with hot air.

infrared *adj.* describes an invisible ray with a wavelength just longer than that of the red light we can see. It can be felt as heat. Infrared rays pass through mist, fog and clouds without being scattered, unlike visible light. Aerial photographs taken with infrared equipment, that can penetrate cloud cover, give better detail than those taken with ordinary cameras.

inhabit *v.* to live in or on a particular place. Whales inhabit the ocean. Squirrels inhabit woodland.

inherit *v.* to gain the characteristics of parents through the sexual reproductive cells (gametes) of parents. *Peter* **inherited** *his father's tall build, but his mother's dark hair and brown eyes.*

inject (1) *v.* to force a liquid from a syringe through the skin into a muscle or blood vessel. *Diabetics* **inject** *themselves with insulin.* (2) injection *n.* the act of injecting. The substance injected. *The doctor gave the cyclist an antitetanus* **injection** *after his road accident.*

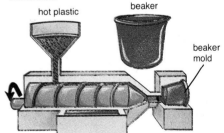

hot plastic · beaker · beaker mold

injection molding a method of shaping plastics by forcing hot, liquid plastic into water-cooled molds. The plastic hardens as it cools.

inner ear in vertebrates, the innermost part of the ear, inside the head. It consists of the cochlea⊔, which has to do with hearing, and three semicircular canals⬚, which have to do with balance. Both these organs contain sensory cells and liquid. When these cells are stimulated by vibrations in the liquid, they send nerve messages to the brain. The brain decodes these messages into sounds, or body movements

inorganic *adj.* describes substances that are mostly of mineral⬚ origin and are not organic⬚.

insect *n.* any of a group of animals with a hard outer skeleton and a body divided into three parts: head, thorax and abdomen. Insects have three pairs of legs, attached to the thorax⬚, and usually two pairs of wings. Bees, ants, butterflies, mosquitoes and beetles are insects.

Butterflies are insects that fly by day. They have a long tubelike mouth part for sucking nectar.

insecticide *n.* a chemical that kills insects and some other pests.

insoluble *adj.* not soluble. Describes a substance that does not dissolve in a given liquid. Some substances that are insoluble in water are soluble in alcohol or other liquids.

instinct *n.* a form of behavior that some animals are born with. It does not have to be learned. *Salmon and eels have an* **instinct** *to swim across the Atlantic Ocean in order to spawn in certain rivers. Birds have an* **instinct** *for building nests.*

instrument (1) *n.* a device used for measuring, or recording, information, e.g. a barometer is an instrument that measures atmospheric pressure. (2) a tool used for doing a particular job, e.g. a pair of scissors. (3) any device that produces musical sounds, such as a guitar, piano or trumpet.

At the top of this barometer the thermometer records room temperature.

insulate *v.* to enclose with a material that prevents the leakage of electricity, or reduces the passage of heat and sound. *Electricity cables are* **insulated** *with rubber. Hot water tanks are* **insulated** *to keep the heat in.*

insulation (1) *n.* the process of insulating. (2) any material in which an electric current will not flow or through which heat and sound cannot easily pass. Most non-metals, and all gases, are good insulators.

insulator (1) *n.* a device, made of glass or porcelain, used to support and insulate electric wires. (2) double-glazing, in windows and doors, makes use of the fact that air is a good insulator. It prevents the loss of heat from a room, and noise from entering.

insulin *n.* a hormone made by the pancreas. It controls the use of sugar by the body. Diabetes⬚ develops if too little insulin is made.

integrated circuit a complicated electrical circuit made up into a single silicon chip⬚. Integrated circuits contain whole systems, rather than single components, and are used in radios, computers, and other electronic devices.

intelligence *n.* the ability to learn, understand and reason, possessed by humans and certain other mammals.

intensity *n.* in physics, the quantity or amount of heat, light, sound or electrical energy present, e.g. the brightness of a lamp, or the loudness of a sound.

intercom (**inter**nal **com**munication) *n.* a radio or telephone system connecting sections of a building, ship or aircraft.

internal combustion a process in which energy is released to do work by burning a fuel-and-air mixture inside a cylinder. Most types of vehicle have internal combustion engines.

internode *n.* in plants, the part of a stem between one leaf and the next.

interval *n.* the space between two objects; the time between two events.

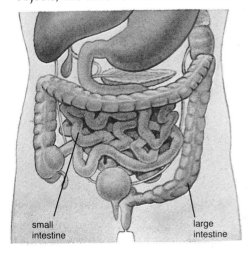

small intestine   large intestine

intestine *n.* part of the alimentary canal. The tube that passes down from the stomach, where food is digested and absorbed. It has two parts. The small intestine leads into the large intestine.

invent *v.* to discover an entirely new process for doing something. To create a new machine. *Alexander Graham Bell* **invented** *the telephone system in 1875.*

A cuttlefish is an invertebrate.

invertebrate (1) *n.* an animal that does not have a backbone. Worms, snails, insects and crabs are examples of invertebrates. (2) *adj.* describes any animal without a backbone.

invisible *adj.* not able to be seen. Air, wind, heat and cold are invisible.

iodine (1) *n.* a nonmetallic chemical element. It consists of shiny, greyish-black crystals, which give off a purple gas when heated. Iodine is used in medicine and in photography. (2) iodine solution is used to detect the presence of starch; it turns a blue-black color.

ion *n.* an atom or group of atoms that has a negative or positive electric charge. Negative ions are formed by atoms gaining electrons☐, and positive ions are formed by atoms losing electrons.

ionosphere *n.* part of the Earth's upper atmosphere which contains many ions. It can reflect radio waves back to Earth.

The gases in the ionosphere are charged with electricity and form ions.

iris (1) *n.* the colorful part of the eye between the cornea and the lens. The iris controls the amount of light entering the eye. (2) a colorful flowering plant that grows from a rhizome⬜.

This eye has a blue iris.

iron *n.* a hard, grey, brittle, metallic chemical element. Iron is the most common and important of all metals. It is essential for plant and animal life. Mixed with other metals, it forms the alloy⬜ steel. Iron has magnetic properties. Iron rusts and corrodes in moist air. It is sometimes coated with zinc to prevent rust (galvanized iron).

irrigate *v.* to water land and crops by using man-made channels or pipes. The water is pumped up from deep wells or diverted from rivers or dams. Irrigation makes it possible to grow crops in dry places.

isobar *n.* a line on a map that connects points on the Earth's surface having the same atmospheric pressure⬜ at a given time.

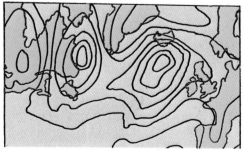

isolate (1) *v.* to set apart or separate. *Doctors* **isolate** *infected persons from others to prevent a disease spreading.* (2) to separate a chemical substance in a pure form from a mixture⬜ of substances or a compound⬜.

isosceles *adj.* describes a triangle with two sides of equal length. (say *i-soss-ilees*)

isotherm *n.* a line on a map connecting points on the Earth's surface that have the same temperature at a given time, or the same mean⬜ temperature. (say *i-so-therm*)

isotope *n.* an atom that is chemically the same as another atom of an element, but has a different number of neutrons⬜ in its nucleus.

isthmus *n.* a narrow stretch of land connecting two larger land masses. It has water on both sides. North and South America are connected by an isthmus. (say *iss-miss*)

J j

jaundice *n.* in humans, a disease of the liver in which there is too much bile pigment in the blood. It causes a yellow color in the eye and skin.

jaw *n.* either of the two bony parts of the mouth in some animals. The jaws hold the teeth in place and give shape to the mouth.

jellyfish *n.* a sea animal with a soft, jellylike body. It has long, threadlike tentacles hanging down from its underside. Some jellyfish have a powerful sting.

The jellyfish uses its tentacles to catch food. The food can be seen inside its transparent body.

jerboa *n.* a small desert rodent⊔, native to North Africa and Asia. It jumps like a kangaroo and has very long, powerful hind legs. It is active at night and sleeps during the day (nocturnal). Many children keep jerboas as pets. (say *jer-boa*)

jet engine a powerful engine used in aircraft and ships. It works by jet propulsion.

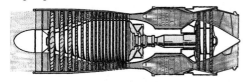

In this jet engine hot exhaust gases are forced out in a powerful jet which propels the aircraft forward.

jet propulsion a method of moving an object, such as a boat or aircraft, forward, by the reaction caused when very hot gases, under great pressure, are released through an opening at the back of the engine.

jet stream (1) a stream of hot exhaust gases from a rocket. (2) very rapid winds that move around the Earth from west to east, at an altitude of 8 to 10 miles (13 to 16 kilometers). *The flight arrived in England ahead of schedule because of a* **jet stream** *over the Atlantic.*

jig *n.* a device used in the toolmaking industry as a guide tool or as a patternmaker for other tools.

joint (1) *n.* a place in the body where two bones are joined (articulated) so that they can move freely. The hip and shoulder joints are examples of ball and socket joints. The elbow and knee are hinge joints. (2) in engineering, a mechanical connection. (3) in plants, a place where a branch or leaf grows from the stem.

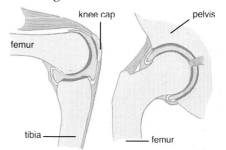

The hinged knee joint *(left)* only allows the leg to bend and straighten. The ball and socket hip joint *(right)* allows the thigh to move in all directions.

joule *n.* a unit of measurement for energy and work. Named after James Joule (1818–89). (say *jewel*)

junction *n.* a place where two or more routes or pathways join or cross, e.g. electric circuit junctions, nerve fiber junctions (synapses), road and railroad junctions.

jute *n.* a strong fiber used for making ropes, sacks and matting. It comes from the stem fibers of a tropical Asian plant.

K k

keel (1) *n.* the main timber or steel beam that runs along the bottom of a ship. It is the main support of the ship, and the hull is attached to it. (2) A flat piece of wood, metal or fiberglass fixed to the bottom of a sailing boat. It keeps the boat steady in the water. (3) *v.* to keel over, or capsize. *The large wave upset the balance of the boat and caused it to* **keel** *over.*

kelp *n.* a large, coarse, brown seaweed; it is a valuable source of iodine. Kelp is used as a fertiliser and soil conditioner.

kernel (1) *n.* the seed inside a hard nut. (2) the stone inside some fleshy fruits, e.g. peach, plum. (3) the grain or seed of wheat, rice, corn, etc.

The stone of a fleshy fruit contains the seed or kernel.

kerosine *n.* a thin, light-colored oil obtained from petroleum. It is used as a fuel for heating, for oil lamps and for jet engines.

key *n.* a chart or list of symbols or facts that solves or helps to explain a problem, such as a key to a map. *A classification* **key** *helps us to identify animals and plants in their correct family, genus and species.* (2) a device that operates a machine.

keyboard (1) *n.* the set of keys on a piano or typewriter. (2) The input part on a computer, on which information is typed in. It looks like a typewriter.

kidney *n.* one of two paired organs in animals with backbones (vertebrates). The kidneys control the amount of water in the body and take out waste substances from the blood. The kidneys pass these as urine into the bladder.

kiln *n.* an oven or furnace. Kilns are used to dry grains and wood. Kilns that heat up to high temperatures are used to bake pottery and bricks.

kilogram *n.* a unit of weight or mass in the metric system, equal to 1000 grams or about 2.2 lb.

kilometer *n.* a unit of length or distance in the metric system, equal to 1000 meters. 1 kilometer is equal to 0.6214 mile.

kilowatt *n.* a unit of electrical power, equal to 1000 watts.

kinetic energy the energy of movement. Wind, moving objects and flowing water have kinetic energy. (say *kin-et-ik*)

kingdom *n.* the greatest unit in the classification system of animals and plants; the animal kingdom; the plant kingdom.

knot (1) *n.* a measure of speed used at sea by sailors. It is equal to one nautical mile per hour. A nautical mile

is equal to 6076.12 feet. *The supertanker was travelling at about 15* **knots**.
(2) a joint on a plant stem, where leaves or branches grow out. (3) in wood, a cross-section through the point where a branch has grown out.

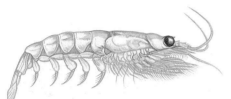

Krill live in the upper plankton layer of oceans.

krill *n.* a small sea animal like a shrimp; an important food for other larger fish and some whales.

L l

laboratory *n.* a place used for practical scientific work and experiments. (say *lab-re-tory*)

lake *n.* a large, inland body of fresh or salt water.

laminate (1) *v.* to build up in thin layers, as in plywood. (2) to press into a thin sheet or layer. (3) to cover with or bond to a thin layer, as in plastic laminate on work surfaces.

lapilli *n.* small pieces of rock (between 4 mm and 32 mm in diameter) that are thrown out of a volcano during a violent eruption. Lapilli means 'little stones' in Latin.

large intestine part of the alimentary canal; the lower part of the intestine. It absorbs water from the waste matter and passes solid feces into the rectum.

larva *n. (pl. larvae)* a part of the life cycle of insects and other animals without backbones. The larva hatches

A caterpillar larva has a soft, segmented body.

out of the egg and has a soft, wormlike body. The caterpillars of butterflies and moths are larvae.

larynx *n.* the 'voice box'; the part of the air passage between the nose and mouth and the trachea (windpipe). The vocal cords are in the larynx. These control the sound and pitch of your voice. To form speech you need lips, tongue and teeth.

laser *n.* a device that produces a very bright, narrow beam of light. In a ruby laser, light from a flash tube excites atoms of ruby crystals or gases such as carbon dioxide, helium or neon. The 'excited' atoms shoot off photons of light of the same wavelength. This produces a very powerful beam of light. Lasers are used in medicine and industry.

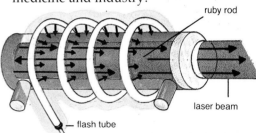

ruby rod
laser beam
flash tube

lateral *adj.* relating to the side. Describes the part of a plant or animal lying at the side. A lateral root branches out to the side of the main root. A lateral bud develops in the axil of a leaf at the side of the stem.

lathe *n.* a machine for holding and turning a piece of wood or metal against a sharp cutting tool. It shapes the wood or metal.

latitude *n.* lines on a globe or map of the world, drawn from east to west, parallel with the equator. Latitude is measured in degrees from the equator going north and south. The equator is latitude O°. The latitude of the Tropic of Cancer is 23½°N.

launch (1) *v.* to send or blast off a rocket or weapon. *Apollo 17 was* **launched** *in 1972 by a Saturn rocket.* (2) to slide the hull of a newly-built ship into the water; to float a vessel. (3) *n.* the act of launching a vessel or rocket.

launch pad the strong, flat base from which a rocket or guided missile is launched. It is also called a launching pad.

lava (1) *n.* the hot liquid (molten) rock that gushes out of an erupting volcano. (2) the hard rock formed from molten lava as it cools.

law (1) *n.* a set of rules that must be obeyed. (2) natural laws: a series of events in nature that always occur in the same way, under the same conditions. (3) physical laws: a similar series of events affecting the Earth and the solar system and the behavior of matter. *Sir Isaac Newton discovered the* **law** *of gravity.*

layer (1) *n.* a single thickness or band of material; a single thickness of cells in living tissue, e.g. the epidermal layer of a leaf, a layer of sedimentary rock, a layer of paint. (2) part of a plant stem that has been pegged down into the soil. The layered stem will root and grow into a new plant. (3) *v.* to produce a layer.

leach *v.* to filter a liquid through a material in order to take out soluble substances. Heavy rains leach the soil by washing away the soluble nutrients. Plants do not thrive on leached soils.

lead (1) *n.* a soft, heavy, dull grey metal. Lead is a chemical element. X-rays cannot pass through lead. Lead is used to make alloys, solder and weights for fishing lines. (2) a lead line (plumb line). It consists of a lead weight hanging on a piece of string. When at rest it is vertical. A lead line is used for measuring the depth of shallow waters, and to test if a wall is vertical. (rhymes with *bed*)

lead *n.* an electrical cable that connects an electrical device to a power supply. (rhymes with *reed*)

lead *v.* to direct or guide along a definite pathway. To conduct gas, water, steam or electricity along a certain course or channel. *Storm drains* **lead** *away rainwater. The exhaust pipe* **leads** *the exhaust gases away from the engine.* (rhymes with *reed*)

leaflet

A compound leaf.   A simple leaf.

leaf (1) *n.* one of the parts of a plant that grows from a node on a stem. A leaf usually consists of a thin flat blade and a stalk. Most leaves contain green chlorophyll cells. They use sunlight energy, water and carbon dioxide to make the plant foods needed for growth (photosynthesis). Leaves also control the loss of water from a plant through special pores (stomata). Leaves have many different shapes. A compound leaf is divided into several separate parts. (2) leaf metal, a very thin sheet of metal.

leaflet *n.* part of a compound leaf.

learning (1) *n.* knowledge that is gained by an animal, from study or from events that have happened in the past (experience). (2) the gaining of a skill through practice. The ability to learn is found in humans and other mammals.

leech *n.* a kind of worm, with suckers. It lives in water or wet earth. Some leeches suck blood. Doctors at one time used them to bleed their patients.

legume (1) *n.* any plant belonging to the pea-flower family, e.g. clover, vetch, broom, pea, bean. (2) any vegetable of the pea and bean type. (3) a long, narrow, dry fruit consisting of two halves. The seeds are fixed along the join. When the pod opens, the seeds fall or may shoot out.

lens (1) *n.* a piece of glass or transparent material that has been given a convex or concave shape. Light rays passing through a convex lens are brought to a focus at a point. Light rays passing through a concave lens are spread out. Cameras, telescopes and spectacles have lenses. (2) the convex lens in the eyes of mammals and other vertebrates (animals with backbones). It focuses an image on the retina at the back of the eye.

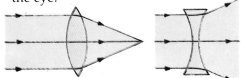

A convex lens *(left)* brings light to a focus; a concave lens *(right)* spreads it out.

lepidoptera *n.pl.* any of a large group of insects that includes butterflies and moths. They have two long feelers (antennae) and two pairs of large wings covered with fine, powdery scales. The larvae of lepidoptera are caterpillars. (say *lep-idop-tera*)

leukemia *n.* a condition in which too many white blood cells (leucocytes) are present in human blood.

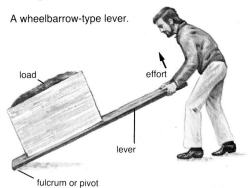

A wheelbarrow-type lever.

load

effort

lever

fulcrum or pivot

lever (1) *n.* a simple machine for lifting weights or prising something open. It consists of a strong, stiff bar that turns about a pivot, like a seesaw. Power is applied at one end, and the weight is lifted at the other end. (2) *v.* to lift a weight or move an object by using a lever. *I was able to* **lever** *the lid off the can with a coin.*

lichen *n.* a small plant without flowers. It is really two plants, an alga and a fungus living together. The fungus protects the alga and stops it drying out and dying. The alga produces sugars which the fungus uses as food. This sharing of life is called symbiosis. Lichens usually grow in damp places, on tree bark and rocks. (say *liken* or *litchen*)

life (1) *n.* the state in which plants and animals grow, develop and reproduce themselves. It distinguishes them from dead organisms and from rocks, metals and other objects. (2) the time between the fertilized egg and death.

life cycle the changes through which a living organism passes in its development from a fertilized egg to an adult. The life cycle of many insects is egg – larva – pupa – adult – egg. The life cycle of a frog is egg (frogspawn) – tadpole – frog – egg. Mammals have a very simple life cycle. They produce offspring that are like themselves.

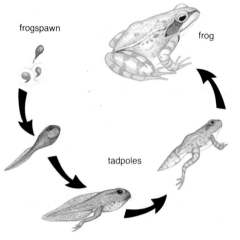

The life cycle of a frog.

life history the stages and changes that an organism goes through in its life cycle from fertilized egg to death.

lift (1) *v.* to raise or pick up an object. *Father* **lifted** *the suitcase onto the roof-rack.* (2) to rise in the air and seem to disappear. *As the Sun* **rose** *the fog lifted.* (3) *n.* the act of lifting. (4) the force, created by the difference in air pressure above and below the wings, that keeps an aircraft in flight. (5) an elevator: a platform or small room, used for carrying people or goods from one floor to another, in a tall building.

ligament *n.* in animals with backbones (vertebrates), (a) a band of strong tissue that connects bones at a joint. (b) a similar band of tissue that holds an organ of the body in place.

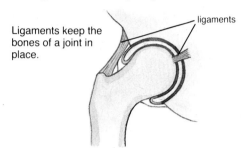

Ligaments keep the bones of a joint in place.

ligaments

light (1) *n.* a form of radiation that makes it possible for animals with light-sensitive organs, such as the human eye, to see objects. It is used by green plants to make their own food. Natural light comes from the Sun, giving daylight. The light of the Moon is reflected sunlight. Artificial light is given off by man-made things such as candles and electric light bulbs. White light is a mixture of different colors, each with a different wavelength. Humans, and some animals, are able to sense color because of special cells in the eye called cones. (2) any object or device that can produce light. *Please turn on the* **light**. (3) *adj.* bright; full of light. *The room was very* **light** *because of the large windows.* (4) pale in color. *She was wearing a* **light***-blue dress.* (5) not heavy; having little weight. (6) *v.* to fill with light or to give light to something. *We can* **light** *the room with candles.* (7) to set fire to something. *Please* **light** *the fire for me.*

light energy energy from light radiation. It may come from a natural source, like the Sun or stars, or from electricity or heat energy, as in electric light and oil lamps.

lightning *n.* A powerful flash of light in the sky. It is a giant electrical spark between two electrically charged clouds or between a charged cloud and the ground.

light year the distance traveled by a ray of light in one year (9.5 million, million km). This unit is used to measure immense distances in the universe. *Our galaxy is about 100,000* **light years** *across.*

lignite *n.* soft, brown coal. It is softer than ordinary coal and is found nearer to the surface of the Earth.

limb (1) *n.* an arm, leg, wing or flipper of an animal. (2) one of the main branches of a tree into which the trunk divides.

lime (1) *n.* a white, powdery chemical compound, calcium oxide, formed by heating limestone. Lime is used to make mortar and cement for building. It is alkaline and is used to neutralize acid soils.(2) a small, sour, green fruit, similar to a lemon. (3) *v.* to apply lime to soil or other surfaces.

limestone *n.* a hard, sedimentary rock made of calcium carbonate and some magnesium carbonate. Limestones are formed from the remains of microscopic sea organisms and rocks that have been gradually broken down into sand, silt and mud. These settle as sediment on the beds of seas and lakes.

linen *n.* a natural material made from the stem fibers of the flax plant. They are spun and woven into cloth.

lining (1) *n.* a layer of material covering the inner surface of an object. *The* **lining** *of some chemical containers is made of glass.* (2) a layer of cells covering the inside of a tube, duct or gland in a living organism. *The* **lining** *of the stomach secretes the gastric juices.*

link (1) *n.* a single unit that forms part of a chain. Something that joins things together. A chemical bond that binds atoms and molecules together. A link in a food chain. (2) *v.* to join objects together.

liquid *n.* a state of matter. All materials are solids, liquids or gases. Liquids flow and always take up the shape of the vessel into which they are poured. This occurs because the molecules of a liquid have weaker bonds than those of solids, and so can move around. Liquids have a definite volume and do not move as freely as gases. Water, milk and oil are liquids.

The small battery that powers a liquid crystal display watch can last for many years.

liquid crystal display (LCD) a system by which the numbers on a calculator or watch are displayed. The lines in the numbers hold liquid crystals. These are visible when an electric current passes through them. LCDs use less electric current than a LED (light emitting diode).

liter *n.* a unit of liquid measure in the metric system. A liter is equal to 1000 cubic centimeters (cm^3) or milliliters (ml). One liter is equal to 1.76 pints.

lithosphere *n.* the outer, solid rock layer of the Earth, also known as the Earth's crust□. The lithosphere also includes the upper layer of the mantle□. (say *lith-o-sfear*)

litmus paper absorbent paper that has been treated with litmus dye. Litmus turns blue in an alkaline solution and red in an acid solution. Litmus paper is used in chemical tests for acids and alkalis.

litter (1) *n.* a number of animals born at the same time to a pig, dog or other mammal. (2) the decomposing leaves and vegetation on a forest floor.

live (1) *adj.* of organisms; to have life, to be able to function, develop and reproduce. (2) carrying an electric current. (3) glowing or burning. *He roasted chesnuts on the* **live** *coals.* (4) an unexploded weapon: a live bullet, a live bomb.

live *v.* to have life.

liver *n.* a large organ in the body of vertebrates (animals with backbones). It has many uses: it destroys poisons; it stores carbohydrates, fats, some vitamins and iron. The liver makes bile, which helps in the digestion of fat. The bile enters the gut through the bile duct. Cod liver oil and halibut liver oil are very rich sources of vitamins A and D.

liverwort *n.* a type of small, low, green, mosslike plant, which lives in shady, moist places. It does not have flowers, and it reproduces by spores. The plant body consists of broad, flattened leaves that lie close to the ground. It depends on moist conditions to carry out its life cycle.

lizard *n.* a type of reptile with a long, slender body and a long tail. It has a scaly skin, and is cold-blooded. Chameleons, iguanas and geekos are all types of lizard.

load (1) *v.* to add weight. (2) to add film to a camera or an explosive charge to a gun. (3) *n.* in mechanics, the weight raised or moved by a lever or other machine. *The helicopter's maximum* **load** *was limited to four persons.* (4) the weight carried by beams and pillars in buildings. (5) the electrical power delivered by a generator, or carried by an electrical circuit.

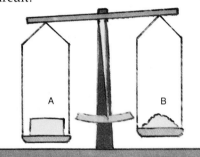

Weights have been loaded on to scale pan A to weigh the material on pan B.

loam *n.* a rich, fertile soil made from fine clays, silt, sand and humus. It is the best soil for growing plants.

lobe *n.* a rounded part that sticks out. The fleshy lower part of the external ear. One of the main parts of an organ, such as the lobes of the lungs, liver and brain.

locomotion (1) *n.* in living organisms, the action of moving or the ability to move from place to place. Walking, swimming and flying are forms of locomotion. (2) the act of moving from place to place with the aid of a machine, e.g. a railway locomotive.

locus *n.* *(pl. loci)* a place. (1) a place on a chromosome where a particular gene is always found. (2) in mathematics, the path of a moving point. The circumference of a circle is the locus of all points at the same distance from the center of the circle.

Locusts have springs in their legs which enable them to jump great distances.

locust *n.* a type of large grasshopper that lives in warm parts of the world. Locusts travel in huge swarms and feed on plants. Locusts are harmful and destroy vast areas of crops and vegetation.

lodestone *n.* a piece of brown rock that contains iron. It is now called magnetite. It acts as a magnet. A lodestone was used as a compass in ancient China.

Lodestones were once used by sailors to magnetize compass needles.

longitude *n.* the east or west location of a position on the Earth, measured in degrees. Lines of longitude are marked on a map or globe, and run from the North Pole to the South Pole. They are numbered in degrees running east and west of a line, known as the prime meridian, which passes through Greenwich, in England.

long sight a defect in sight. A person with long sight can see objects clearly at a distance, but things close to look blurred. This occurs because the eye cannot focus near objects onto the retina. Long sight can be corrected by convex lenses in eyeglasses.

long wave a radio wave, usually longer than 1000 meters and of low frequency□. Radio waves can travel across oceans and continents.

loop (1) *n.* in computers, a loop is the means by which a computer process may be repeated a fixed number of times, before the process is ended. (2) a complete vertical circle made by an aircraft. *The pilot* **looped** *the* **loop** *in the air display.*

loudspeaker *n.* an instrument that changes electrical signals into sound loud enough to be heard. Headphones are a type of loudspeaker.

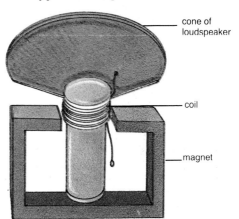

cone of loudspeaker

coil

magnet

Changing electrical signals from an amplifier make the coil vibrate. These vibrations are passed on to the cone which produces sound waves.

louse *n.* *(pl. lice)* a small insect with no wings. It has a flat body and short legs with claws, which it uses to cling to the host animal. It lives on mammals, by biting and sucking blood. The eggs of lice, called nits, are attached to body hairs. Lice spread diseases, such as typhus fever.

low pressure (1) having a low barometric pressure. (2) a region of air near the Earth's surface which has been made lighter by heat from the Sun. Warm air is lighter than cold air. Where the Sun's rays are strongest, near the equator, a band of low pressure is always present.

low tide (1) the lowest level reached by the falling (ebbing) tide. (2) the time when this level is reached. Tides are caused by the pull of the Moon at different phases and the rotation of the Earth.

lubricant *n.* a slippery substance, such as oil or grease, used to coat the surfaces of the moving parts of a machine. It allows them to move smoothly against each other and reduces friction and wear. Powdered graphite is also used as a lubricant in some machines.

Lubricants are used to reduce friction and wear between moving parts.

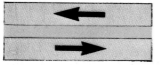

lubricate *v.* to apply oil or grease to the moving parts of a machine so that they will move freely.

lumen (1) *n.* the space inside a hollow organ or tube, such as in a plant cell, blood vessel or water pipe. (2) a unit of measurement of light intensity.

luminous (1) *adj.* giving out light. (2) glowing in the dark as in the effect produced by glowworms and luminous chemicals.

lunar *adj.* to do with the Moon. *The* **lunar** *landscape is pitted with craters. Astronauts explored the surface of the Moon from the* **lunar** *module.* A lunar month is the time it takes for the Moon to go around the Earth (approximately 28 days).

lung *n.* the organ for breathing air in most vertebrates (animals with backbones). There are two lungs, one on each side of the chest, or thorax. In the lungs oxygen passes into the blood, and carbon dioxide is taken from the blood.

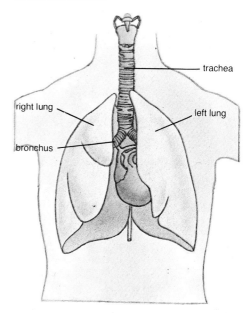

The lung is made of spongy tissue full of tiny air sacs. Air passes into the lungs through the bronchus.

luster *n.* the quality of light reflected by a mineral. Silver, gold and other metals have luster, so also do gems and precious stones.

lymph *n.* a clear, watery liquid formed in the bodies of vertebrate animals. It contains white blood cells, mainly lymphocytes. It flows around the body in lymph vessels, which collect together and empty into the blood system.

M m

machine (1) *n.* a device that uses energy or effort to do work. A machine enables the user to do a piece of work with less effort. Some simple machines are levers, wheels, pulleys, screws and inclined planes. Other machines consist of many different moving parts with gears and wheels put together in a particular way. A robot is a machine. (2) *v.* to shape something with a machine tool.

machine code a programming code, based on the binary system that is directly obeyed by a particular computer. The computer translates high-level language programs into machine code.

machinery (1) *n.* the parts of a larger machine. (2) a group of machines, such as in a car assembly factory.

machine tool a power-driven tool used to shape metal parts of other machines. A drill and lathe are machine tools.

Mach number a comparison between the speed of an aircraft and the speed of sound in air. Since the speed of sound varies according to altitude, the Mach number varies with it. Mach 3 represents a speed three times that of sound. It was named after Ernst Mach (1838-1916). (say *Mak*)

maggot *n.* the soft, thick, worm-like body of an insect larva. The larva of a housefly.

magma *n.* the hot, liquid (molten) rock found in the Earth's mantle, just below the crust. The large plates of crust float on the molten magma. During some volcanic eruptions magma is forced out of the Earth's crust.

magnet *n.* a piece of iron that can attract iron or steel. A magnet will attract or repel other magnets. When able to turn, a magnet will always point in a north-south direction.

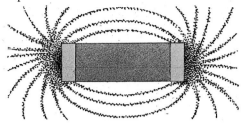

magnetic field the space around a magnet within which its magnetic force acts.

magnetic tape a thin, plastic tape, coated on one side with a magnetic powder. It is used to store signals that can be changed into sounds or pictures. Computers at one time used magnetic tape to store information, but now floppy disks and hard disks are used.

magnetism *n.* the property of iron, steel and some other metals to attract or repel a piece of iron, or an electric conductor placed close to it.

magnetite *n.* a brownish rock. A type of iron; it acts as a natural magnet.

magnify *n.* to make an object appear larger than it is by using a convex lens or a system of lenses, as in a telescope or microscope.

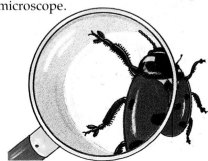

M

magnifying glass a hand lens. A convex lens used to make objects or print look larger. Rays of light are reflected from the object and pass through the lens to the eye. The image in the eye looks larger than the object.

magnitude (1) *n.* greatness of size, strength and importance. *Seismographs record the* **magnitude** *of earthquakes.* (2) in astronomy, the brightness of a fixed star. The brightest stars are those of the first, or greatest, magnitude. The faintest stars belong to the sixth magnitude.

main (1) *n.* any of the larger pipes or lines in a system, from which smaller pipes carry water, gas or electricity to buildings. *The water* **main** *has burst and the street is flooded.* (2) *adj.* the most important or largest part of an object or system. *The aorta is the* **main** *artery in the body.*

maize (1) *n.* the corn plant, a type of grass. (2) the grain produced by the corn plant. The grain grows in tightly packed rows on large ears. Several ears are carried on each stem.

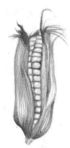

The large ears of maize are called cobs; they are protected by the outer leafy husks.

malaria *n.* an infectious disease of humans that causes repeated attacks of high fever, chills and sweating. Malaria is caused by a microscopic parasite, which is carried by a type of mosquito. The female mosquito picks up the parasite when it sucks the blood of an infected person. It passes this on to other humans each time it bites. The malaria parasite lives in the red blood cells of humans. It kills the cells and this can cause severe anemia. World health authorities have stamped out malaria in many parts of the world by draining the marshes and stagnant waters where mosquitoes breed.

male *adj.* to do with the sex of living organisms. A male organism produces male gametes (sex cells); e.g. the male organ of a flowering plant is the stamen, which produces the male sex cells or pollen grains.

malignant *adj.* in living organisms, it describes cells that multiply very rapidly, forming lumps or tumors. Malignant cells invade other tissues and can spread throughout the body in the lymph and blood. Cancer cells are malignant.

malnutrition *n.* a condition in which animals do not get enough of the right kinds of food for healthy growth and development. *When the harvest failed many people suffered from* **malnutrition**.

mammal *n.* a vertebrate animal that is warm-blooded and usually covered with hair or fur. A mammal has a well-developed brain and a heart with four chambers (two auricles and two ventricles). The female mammal produces live young and feeds them on milk from mammary glands. Humans, lions, bats and whales are examples of mammals.

mammary glands the glands in female mammals that produce milk for the young. In four-legged animals the glands are arranged in pairs down each side of the underbelly. Humans have only one pair.

mammoth *n.* a very large, extinct mammal. A type of hairy elephant with long curling tusks and a trunk. Mammoths became extinct about 10,000 years ago.

man (1) *n. Homo sapiens;* the human species as a whole. Man has a highly developed brain and walks erect. Man differs from other primates in being able to make tools and communicate by means of language. (2) a single male adult. (3) *v.* to operate a machine or boat; to provide humans as a work force.

mandible (1) *n.* the lower jaw of a vertebrate. (2) a special mouth part found on the head of certain arthropods, such as insects. It is used for cutting and crushing solid food before it is eaten.

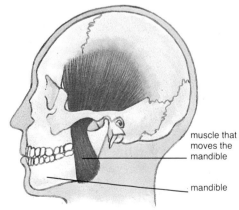

muscle that moves the mandible

mandible

manned *v.* operated by humans instead of by machines. *Spacecraft are* **manned** *by astronauts.*

mantle (1) *n.* part of the Earth's structure; it lies between the Earth's crust and the core of the Earth. The mantle is divided into two parts, the lower mantle and the upper mantle. (2) a gas mantle: a fine, meshed hood which glows white hot and gives out light when heated. (3) a fold of skin that covers most of a mollusc's body. It secretes (gives off) the substance that makes the shells of some molluscs, such as a snail.

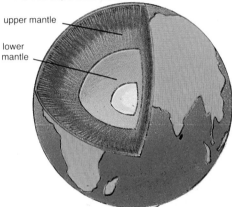

upper mantle

lower mantle

A section through part of the Earth showing the upper and lower mantles.

manual (1) *adj.* to do with the hand, e.g. a manual gear change in a car, as opposed to an automatic gear change. (2) *n.* a handbook of instructions or information which explains how to do a particular job.

manufacture *v.* to make by hand or with the help of machines, e.g. clothing, cars and furniture are some things which are manufactured.

manure *n.* a material put into the soil to increase its fertility; animal dung, mixed with straw bedding or wood shavings. Manure increases the humus and minerals in the soil.

M

marble *n.* a hard, metamorphic limestone rock. It may be white or colored, or streaked with color. Marble can be highly polished and is used in buildings and sculpture.

marine *adj.* to do with the sea. Describes something that lives in the sea or is formed by the sea. *The seashore is populated by* **marine** *organisms.*

marrow (1) *n.* the soft tissue found within the bones of mammals. Yellow marrow contains fat and is found in the long bones. Red marrow produces red blood cells. (2) a large, fleshy vegetable belonging to the melon, cucumber and gourd family.

A vegetable marrow.

marsh (1) *n.* an area of low, wet, soft land; a bog or a swamp. Rushes, sedges and reeds are common marsh plants. (2) salt marsh: a similar area fed by salt water.

marsupial (1) *n.* a mammal with a pouch, belonging to the order Marsupialia. Kangaroos, koala bears and opossums are marsupials. (2) *adj.* belonging to an order of mammals whose young are born very small and immature. They spend the first six months of life in a pouch on the female's abdomen. The young marsupial animal feeds from milk glands in the pouch. Marsupial mammals are found only in Australasia and North and South America. (say *mar-soup-eeal*)

A koala bear is a marsupial. It eats only eucalyptus leaves.

mass *n.* the measure of the amount of matter in a body. It is not the same as weight. The mass of a body always remains the same, even in space, where its weight is less than on Earth.

material *n.* any matter from which other things can be made. Stone, wood, leather, fabric and rubber are all materials. Materials do not have an exact composition like chemical substances.

mathematics *n.* the science that deals with numbers, shapes, measurements and quantities, and how they relate to each other. Arithmetic, geometry and algebra are all part of mathematics.

matrix *n.* that within which something is formed or embedded. (1) in biology, the material in which living cells are supported or enclosed. Bone matrix consists of hard calcium salts and tough collagen fibers. Fine channels in the hard matrix link the living bone cells. (2) the cells from which a nail or tooth grows. (3) in geology, the rock that surrounds crystals or fossils.

matter (1) *n.* the material of which all things in the universe are made. (2) grey matter and white matter: two types of nervous tissue found in the brain and spinal cord of vertebrates (animals with backbones).

maximum (1) *n.* (*pl. maxima*) the greatest amount or number of something that is possible or allowed. (2) *adj.* describes the greatest possible. *The car was travelling at its* **maximum** *speed.*

mean *n.* a middle point; a value or point halfway between extremes. *The* **mean** *temperature for the day was 72°F, between a high of 78°F and a low of 66°F.*

measles *n.* an acute, infectious disease caused by a virus. It produces fever, a skin rash of small red spots and the symptoms of a heavy cold, with sore eyes. German measles: a similar but milder disease. It is important for all women to be protected against German measles, because it can cause severe defects in unborn babies if the mother catches the virus during the first three months of her pregnancy.

measure (1) *n.* any unit used to stand for the size, quantity or volume of something. *A kilogram is a unit or* **measure** *of weight.* (2) an instrument, container or device used for working out the size, quantity or volume of something, e.g. a chemical balance or a measuring cylinder. (3) *v.* to find the size, weight, volume or amount of something. *We* **measured** *the floor area before ordering the carpet.*

mechanical energy a form of energy by which a machine is able to do work or create another form of energy; e.g. the mechanical energy of a moving turbine may be turned into electrical energy.

mechanics *n.* the science that deals with movement and the effect of forces acting on a body.

medicine (1) *n.* the scientific study of diseases; how to detect, treat and prevent them. (2) the branch of this science which uses drugs, and means other than surgery, in the treatment of disease. (3) any substance taken by mouth or injection that is used to treat illness or pain.

medium (1) *n.* a substance in which cultures of microorganisms are grown in a laboratory, e.g. agar jelly. (2) anything through which a force acts. *Copper is a good conducting* **medium** *for heat and electricity.* (3) a liquid in which other substances are dissolved or suspended, e.g. as in ink, paints, varnishes and aerosols. (4) *adj.* average, intermediate (in the middle) in quality, amount, size, etc.

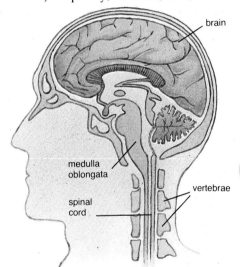

A section through a human brain.

M

medulla (1) *n.* the inner part of a plant stem or root. (2) the inner part of an animal tissue, especially in the kidney. (3) medulla oblongata: part of the hind brain in vertebrates (animals with backbones). It is continuous with the spinal cord. The medulla oblongata controls the automatic activities of the body, such as breathing, heartbeat, swallowing and the amount of blood flowing into a tissue.

megabyte *n.* in computers, a unit consisting of one million bytes. A megabyte store is a computer memory that can store up to one million bytes.

melanin *n.* a brownish-black pigment found in the hair, fur and skins of animals. Lack of melanin causes fair skin and hair. An albino animal, with white hair and skin and pink eyes, has no melanin in its body.

melt *v.* to change a solid into a liquid by heating it. Ice melts into water when it is warmed. Metals are melted in furnaces.

membrane *n.* a thin layer of tissue in living organisms. Membranes cover, separate or line plant and animal organs. *Mucous* **membranes** *line the nose, throat and lungs.* (say *mem-brain*)

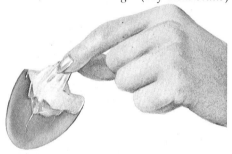

The membrane lining an egg protects the egg inside.

memory (1) *n.* the ability to remember. The power of storing facts and experiences in the mind and bringing them back when needed. (2) something that is remembered. (3) in computers, the primary memory provides a permanent set of instructions to the computer (ROM — read only memory), and access to all the information in the computer (RAM — random access memory). Primary memories cannot be separated from the computer. Peripheral memories, in the form of disks, can be used, removed or transferred from one computer to another.

menstrual cycle the female reproductive cycle that occurs in humans and other primates. In humans the cycle lasts about 28 days. It is repeated continuously from puberty to the menopause (change of life), except during pregnancy. The menstrual cycle is controlled by female hormones. These are chemical substances which stimulate the ovaries to shed an ovum and the uterus to prepare the lining to receive it. If the ovum is not fertilized, the uterus sheds it and the lining, causing menstruation, the regular monthly bleeding.

menstruation *n.* the periodic loss of blood from the uterus during the menstrual cycle◻. It occurs about every 28 days, from puberty to the menopause (change of life). The bleeding lasts about 4 to 5 days.

mental (1) *adj.* to do with the mind. Mental ability is the power of a person to learn, reason and work out problems in the mind, e.g. mental arithmetic. (2) mental age: the mental ability of a person, expressed in years. *Alice is only six years old, but she has the* **mental** *age of an eight-year-old. She is very advanced for her age.* (3) mental illness: a condition in which the normal activity of the mind is disturbed and the person behaves in a strange way. There are many different forms of mental illness.

mercury (1) *n.* a heavy, silver-colored metal, which is liquid at room temperature. Mercury is a chemical element. It is called quicksilver because of the way it moves. Mercury is used in scientific instruments, such as thermometers and barometers. Mercury dissolves other metals to form amalgams. An amalgam is used in dentistry to fill tooth cavities. (2) Mercury is the smallest planet in our solar system. It is the closest to the Sun, and it takes only 88 days to complete its orbit, whereas our Earth takes 365 days.

A mercury thermometer.

meridian (1) *n.* an imaginary line that circles the Earth, passing through the geographical poles. (2) half such a line, known as a line of longitude. The prime meridian passes through Greenwich, England. (3) the highest point reached by a heavenly body along its course. *The Sun reaches its* **meridian** *about noon.*

metabolism *n.* all the chemical and physical processes that occur continuously in living organisms. Metabolism includes the taking in and breaking down of complex food substances into simpler, soluble ones that the body can use for energy, growth and repair, and the removal of waste products.

metacarpal bone (1) in primates (humans, apes, monkeys) one of the five bones in the hand that join the bones in the thumb and fingers to the carpal bones (wrist bones). (2) a similar bone in the forefoot of amphibians, reptiles, birds and other mammals.

metacarpal bone

metal (1) *n.* a shiny, mineral substance. All metals, except mercury, are solid at ordinary temperatures. Metals conduct heat and electricity. Metals can be pulled out into thin wires and can be beaten into shapes. In chemical reactions the atoms of metals form positive ions. Certain metals can be melted together to form alloys, such as brass and bronze. (2) **metallic** *adj.* having the characteristics of a metal.

metallurgist *n.* a scientist who deals with the separation of a metal from its ore (by smelting and refining processes) for use in industry. (say *metal-ler-jist*)

metamorphic *adj.* describes a change of form in inorganic materials and in living organisms. In geology, metamorphic rocks are rocks that have been changed by great heat or pressure. *Marble is a* **metamorphic** *rock.* (say *meta-more-fik*)

metamorphosis *n.* the change of form in some animals during their development from egg to adult; e.g. butterflies and moths undergo metamorphosis. They change from egg to caterpillar (larva), to chrysalis (pupa), to adult. (say *meta-more-fisis*)

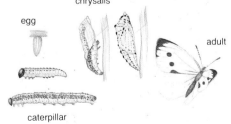

The metamorphosis of a butterfly.

metatarsal bone (1) in humans and other primates, one of the five long bones that join the ankle bones to the toe bones. (2) in other vertebrates, the part of the hind limb, between the tarsus and the toe bones.

M

meteor *n.* a small piece of matter traveling around the Sun. When it enters the Earth's atmosphere, it is burnt up as a result of friction⬜. We see this as a shooting star. Larger meteors do not burn up completely and fall to Earth as meteorites⬜.

meteorite *n.* the remains of a large meteor that has not been completely burned up as it falls through the Earth's atmosphere. It falls to Earth as a mass of metal or stone.

meteorology (1) *n.* the science that deals with the study of the weather patterns throughout the world. It provides the information on which weather forecasts are made.
(2) **meteorologist** *n.* a scientist who studies weather. (say *meet-eor-ol-ogee*)

meter (1) *n.* a unit of length in the metric system of measurement. There are 100 centimeters in 1 meter. 1000 meters equal 1 kilometer.
(2) an instrument or device used for measuring. For example, a gas meter measures the amount of gas used, an altimeter measures height above sea level, a parking meter measures the time a vehicle is allowed to park.

methane *n.* a gas that has no smell or color and easily catches fire. Methane is present in natural gas, marsh gas and fire damp, which is the gas that sometimes causes explosions in coal mines.

method (1) *n.* an orderly way of doing something, such as teaching or demonstrating scientific facts or experiments. (2) a system of doing things, e.g. the stages in the methods for extracting and refining metals for industry.

metric system a system of measurement of weight, length and capacity, based on units of ten. The basic unit of length is the meter, of weight, the gram (the weight of 1 cubic centimeter of water). The prefix kilo on any of these units means a thousand units; e.g. 1 kilogram equals 1000 grams, 1 kilometer equals 1000 meters. The prefix milli on any of these units means a thousandth part; e.g. 1 milligram equals 1/1000 gram, 1 millimeter equals 1/1000 meter. The centigrade or Celsius temperature scale is part of·the metric system. It was invented in 1742 by a Swedish astronomer, Anders Celsius.

mica *n.* one of a group of minerals, some being formed from compounds of iron and magnesium. The molten rock, containing the compounds, cooled slowly, forming thin layers of crystals, which split easily into fine bendable sheets that are almost transparent. Mica will not burn and is used in the doors of closed stoves. Mica does not conduct electricity.

microbe *n.* a tiny living organism that can be seen only through a microscope.

microchip *n.* a system of many integrated circuits, etched into a thin wafer of silicon⬜ and used in computers.

microcomputer *n.* a very small computer containing a single-chip microprocessor. It may be used to control a tool or instrument.

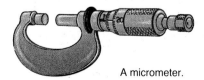

A micrometer.

micrometer *n.* an instrument used for measuring very small angles and distances accurately.

microorganism *n.* a very small organism that can be seen only through a microscope. Bacteria are microorganisms.

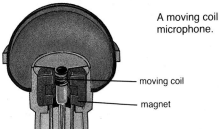

A moving coil microphone.

moving coil

magnet

microphone *n.* an instrument that changes sound into electric signals. It contains a thin disk that vibrates under pressure from sound waves.

microprocessor *n.* a single integrated circuit etched into one silicon chip. It is used in a wide range of electronic products and pocket calculators.

microscope *n.* an instrument that uses a system of magnifying lenses in order to make very small objects, which cannot easily be seen with the naked eye, appear larger.

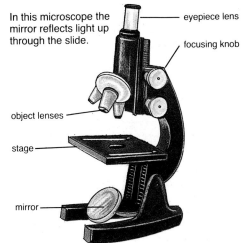

In this microscope the mirror reflects light up through the slide.

eyepiece lens

focusing knob

object lenses

stage

mirror

microscopic *adj.* describes any tiny particle or organism that is so small that it can only be seen through a microscope.

microwave *n.* radiation in which the wavelengths range between very short radio waves and the infrared waves of the spectrum. In microwave ovens food is cooked by the heat given off by microwaves.

middle ear the part of the ear found in humans and most four-legged animals with backbones. It lies between the eardrum and the cochlea in the inner ear. The middle ear is filled with air and contains three tiny bones (ossicles), the hammer (malleus), anvil (incus) and stirrup (stapes). These receive sound vibrations from the eardrum and increase their strength as they transmit them to the cochlea through a membrane called the oval window. See **eardrum**.

migrate (1) *v.* of animals, to move from one place to another over long distances, usually at a certain time of year. Animals, especially birds, migrate to warmer regions to escape harsh winters which lead to a food shortage. The snow goose breeds in Alaska and Siberia but spends the winter in California. Some animals, such as turtles, eels and salmon, travel thousands of miles to breed in particular areas. (2) **migration** *n.* the act of migrating.

mildew (1) *n.* a greyish-white coating that forms on damp objects made of natural materials, such as cotton, paper or leather, which has a characteristic musty smell. It is caused by a fungus. (2) a disease in plants caused by a fungus.

mile *n.* a unit of length or distance. It is equal to 1760 yards or 1609.34 meters.

M

milk (1) *n.* a whitish liquid secreted by the mammary glands of female mammals as a food for their young. Milk provides the young mammal with all the substances it needs for the first few weeks or months of life. It also gives the young human baby some immunity against certain infectious diseases. (2) the milk of cows used as a food by humans. (3) the fluid inside a ripe coconut. (4) *v.* to take milk from a cow, goat or other mammal.

milk teeth the first set of teeth in most young mammals, including humans. They are shed during the early years as the permanent teeth push through the gum. There are no back molars in a set of milk teeth.

The grinding stones of a windmill grind grain into flour.

mill (1) *n.* a machine used for grinding any grain or solid material into a powdery form. (2) a machine used to form a ridged edge or surface in metal objects. (3) a building with machines where things are made, e.g. a textile mill, a steel mill, or a paper mill. (4) *v.* to crush, grind or form something. *Grain is* **milled** *to produce flour.* (5) to raise or produce a ridged edge, as in some coins.

millibar *n.* a unit used for measuring atmospheric pressure. One millibar is equal to one-thousandth (1/1000) of a bar. One bar is roughly equal to the pressure of the atmosphere at sea level.

milligram *n.* a unit of mass or weight in the metric system, equal to one-thousandth (1/1000) of a gram.

milliliter *n.* a unit of liquid capacity measurement in the metric system equal to one-thousandth (1/1000) of a liter.

millimeter *n.* a unit of length in the metric system equal to one-thousandth (1/1000) of a meter.

mimicry *n.* the imitation, by one species, of the color, shape or sound of another. Some harmless, edible animals gain protection from predators by copying the appearance of other, dangerous, poisonous or inedible animals. The owl butterfly has markings on its wings that look like the large eyes of an owl—a trick that may discourage predators. Many different species of harmless insects have developed the same markings as those that are poisonous to other animals. Predators have learned to avoid eating these poisonous animals, and so all the 'look-alike' species are also protected.

mind (1) *n.* the part of a living human being that thinks, reasons, learns, remembers, feels emotions, imagines and dreams. All the processes of the mind are carried out by the brain. (2) intelligence; the intellect. A sharp or clear mind shows a quick understanding or intelligence. *A person may have a good* **mind** *for figures.*

mine (1) *n.* an area of land underground from which rocks and minerals are extracted. (2) *v.* to dig out or remove from underground.

Diamonds, mineral rocks and coal are materials which are mined. (3) to place explosive devices underwater or underground in order to cause damage by explosion.

mineral (1) *n*. any natural material found in the ground that does not come from animals and plants, e.g. iron, rock salt and limestone. Coal is considered to be a mineral, although it was formed from plants. Each mineral has a known chemical composition and typical chemical and physical properties. (2) *adj*. to do with minerals, e.g. mineral salts, mineral oils.

mineral salts (1) chemical compounds containing a mineral acid. They have a known chemical composition and characteristic physical and chemical properties. (2) soluble mineral substances needed by living organisms in order to stay alive. For example, iron is needed to make the red pigment in red blood cells, which carry oxygen around the body.

minute (1) *n*. a unit of time: one-sixtieth (1/60) of an hour, equal to 60 seconds. (2) a unit of measurement of an arc of a circle, equal to one-sixtieth (1/60) of a degree.

mirage *n*. a reflected image, usually seen in the desert or at sea. It is created by light rays being refracted (bent) through layers of air of different densities. If these layers are above the observer, he or she may see in the sky upside-down images of objects which may be hidden over the horizon; or the mirage appears as a sheet of water in the distance, in which objects are reflected. In Arctic regions, mirages of glaciers hanging down from the sky may be seen. (say *meer-ahj*)

mirror *n*. a smooth, polished surface of metal or glass, with a silvered backing, which reflects light. A mirror produces an image that appears to come from a point as far behind the mirror as the object is in front. The image is also reversed left to right (a mirror image). This is caused by the angle of reflection of the light rays from a flat or plane mirror. Curved mirrors produce other effects. A concave mirror, such as the inside of the bowl of a spoon, will produce an upside-down distorted image. A convex mirror, such as the outside of the bowl of a spoon, produces an image that is the right way up. The convex mirror also reflects more of the surroundings.

In the mirror image this girl's right hand appears as her left.

missile *n*. something that is discharged or launched into the air, e.g. bullets, shells from big guns, boomerangs and rockets.

mist *n*. a cloud of fine water droplets formed at ground level. It is caused by condensation☐ of water vapor when warm, moist air is suddenly cooled. *When I breathe on the cold window,* **mist** *is formed.*

M

mite *n.* a tiny animal belonging to the spider family (arachnid). Some are free living and are found in food, but most are parasites, living off particular host plants or animals. Some mites transmit diseases such as typhus.

mixture *n.* a material formed by adding together two or more substances. They can be separated again by physical means. Mixtures may consist of solids, liquids or gases. Air is a mixture of nitrogen, carbon dioxide, oxygen, water vapor and very small amounts of other gases. Mortar is a mixture of cement, sand and lime.

mobile *adj.* able to move from place to place. Animals are mobile organisms. Robots and vehicles are mobile machines when switched on or driven.

model (1) *n.* a small, exact copy of an object such as a building, boat or machine. (2) *v.* to form or shape an object.

modify *v.* to change or alter the form, quality or degree of something. *In plants, some leaves are* **modified** *to form tendrils or spines.*

modulation *n.* the process of adding electrical signals onto a radio wave, which carries them (carrier wave). There are two ways of doing this: (i) amplitude modulation (AM), in which the size of the carrier wave is changed to match the signals being sent, and (ii) frequency modulation (FM), in which the frequency of the carrier wave is changed in step with the signals being sent.

module (1) *n.* in electronics, a machine that is complete in itself but that can become a unit of another machine such as a computer. Modules can be interchanged without affecting the computer. (2) part of a spacecraft that can be separated from the main craft to carry out operations in space on its own, e.g. the lunar module which landed on the Moon. (say *mod-jewel*)

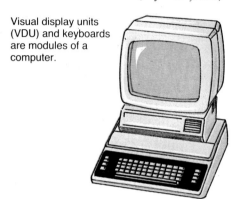

Visual display units (VDU) and keyboards are modules of a computer.

moist *adj.* slightly wet, damp.

moisture *n.* dampness; water that is present in the air as water vapor or mist, as tiny droplets in the soil or as condensation on cold surfaces.

Section of a human molar

enamel

dentine

roots

molar *n.* any of the large teeth, found at the back of the mouth in mammals. They have three roots and a large flat or ridged surface for crushing and grinding food. Molars are only present in the permanent teeth.

mold (1) *n.* a grey or white feltlike growth of a fungus over the surface of a living or dead organism, e.g. food, leather or paper. It causes the decay of the organic matter. Molds reproduce by spores☐. (2) a hollow container of a particular shape, used for forming objects.

molecule *n.* the smallest particle of an element☐ or compound that can exist by itself and still have all the properties of that element or compound. It consists of atoms. *A molecule of water consists of two hydrogen atoms and one oxygen atom.* (say *moll-e-cule*)

A molecule of water.

mollusc *n.* any one of a large group of animals, without a backbone, with a soft, muscular body divided into a head and a foot for movement. Many molluscs are protected by hard shells. Most live in water, e.g. mussels and clams. Squid and octopuses are molluscs that do not have shells.

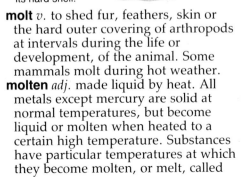

When a snail is in danger it withdraws into its hard shell.

molt *v.* to shed fur, feathers, skin or the hard outer covering of arthropods at intervals during the life or development, of the animal. Some mammals molt during hot weather.

molten *adj.* made liquid by heat. All metals except mercury are solid at normal temperatures, but become liquid or molten when heated to a certain high temperature. Substances have particular temperatures at which they become molten, or melt, called the melting point. Ice melts at 0°C. Copper melts at 1083°C.

momentum *n.* the force produced by a moving body. It is equal to the product of the mass of the body and its velocity (speed), e.g. an object with a mass of 10 kg moving at a speed of 6 m/s (meters per second) has a momentum of 60 kg m/s.

monkey *n.* any one of the small long-tailed primates. They have long arms and legs with grasping digits on hands and feet. They live mainly in the upper tree layers in tropical rain forests and eat plants, fruit and nuts.

monocotyledon *n.* a flowering plant (angiosperm) that has only one cotyledon (seed leaf) in its seed. The leaves of monocotyledons usually have parallel veins, unlike the net-veined leaves of dicotyledons (two seed leaves). Grasses and palm trees are monocotyledons.

monsoon *n.* a regular seasonal wind that blows over the Indian Ocean and southern Asia. From April to October it blows off the ocean. The monsoon is caused by convection currents of warm air rising off the very hot land masses of India and Asia. Cooler, moisture-laden air is drawn in over the land from the sea, creating the southwest monsoons. The opposite conditions, cool land and warmer sea, occur during the winter, and the monsoon blows from the northeast.

month (1) *n.* any one of the twelve parts into which the calendar year is divided, e.g. January, February, etc. (2) a lunar month: the time taken for the Moon to make a complete revolution of the Earth, approximately 28 days. (3) one-twelfth of the solar year, approximately 30 days.

M

moon (1) *n.* any satellite of any planet. Jupiter has four bright moons. (2) Earth's satellite Moon: a small world with no water and no atmosphere; it orbits the Earth approximately once every 28 days. The same part of the Moon always faces the Earth. The Moon is held in orbit by the Earth's gravity, which is five times as great as the Moon's gravity. The Moon does not give out light; it reflects the light from the Sun.

moraine *n.* a huge mass of rocks, gravel, sand and clay that has been moved by glaciers or ice sheets. A moraine may have been left behind by the moving glacier or pushed in front of it (terminal moraine).

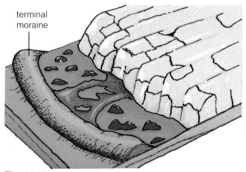

terminal moraine

The glacier has moved, exposing the moraine.

mortality (1) *n.* the condition of being mortal, and bound to die. (2) **mortal** *adj.* having a limited life span.

mortar (1) *n.* a mixture of sand, lime and cement, which, when mixed with water, forms a material that dries hard. It is used in building, to bond bricks and stones together. (2) a bowl in which certain solids are ground to a fine powder by a pestle.

mosquito *n.* (*pl. mosquitoes*) any one of a number of species of small insects with two wings. The female has a piercing mouth part (proboscis) and sucks blood. Mosquitoes breed in ponds and marshland, and the larvae are aquatic. Some species of mosquito transmit diseases, such as malaria and yellow fever.

moss *n.* a small, green, tufted, low-growing plant, belonging to the class Musci. Mosses form coverings and dense mats of green on trees, stones, paths, fences, and the ground. The plant body consists of fine stems, leaves and rootlike rhizoids. Mosses do not bear flowers. They reproduce in two ways, by forming gametes or spores.

moth *n.* an insect belonging to the same order as butterflies (Lepidoptera). Moths have four wings and the antennae are not clubbed as in butterflies. Sometimes the antennae are feathery. The body and wings are covered with fine scales, often brightly colored. Most moths fly at night. The moth goes through a complete metamorphosis during development: egg larva, pupa, imago (adult moth). A moth larva is a caterpillar.

A garden tiger moth with feathery antennae.

motile *adj.* describes animal microorganisms that are able to move about in water by means of flagella⬚, cilia⬚ or contracting movements of the body.

motion *n.* movement: of an animal from place to place, of a limb or part of a body, of a machine.

motor (1) *n.* a machine that moves or causes movement. An internal combustion engine which drives a vehicle or other machine, such as a lawnmower. (2) a machine that changes electrical energy into mechanical energy. (3) *adj.* producing motion or being powered by a motor, e.g. a motor vehicle. (4) *v.* to travel by car.

motor nerve (motor neuron) a nerve that carries messages (impulses) from the brain to all parts of the body, such as muscles, causing them to contract, and to the digestive glands, causing them to produce digestive juices.

mountain range a group or chain of very high mountain peaks linked together by the surrounding high ground. The Alps, Rockies and Himalayas are mountain ranges above ground. There are also mountain ranges running under the oceans, which are higher than Mt Everest in places, and form chains of islands and volcanoes. Mountain ranges are formed by movements in the plates of the Earth's crust.

mouth *n.* in animals, the opening in the body through which food is taken in. In vertebrates, the space behind this opening which contains the teeth and tongue. It has a roof (the palate) and a floor. The sides are edged by the jaws, which bear the teeth. The tongue and teeth prepare food for swallowing. In mammals it is mixed with saliva, produced by glands that open into the mouth through ducts. Sounds are made through the mouth of mammals and certain other vertebrates.

move (1) *v.* to change, or cause to change, the position of an organism or object from one place to another. (2) in animals, to change the position of part of the body, such as bending an arm or turning the head. (3) in plants, to alter the position of part of a plant in response to a stimulus such as light or gravity, e.g. the leaves of plants turn to face the light.

movement (1) *n.* a change in position of part of an animal or plant, such as the wave of a hand or the opening and closing of a flower. (2) the moving parts of a mechanism, such as the wheels of a watch or clock.

mucus (1) *n.* a clear, slimy fluid produced by the mucous membranes which line the mouth, nose, lungs and gut of mammals and some other vertebrates. The mucus moistens and protects the linings. (2) a similar substance produced by fish and some invertebrates, e.g. snails, slugs. (3) an unpleasant, slimy substance produced by the moist skin of some cold-blooded vertebrates, such as toads. It makes them distasteful as food for other animals, and so helps to protect them.

mulch (1) *n.* any plant material such as leaves, grass cuttings, peat or tree bark, that is spread on the soil around plants to keep the soil cool and moist, and to stop the growth of weeds. As the mulch decays, it adds plant nutrients to the soil. (2) *v.* to spread such material on the ground.

multicellular *adj.* describes living organisms consisting of many cells. (say *multi-sell-ular*)

M

multiply (1) *v.* to increase in number. Cells multiply by simple cell division, a process in which one cell divides into two identical halves. Each half becomes a new cell. Different animals multiply or reproduce by different processes, which may be sexual or by other means. Mammals multiply sexually. A simple organism such as a hydra may multiply by budding off a new animal from its body. Plants may reproduce sexually with the germination of seeds or by spores or vegetative means, by layers or cuttings. (2) to obtain the product of two or more numbers or values.

mumps *n.* an infectious disease, caused by a virus, common in children. It causes fever and painful swelling of the salivary glands in the mouth and in front of the ear. It is painful to eat and swallow with mumps.

A striped muscle; the enlargement shows muscle fibers as seen through a microscope.

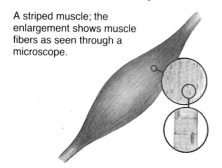

muscle *n.* a special tissue in animals, made of cells, which when stimulated by a nerve impulse can shorten and become wider (contract). Some muscles work in pairs. As one is made to contract, it causes its partner to relax or lengthen. If the relaxed muscle then receives an impulse, it will contract. It is the tissue that causes motion and movement of parts of the body.

muscle fiber a muscle cell: one of three different types (striated, cardiac and smooth) which make up the muscle tissues in animals. Striated (striped) muscle fibers occur in vertebrates (animals with backbones). They form the muscles that move the joints of the skeleton. The striated muscles are controlled by the brain. Cardiac muscle fibers form heart muscle. They contract more slowly than striated muscle, and do not normally become fatigued. Smooth muscle fibers are controlled by the autonomic nervous system. They occur in vertebrates and form the walls of hollow organs such as the bladder, intestine and blood vessels.

muscular (1) *adj.* describes a tissue made of muscle fibers. (2) describes an animal or human with well-developed, powerful muscles.

mushroom *n.* a white, umbrella-shaped fungus; an organism without true stem, leaves or green pigment (chlorophyll). Fungi cannot make the substances needed for growth; they take them from decaying vegetation. Mushrooms grow very rapidly from spores, produced in raylike gills on the underside of the cap. The cap is supported by a thick,

fleshy stalk (stipe). Some mushrooms can be eaten; others are very poisonous.

mutation *n.* the process by which living organisms suddenly produce offspring with different or varied characteristics from the parent. Mutation is caused by a change in the form of genes or behavior of chromosomes. This may occur spontaneously or be caused by chemicals or radiation. For example, a plant that normally produces red flowers may suddenly produce blue flowers. Such a plant is a mutant.

myopia *n.* short sight. A condition of the eye in humans in which images of distant objects look blurred, whereas images of near objects are clear and sharp. Suitable concave lenses correct myopia. (say *my-ope-eea*)

N n

nail (1) *n.* one of the hard plates made of keratin at the ends of digits in some mammals; similar to claws, but flat. They are formed by special cells in the skin at the base of the nail and grow continuously during life. In wild mammals they are worn away naturally, but in humans they have to be cut regularly. (2) a thin, pointed rod of metal with a flat head, used for joining pieces of wood. It is forced into the wood with hammer blows to the head. (3) *v.* to fix things together by using nails.

nanometer *n.* a unit of microscopic measurement in the metric system, equal to one-thousand-millionth of a meter.

narcotic *n.* any drug that causes sleep or dulls pain and other feelings. People can become dependent on narcotics. If taken regularly they damage health and may cause death. Opium, heroin and morphine are powerful narcotics.

nasal cavity in vertebrates (animals with backbones), the space inside the head which contains the sense organs for smell. In land vertebrates, air passes through the nasal cavity before entering the windpipe (trachea). The mucous lining produces a sticky liquid which traps dust and germs. Tiny hairs called cilia carry the mucus toward the nostrils, where it is removed. Pockets of air in the skull (sinuses) open into the nasal cavity.

natural *adj.* produced by nature; not made by humans; not artificial. Wild animals and tropical rain forests are natural things. *Cotton, wool and silk are* **natural** *fibers. Stone and wood are* **natural** *materials.*

natural gas a gas found naturally in pockets near mineral oil deposits underground. It is used as a fuel. Natural gas consists mainly of methane and some other hydrocarbon gases. Large pockets have been found in the North Sea and around the British Isles.

naturalist *n.* a person who studies plants and animals.

natural selection a gradual process in evolution in which some organisms survive and reproduce, whereas others become extinct. The organisms that survive are those that develop new characteristics that help them to adapt to changing surroundings. These characteristics are passed on to future generations. Charles Darwin, a famous naturalist, called this process of natural selection 'the survival of the fittest'.

N

nausea *n*. an unpleasant feeling of sickness in the stomach which is often followed by vomiting.

nautical *adj*. to do with ships, sailors and navigation. *The captain of the trawler had great **nautical** experience.*

nautical mile an international measurement of distance used by sailors, roughly equal to 1852 meters, or 6076 feet.

navigation (1) *n*. the means by which a traveler is able to work out his or her position on land or sea, in air or in space, and to plan and direct a course. Until about 70 years ago, the only instruments of navigation were a compass, a sextant, a chronometer, a gyroscope and an almanac. The almanac is a book that shows the positions of the Sun, stars and planets for each day of the year. Nowadays ships and aircraft have very efficient radar, and a **long range navigation** system (LORAN). The systems can be linked to navigation satellites through computers, and the course and position are shown on a screen. (2) the act of planning and directing the course or route of an aircraft or ship.

Neanderthal man primitive humans who lived in Europe and the Middle

East some 70,000 to 60,000 years ago. They were short and stocky and walked upright. Their brains were smaller than those of modern humans, and their skulls were a different shape. Neanderthal man was a skilled hunter with weapons of flint and bone. They buried their dead under huge burial mounds. (say *knee-an-der-thal*)

neap tide a very low sea tide which occurs twice a month, just after the Moon is in its first or third quarter. At neap tide there is the smallest difference in level between high and low water. Neap tides occur when the axis of the Moon is at right angles to the Sun, and they are pulling against each other.

nebula *n*. (*pl. nebulae*) a cloud of dust and gases in space. Stars are born inside nebulae, which are often called stellar nurseries. Many nebulae are visible with telescopes from Earth.

neck (1) *n*. in animals with backbones, the narrow part of the body that joins the head to the shoulders. (2) a narrow strip of land connecting two larger land masses; a strait. (3) the long, narrow part leading into a flask, bottle or other container.

nectar *n*. a sweet liquid made by a tiny gland (nectary) deep inside some flowers. Nectar attracts insects. As they push their mouth parts into the flower, pollen grains stick to their bodies and are carried to other flowers, causing pollination☐.

negative (1) *adj*. in mathematics, less than nothing, minus. Measured in the opposite direction to positive. (2) in electricity and magnetism, there are positive and negative electrodes☐ in an electrical device. The south-seeking pole of a magnet has a negative charge. (3) in plants, describes a response made away from a stimulus. Plant stems show a negative response to gravity and grow upward against the force of gravity. (4) *n.* an exposed film, before it is printed. The dark and light areas on the object are reversed in a negative; black appears white and vice versa.

nematode *n.* a round worm; an animal with a long, narrow, tubelike body covered with a thin cuticle⬚. Its body is not segmented. The digestive tube is a single tube open at both ends. Nematodes are found in fresh and salt water, in the soil, and as parasites on other animals, e.g. hookworm and pinworm. (say *nema-toad*)

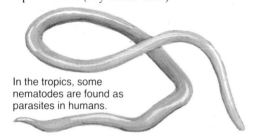

In the tropics, some nematodes are found as parasites in humans.

neon *n.* a gas that has no color or smell, which occurs in minute amounts in the atmosphere. Neon is an inactive chemical element, but it has been made to react with fluorine, the most reactive element of all. When an electric current is passed through a light bulb filled with neon gas, it glows with an orange-red color. Neon is widely used in electric signs.

nerve *n.* a bundle of nerve fibers (axons and dendrons) surrounded by a protective, fatty sheath with its own blood supply and supporting tissues. Nerves carry messages (impulses) between the brain and spinal cord, and all other parts of the body.

A nerve cell.

axon

A nerve end plate in muscle fibers.

nerve cell a neuron; the cells that make up the nervous system in all animals made of more than one cell (multicellular). A nerve cell has a cell body with a nucleus surrounded by cytoplasm⬚. Cell bodies are found in the grey matter in the brain and spinal cord. A number of fine threads or fibers project from the cell body, usually one long one (axon) and several shorter ones (dendrons) with branching twiglike ends (dendrites). These fibers form the white matter of the brain and spinal cord.

nerve fiber an axon⬚ or dendron⬚ with a fatty protective sheath; one of the neuron fibers which make up a nerve. An axon carries messages away from the cell body to an organ, such as a muscle. The dendrons carry messages toward the cell body from the sensory receptors, such as the skin, eyes and ears, or from other axons. *See* **nerve cell**.

nervous system the system of nerve cells which controls all the actions and reactions of animals. Plants and single-celled animals do not have nervous systems. In simple organisms such as jellyfish, the nervous system consists of a network of connecting

N

nerve cells. In more complex animals, such as worms, insects and spiders, the nervous system consists of a thick cord of nerve fibers running the length of the body, with a swelling (ganglion) in each body segment. Mammals such as humans have a highly developed central nervous system consisting of a large brain and spinal cord. This system controls all the actions and reactions of the body. The peripheral nervous system consists of all the nerves that carry messages from all parts of the body to and from the brain. All sense organs, such as eyes, ears and skin, are part of the peripheral nervous system. So also are the special nerve endings in the muscles and glands.

nest (1) *n.* a shelter made or chosen by birds, in which they lay their eggs and rear their young. Nests may be made from twigs, leaves, reeds, grasses, moss, hair or mud. (2) Any shelter or place used by insects, fish, amphibians, reptiles or other animals for breeding. (3) *v.* to live in or build a

The nest of the weaver bird is woven from grasses and leaves.

nest. *Woodpeckers* **nest** *in holes in trees. Kingfishers* **nest** *in holes in river banks. Many sea birds* **nest** *on rocky ledges.*

network (1) *n.* any system of threads, fibers, wires, canals or roads which connect or cross at intervals to form a mesh. (2) in animals, the network of capillary blood vessels in the tissues; the network of nerve cells and fibers in the brain, spinal cord and all nervous tissue. (3) the network of radio and television channels. (4) a computer network: a series of linked computers which share information.

neural *adj.* to do with a nerve or the nervous system. The neural canal is the hole in the vertebral column (backbone) that contains the spinal cord.

neuron, neurone *n.* the scientific name for a nerve cell. It consists of the cell body and all its processes (dendrites and axon). See **nerve cell**.

neutral (1) *adj.* describes a chemical substance or solution, which is neither acidic nor alkaline. The pH scale measures from pH0 (strongly acidic) to pH14 (strongly alkaline). A neutral solution has a pH of 7. (2) not having a positive or a negative electrical charge; uncharged. (3) an atom with equal numbers of positively and negatively charged particles is said to be neutral. (4) in mechanical engines, the position of the gears when they are not connected and cannot transmit power to the drive. (5) in biology, the same as neuter: having undeveloped or no sexual organs.

neutralize (1) *v.* to remove the electrical charge on a particle or body. (2) to change the alkaline properties of a substance or solution so that it does not behave like an acid or an alkali. To produce a pH of 7 in a solution.

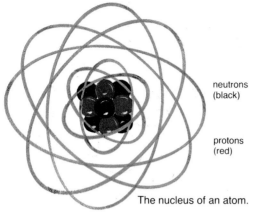

neutrons
(black)

protons
(red)

The nucleus of an atom.

neutron *n.* one of the tiny particles in the nucleus of all atoms, except hydrogen. It has no electric charge.

newt *n.* one of several species of small, long-tailed, amphibian vertebrates (animals with backbones) belonging to the salamander family. The newt is related to frogs and toads and hatches as a tadpole from spawn (eggs) laid in ponds. It develops lungs and front and back legs, like frogs and toads, but does not lose its tail. Newts are able to grow new toes or tails after injuries.

nibble (1) *n.* in computers, a number made up of four digits. (2) *v.* to take small, quick bites with the front teeth (incisors). *Rats, squirrels and sheep* **nibble** *when they eat.*

niche (1) *n.* the special function or position of an organism in its natural community. (2) the particular habitat of an organism in its natural environment.

nickel *n.* a hard silvery-white metal; a chemical element. It is easily beaten into shapes. Nickel is used to coat other metals to prevent corrosion☐ and is one of the metals commonly used in alloys. An alloy of nickel and copper is used as a metal for making coins.

nicotine *n.* a poisonous chemical substance found in tobacco leaves. It stimulates the nervous system and increases the rate of heartbeat when taken in by the body.

nipple *n.* the teat of a mammary gland☐ through which young mammals suck milk. Nipples are small, paired swellings in the skin on the front or underside of the mammal. The milk ducts of the mammary gland open into the surface. Humans and other primates have one pair of nipples, but mammals such as cats, which produce large litters of young at one time, may have many pairs.

nitrate *n.* a salt; a chemical compound formed by the reaction of a metal or base with nitric acid. Certain nitrates are used as soil fertilizers.

nitrogen *n.* a gas with no smell, color or taste; a chemical element. Unlike oxygen, nitrogen will not allow things to burn. Nitrogen makes up almost four-fifths (4/5) of the Earth's atmosphere. Nitrogen, in the form of protein and amino acids, is found in all living organisms. (say *nigh-tro-jin*)

noble gas one of a group of inert (inactive) gases found in minute amounts in the Earth's atmosphere. Helium, argon and neon are noble gases. They are said to be inert because they do not react easily with other elements or substances. They have no color, smell or taste. Argon is used in electric light bulbs to prevent the thin wire filament from burning away. Neon is used in electric signs.

nocturnal *adj.* active or happening at night. It describes an animal which feeds and moves around during the night and sleeps during the day. Owls and bats are nocturnal animals.

N

node (1) *n.* in plants, the part of the stem from which leaves or aerial roots may grow. (2) a point along a wave where there is no amplitude☐ of vibration.

nodule (1) *n.* a small, rounded swelling on the surface of an organ or organism. (2) tiny swellings on the roots of leguminous plants, such as pea, bean, clover and lupin. These contain bacteria which are able to take in the free nitrogen in the soil and turn it into protein, used by the plant for growth. The bacteria, in return, receive food substances from the plant. (3) small lumps of rock found on the floor of deep oceans. They contain manganese, copper and nickel. Scientists are not sure how they are formed. Manganese nodules consist of rock surrounded by layers of manganese oxide. They appear to have been built up gradually.

noise (1) *n.* a loud or undesirable sound. Loudness is measured in decibels (dB). A soft whisper is measured at 0 dB. A sound of 140 dB causes pain to the human ear. Noise is a form of environmental pollution. In many countries there are laws that control the level of noise allowed. (2) any unwanted electrical signal within a communication system, such as radio or telephone. *There is a lot of* **noise** *on this telephone line. I shall hang up and try again.*

nonconductor *n.* a substance or material that does not readily conduct certain forms of energy, such as electricity, sound or heat. Glass and most nonmetals are nonconductors of electricity.

nonmetal *n.* a chemical element that does not behave like a metal. It does not conduct heat or electricity.

Nonmetals may be solids or gases, apart from bromine, which is a liquid. Solid nonmetals are usually hard and brittle and will not bend like metals. Carbon is the commonest nonmetal, but in its crystalline form, graphite, it behaves like a metal and conducts electricity.

North Pole *n.* the point on the Earth's surface that lies at the north end of the Earth's axis.

nose *n.* the sense organ for smell in land vertebrates; the snout or muzzle. It lies at the front of the head. The nose contains two openings (nostrils) through which air is breathed. It contains fine hairs which filter out the dust in the air before it reaches the lungs.

nose cone the cone-shaped front part of a spacecraft. It has a heat-resistant shield that prevents the spacecraft from burning up during its reentry into the Earth's atmosphere.

A nose cone casing being discarded by a satellite.

nostril *n.* one of a pair of small openings in the nose of land vertebrates through which air is breathed.

nourishment *n.* food or other substances taken in or eaten by living organisms, which provide the substances needed for health and growth. *Milk provides all the* **nourishment** *needed by my young baby.*

nova *n.* a star that suddenly shines more brightly for a short period and then fades over the next few months or years. It is caused by a tremendous disturbance inside the star. (say *no-va*)

nuclear energy also known as atomic energy. The energy that is released during the fission (splitting) or the fusion (joining) of the nuclei of atoms.

nuclear fission the splitting of a heavy atomic nucleus by bombarding it with neutrons☐. Nuclear fission produces enormous amounts of nuclear energy.

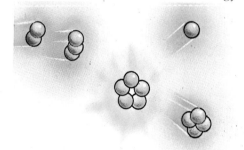

Two forms of hydrogen atoms join to produce energy, one atom of helium and a free neutron.

nuclear fusion a process in which the nuclei of light atoms such as hydrogen are joined to form heavier atoms. This releases enormous amounts of energy, as in the case of the hydrogen bomb. Nuclear fusion occurs naturally in stars such as the Sun. As a source of energy, nuclear fusion would be better than fission because there are unlimited supplies of hydrogen, and there would be no radioactive waste to dispose of.

nuclear reactor a device that uses the controlled fission of the nuclei of a radioactive substance, such as uranium, to produce energy. Nuclear reactors are used in nuclear power stations to provide energy.

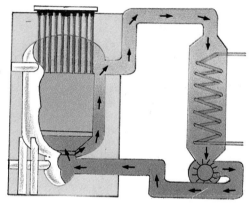

Heat from the reactor is led off by water or gas circulating through a heat exchanger.

nucleus (1) *n.* the center of an atom, which contains the tiny particles called protons and neutrons. The nucleus contains nearly all the mass of an atom. (2) a small, dense mass of cell matter, surrounded by a thin membrane, which is found in nearly all living plant and animal cells. The nucleus controls the growth and reproduction of the cell. A cell dies if the nucleus is damaged.

nut (1) *n.* a fruit that contains one seed, or kernel. The outer layer of the fruit forms a tough coat or woody shell, e.g. a chestnut or a cobnut. The kernels of many nuts are edible. (2) a flat, square-shaped or many-sided metal block with a threaded hole in the middle, which is used for fixing bolts in position. *The* **nut** *was loose on the bolt, so John tightened it with a wrench.*

nutrient (1) *n.* any substance that is nourishing or provides food for a living organism. (2) *adj.* describes anything that is nourishing, such as bread, meat and fruit. (say *new-tree-ent*)

nutrition (1) *n.* the processes of eating, digesting and absorbing food by living organisms. (2) the scientific study of a healthy diet. (say *new-trishun*)

nylon *n.* a very tough, flexible, plastic substance used in the manufacture of strings for tennis rackets, ropes, textiles and many other industrial and household goods. Nylon was the joint product of scientists working in **New York** and **Lon**don, hence its name.

nymph *n.* one of the stages in the development of some insects, such as dragonflies, before they become adult. A nymph has similar eyes and mouth parts to the adult insect, but it has either no wings or undeveloped ones. A nymph may molt several times before it becomes adult. Some nymphs are aquatic.

O o

oasis *n.* (*pl. oases*) an area in a desert where water is nearly always present. Palm trees and other plants grow well in the moist sand. Some large oases

situated in old river valleys support whole villages. Here the water is often underground and has to be brought to the surface. (say *o-a-sis*)

obesity *n.* a condition of being too fat that occurs in humans and other mammals. Obesity may be due to overeating or to certain diseases of the ductless glands (endocrine glands).

object glass a magnifying lens found in optical instruments such as microscopes and telescopes. It is situated at the opposite end to the eyepiece, and is nearest to the object being looked at.

objective *n.* the lens or system of lenses found at the end of a microscope nearest the object. The image produced by the objective can be seen through the eyepiece, which magnifies it many times.

observation (1) *n.* the act of noticing or watching something very closely. Observation is very important in scientific study. *The student wrote an excellent paper on the behavior of young otters based on his own* **observations**. (2) something that is noticed. (3) in navigation, a reading, for example, of the altitude of the Sun, taken in order to plot a position or course on land, at sea or in the air.

observatory *n.* a building especially designed and placed to give a wide

An astronomical observatory.

view of the surrounding land or the sky. An astronomical observatory has a large dome-shaped roof made of sliding panels. The very large telescopes inside the dome are used to study the stars, planets, galaxies and other bodies. A meteorological observatory is used to study the weather.

observe *v.* to notice or watch carefully. *The bird watcher* **observed** *the flocks of migrating snow geese.*

ocean (1) *n.* a large area of deep, salt water. The oceans cover three-quarters of the Earth's surface. (2) one of the following: Arctic Ocean, Atlantic Ocean, Pacific Ocean, Indian Ocean or Antarctic Ocean.

octagon *n.* a flat figure having eight sides and eight angles. If all the sides and angles are equal the figure is called a regular octagon.

octopus *n. (pl. octopuses)* a sea animal with a soft, rounded, muscular body and eight arms, or tentacles. Each tentacle has two rows of suction pads which grip rocks and prey. An octopus has two eyes and a mouth at the base of its body. An octopus is a cephalopod☐ and belongs to the same family as squid and cuttlefish. Some, found in the Pacific Ocean, have tentacles 10 feet long. Smaller octopuses are found in the Mediterranean Sea and some warm, inshore waters. They live among the rocks and feed on molluscs and crustaceans.

ocular (1) *adj.* to do with the eye.(2) *n.* the eyepiece of a microscope or telescope or other optical instrument.

odor *n.* a smell, scent or fragrance. It may be pleasant, like the fragrance of flowers, or unpleasant, like the smell of rotten eggs. Many animals have a particular odor which enables other animals to detect their presence. Certain animal odors are produced at mating time to attract males and females. They also mark out animal territories.

offspring *n.* the young produced by living organisms. *Kittens are the* **offspring** *of cats. Leverets are the* **offspring** *of hares.*

ohm *n.* the unit of measurement of electrical resistance☐. When an electrical force of 1 volt is needed to produce a current of 1 ampere, a resistance of 1 ohm is set up in the circuit wire. The unit was named after G.S.Ohm, a German physicist (1787–1854). (say *ome*)

oil (1) *n.* any of a number of fatty or greasy substances that are normally liquid at room temperature. Oils are obtained from certain plants, animals and mineral oil deposits in the Earth. They burn readily, giving off a black, sooty deposit of carbon. Oils dissolve in alcohol but not in water. They are lighter than water and float on the surface. Certain oils, obtained by the distillation of flowers, are used in making perfumes, e.g. lavender oil. Other vegetable oils are obtained by crushing seeds or heating them with steam, e.g. olive oil, coconut oil and linseed oil. Cod liver and halibut liver oils are rich in vitamins A and D. Petroleum, diesel oil and kerosene are obtained from mineral oil deposits. Oil is a good lubricant; it is used to coat the moving parts of machinery. This reduces friction and so helps the parts to move more freely.
(2) *v.* to coat with oil; to lubricate. *The mechanic* **oiled** *the rusty lock on the old door so that the key would turn more easily.*

O

oil field an area of land or sea beneath which are large deposits of mineral oil. Oil fields are found in many parts of the world, e.g. the Middle East, the North Sea and America.

oil platform a large structure that is used in offshore oil production. Oil platforms may be fixed to the seabed or floating and anchored by chains. They gather and store oil from several wells and process it in readiness for shipping it ashore.

oil pollution the harmful presence of a thick layer of oil on the surface of the sea. It is sometimes driven ashore by wind and tide; it kills sea birds and fish and damages the shore. Oil pollution is caused by oil spilled from tankers.

This floating drilling rig is anchored to the sea bed by chains.

oil rig a drilling platform, anchored offshore, used for obtaining oil from under the seabed.

oil well a hole bored into the ground to obtain oil.

olfactory *adj.* to do with the sense of smell. The nose, with its internal passages, is called the olfactory organ. The olfactory nerve transmits impulses from the sensory endings in the upper part of the nose to the brain.

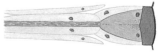

A single ommatidium. The compound eye of a bee contains 15,000 ommatidia.

ommatidium *n.* (*pl. ommatidia*) one of the individual units that make up a compound eye. Each ommatidium has a separate lens that focuses light on only a few cells. It is separated from other ommatidia by black pigment⬜, which keeps light from passing from one unit to another. Movement of the pigment in the ommatidium controls the amount of light entering it. Insects, such as bees and flies, have compound eyes. (say *omma-ti-deeum*)

omnivore *n.* an animal that eats plants and animals. Humans are omnivores. (say *om-ni-vore*)

opaque (1) *adj.* describes any substance that does not let light pass through it. Wood and bricks are opaque. (2) dull or light-absorbing; not reflecting light. (say *o-pake*)

opencut *adj.* in mining, the cutting or digging out of coal or ores on the surface, rather than from underground.

operate (1) *v.* to cause a piece of machinery to work and to control it. *The dockworker* **operated** *the crane skillfully.* (2) to perform a surgical operation.

operation (1) *n.* the working or method of action of a machine. *The pilot explained the* **operation** *of the flight controls to the air cadet.* (2) the act of performing surgery. *The* **operation** *on Scott's knee was successful and he was soon able to run again.*

opium *n.* a powerful, narcotic drug that relieves pain and causes sleep. It is made from the milky juice found in the seed of the opium poppy, which grows wild in the mountains of China, India and Pakistan.

optic *adj.* to do with the eye or sense of sight, e.g. the optic nerve.

optical illusion something that is seen but that is not really as it seems. Certain patterns of lines, shapes and colors play tricks on the eye and brain.

Weather satellites orbiting the Earth take photographs which are used to make accurate weather forecasts.

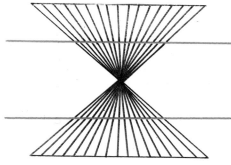

The two red lines appear to bend, but they are straight. This is an optical illusion.

optic nerve the nerve that transmits impulses from the light-sensitive retina at the back of the eye to the base of the brain.

oral *adj.* to do with the mouth. **Oral** *hygiene is important in preventing tooth decay.*

orbit (1) *n.* the path of a satellite or planet as it moves around another body in space under the effect of gravity. (2) the path of an electron☐ as it moves around the nucleus☐ of an atom. (3) in animals with backbones (vertebrates), the bony hollow containing the eye. (4) the skin or border around the eye of a bird, reptile or insect. (5) *v.* to move in an orbit. *The Earth* **orbits** *the Sun; the Moon* **orbits** *the Earth.*

orbital velocity the speed that must be reached by a satellite or spacecraft for it to go into orbit around the Earth or other body.

order *n.* in biology, one of the groups in the classification of animals and plants; a unit into which classes are divided. An order is divided further into families. *Butterflies and moths belong to the class Insecta and the* **order** *Lepidoptera.*

ore *n.* any mineral found in the Earth from which metals can be extracted, e.g. aluminum is obtained from the reddish-brown ore bauxite.

organ *n.* in multicellular animals and plants, a distinct part made of specialized tissues, which has a particular function, e.g. the brain, kidney and ovary are all organs.

O

organic (1) *adj.* to do with the organs of an animal or plant. The production of insulin and digestive juices is the organic function of the pancreas⬜. (2) any material produced by or from living organisms. Fungi feed on decaying organic matter. (3) any compound that contains carbon is said to be organic. Carbon compounds are found in all living cells.

organism *n.* a living animal or plant. Seaweed, insects and frogs are all organisms.

orifice *n.* an opening into a cavity or onto the surface. (say *or-i-fis*)

origin (1) *n.* the source or the beginning of something. (2) a place on a bone to which one end of a muscle is fixed. (3) in mathematics, the point at which two axes meet or intersect.

osmosis *n.* the movement of molecules of solvent⬜ through a semipermeable membrane which separates two solutions of different concentrations. The molecules pass from the less concentrated solution to the more concentrated solution until the concentration on both sides of the membranes is the same. (say *oz-mo-sis*)

ossicle (1) *n.* a very small bone. (2) one of three small bones found in the middle ear: the hammer (malleus), the stirrup (stapes) and the anvil (incus). (3) one of several hard, limestone plates in the skin which make up the skeleton in certain animals such as sea urchins.

Otto cycle the four-stroke cycle in an internal combustion engine. Named after the inventor, Nikolaus Otto (1832–91). At stroke 1, a mixture of fuel and air is sucked into the cylinder; at stroke 2, the mixture is compressed; at stroke 3, the mixture is ignited and explodes, forcing the piston downward; at stroke 4, exhaust gases are forced out of the cylinder.

The four stages of the Otto cycle.

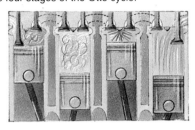

outcrop *n.* part of a layer or stratum of rock that is exposed on the surface.

outer ear the part of the ear that can be seen at the side of the head, the pinna; and the narrow passage that leads from the pinna to the eardrum (tympanum). The function of the outer ear is to collect and funnel sound waves toward the eardrum.

outer space the vast expanse of space beyond the Earth's atmosphere and outside the solar system.

output (1) *n.* the work done by, or energy produced by, a machine. (2) in computers: the information produced in response to coded instructions; any part of the machine or process that takes part in delivering the information. (3) the electrical current, produced by an electrical device, such as a generator, which can be used.

ovary (1) *n.* the sex organ in female

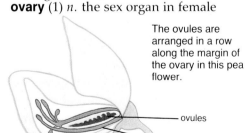

The ovules are arranged in a row along the margin of the ovary in this pea flower.

ovules

ovary

animals which produces the egg cells (ova). (2) the female sex organ in flowering plants, which produces the ovules (seeds). The different forms of plant ovaries play an important part in the dispersal (scattering) of ripe seeds.

oviduct *n.* in female animals, a narrow tube along which egg cells (ova) pass from the ovary. In some animals the egg cells are fertilized in the oviduct. In other types, such as fish and amphibians, they are fertilized outside the body.

ovulation *n.* the releasing of a ripe egg cell (ovum) from an ovary. It passes into the oviduct, or into the Fallopian tube⬜ in mammals. In certain animals such as fish and insects, hundreds of eggs may be released. A cod can lay millions of eggs at one time.

ovule *n.* a female reproductive cell produced by flowering and cone-bearing plants. An ovule becomes a seed after fertilization by a male pollen cell. The ovules of flowering plants have an outer protective covering, which becomes the seed coat. This covering may surround more than one ovule.

ovum *n. (pl. ova)* a mature female animal gamete (egg cell). Ova are large cells formed in an ovary. They contain yolk, which provides food for the developing embryo after fertilization⬜.

oxidation *n.* a chemical reaction in which a substance combines with oxygen; e.g. when carbon burns with oxygen, carbon dioxide is formed.

oxide *n.* a chemical compound of oxygen and one other element. Ferric oxide (rust) is a compound of iron and oxygen. Water is hydrogen oxide. Most ores are oxides of metals.

oxidize *v.* to cause a substance to join with oxygen by burning or by a chemical reaction, such as the rusting of iron in moist air.

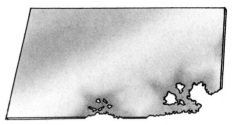

Rust forming on a sheet of iron.
Rust is an oxide of iron.

oxygen *n.* a gas that occurs in air and water. One-fifth of air is oxygen. Oxygen has no color, taste or smell. It is a chemical element necessary for plant and animal life. (say *ox-ih-jin*)

ozone *n.* a pale blue gas with a sharp smell. It is a form of oxygen which is found naturally in the Earth's upper atmosphere. Ozone filters out the dangerous ultraviolet rays sent out by the Sun. (say *o-zone*)

P p

pacemaker (1) *n.* in vertebrates, a group of specialized heart muscle cells. The pacemaker sends out impulses which start each heartbeat and keep the heart beating at a steady pace. In mammals the pacemaker is found in the walls of the right auricle⬜. (2) an electronic device, used in medicine, to regulate the heartbeat when the natural pacemaker is damaged by disease. It is usually placed under the skin and is connected to the heart through an artery.

pad (1) *n*. in biology, a paw; the soft, fleshy part under the feet or toes of some vertebrates. The pad is covered with thick skin. Cats, dogs and foxes have pads. (2) the large floating leaf of a water plant, such as the waterlily.

pain *n*. an unpleasant feeling of hurt in animals with highly developed nervous systems. It may be caused by an injury, such as a cut or burn, or by a disease of the body. Pain helps to protect animals from harm by means of a reflex (automatic) action. For example, when a nerve message from a painful stimulus, such as a pinprick, reaches the nervous system, it causes nerve messages to pass to the muscles of the arm. These immediately contract, pulling the arm away from the harmful stimulus.

palate *n*. in vertebrates, the bony roof of the mouth; the hard palate. It separates the mouth from the nasal air passages. In land mammals and certain other vertebrates, a muscular flap, covered with mucous membrane, is attached to the back of the hard palate. This is called the soft palate. It keeps food from entering the air passages in the nose when one is swallowing.

palm (1) *n*. one of a group of subtropical or tropical trees with a tall trunk, no branches and a growth of broad leaves at the top, e.g. the coconut palm, date palm and oil palm. Palm trees are a rich source of vegetable oils and fiber for ropes and matting. (2) the soft, inner surface of the hand

between the fingers and the wrist in primates such as humans and apes. (3) the flat blade of a deer's antlers.

pancreas *n*. in vertebrates, a gland in the abdomen that produces digestive juices and insulin. The pancreas opens into the duodenum through the pancreatic duct. Insulin controls the way the body uses sugar. Lack of insulin causes the disease diabetes.

parachute (1) *n*. a large umbrella-shaped device made of fabric that is used to slow down the speed at which a person or object falls through the air. The parachute is folded into a pack which is strapped to the person or object. It is opened by a pull of the ripcord. As the parachute opens, its large surface area offers great resistance to the upward pressure of the air. This reduces the effect of gravity on the falling person or object. (2) a structure made up of a mass of fine threads, which spreads out from a point on a small seed or fruit. It helps the seeds to be carried by the wind over a wide area; e.g. willow herb and dandelion have seed parachutes.

parallax *n*. the change in position of an object which seems to occur when it is seen from different positions. For example, if a pencil is held up at arm's length and it is seen first through one eye and then the other, it will seem to move to the left or right depending on the eye used. Parallax occurs when a star is viewed from two different positions on the Earth's surface. It is used to calculate the distance of nearby stars.

parallel *adj.* describes lines or surfaces lying in the same direction or plane which remain the same distance apart, such as railway lines. Parallel lines will never meet. In a parallelogram, such as a rectangle, the opposite sides are parallel.

paralysis *n.* a loss of feeling (sensation) and the power to move in a part of the body. It is caused by damage to the nervous system☐ through accident or disease, e.g. a fractured spine or poliomyelitis. (say *pa-ral-esis*)

parasite *n.* an organism that lives inside or on the surface of another living organism (the host) and gets food and shelter from the host. Parasites are often harmful to the host, and may spread disease; e.g. the louse is a parasite that transmits the disease typhus.

A louse.

parent *n.* any living organism, either plant or animal, that has produced living offspring. In humans and some other mammals the female parent is usually called the mother, and the male parent, the father.

particle (1) *n.* in physics, a very small, invisible piece of matter, such as a molecule or an atom. Inside atoms, there are even smaller particles of matter: neutrons, protons and electrons. (2) a small, visible fragment of material, such as a grain of sand or dust particle. *The doctor removed a* **particle** *of dust from my eye.*

passive *adj.* in chemistry, describes the surface of a metal that has become inactive. This means that it is able to resist corrosion (rusting) as a result of treatment.

pasteurize *v.* to heat liquids, especially milk, to a temperature high enough to kill harmful bacteria. The process of pasteurization was named after a famous French scientist, Louis Pasteur (1822-95).

patella *n.* the kneecap. A small disk of bone at the front of the knee joint in most mammals and some other vertebrates. The patella protects the knee joint.

paw *n.* the foot of a four-legged animal that has claws or nails. The claws may be extended or pulled in by muscles. Foxes, cats and lions have paws.

peak (1) *n.* a high point of land; the pointed top of a mountain; a mountain. (2) *v.* to reach maximum performance, especially of engines. To reach a high number or value. *The engine of my car* **peaks** *at 5000 revolutions a minute.*

peat *n.* a compact, dark brown material found on the surface in boggy areas of land. It is formed from layers of decaying plants. Peat is cut, dried and used as a fuel; it is the first stage in the formation of coal.

pectoral *adj.* to do with the chest in vertebrates. For example, the pectoral girdle is the group of bones that connects the trunk and forelimbs at the shoulder joint. In birds, the chest muscles are called pectoral muscles. They are well developed and are used in flying. Pectoral fins are found in fish.

P

pedigree *n.* a record of the family history of certain animals, such as humans, showing many generations of ancestors. Pedigree is very important in the breeding of some animals, e.g. dairy and beef cattle, race horses and racing pigeons.

pelvis *n.* in humans and other erect mammals, a cavity surrounded by the bones of the pelvic girdle, found at the base of the abdomen, above the legs. The pelvis contains and protects the bladder and the rectum. The female pelvis also contains the uterus, Fallopian tubes and ovaries.

pendulum *n.* a weight hanging from a thread, chain or rod, which can swing freely to and fro, with a regular rhythm. The time taken to complete a swing changes with the length of thread. The longer the thread, the longer the time taken. Pendulums are used in many large clocks to drive the toothed gears that move the hands.

penicillin *n.* a substance produced by certain molds (fungi). Penicillin is a

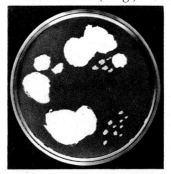

Penicillin mold growing on agar jelly.

powerful antibiotic which destroys harmful bacteria. The effect of penicillin was discovered by Sir Alexander Fleming in 1929. (say *penih-sillin*)

peninsula *n.* a long, narrow strip of land that is almost entirely surrounded by water. It is joined to a larger mass of land at one end.

penis *n.* the male sexual organ of all mammals and certain other vertebrates. It contains muscle and a special tissue which becomes firm so that the male animal can enter the female and deposit sperm⊡. In mammals the penis also contains a narrow tube down which urine passes from the bladder to the outside.

perennial *adj.* describes plants that have a life cycle of more than two years. Some perennial herbs⊡ grow up, flower, produce seed and die down, year after year. Woody perennial plants such as shrubs and trees do not die down to ground level but grow on from stems and branches each year, getting larger and larger. Azaleas and lilac trees are woody perennials.

perfume *n.* a pleasant smelling substance, usually a liquid, produced artificially from sweet-smelling chemicals or obtained naturally from flowers and scented leaves.

perimeter (1) *n.* the outer boundary of an area of land or a figure such as a rectangle. (2) the length of such a boundary; e.g. the perimeter of a rectangle is equal to the sum of the lengths of the four sides.
(say *pa-rim-iter*)

period (1) *n.* a portion of time, such as an hour, a century, a month. (2) one of the twelve portions into which the geological time scale is divided, e.g. the Carboniferous period. Each period can be identified by its characteristic rocks and fossils. (3) the time taken for a pendulum to complete one full swing. (4) the time taken for a complete cycle of events to take place, e.g. the menstrual cycle or period; the cycle of phases of the Moon from new moon to full moon and back to new moon.

periodic table an arrangement of the elements☐ in order of their increasing atomic numbers. They fall into nine groups. The elements in each group have similar chemical properties.

periscope *n.* an optical instrument consisting of a long, thin tube fitted with lenses and reflecting mirrors or prisms. It is used for seeing objects that are distant and above eye level. Periscopes are used in submerged sub-marines for scanning the surface of the sea, the shore and the horizon. *The small child used a* **periscope** *to see the march over the heads of the crowd.*

A submarine periscope.

peristalsis *n.* the wavelike contraction of the muscles in the walls of the intestines☐ which forces food along the alimentary canal☐.

permeable *adj.* porous; describes any material through which liquids or gases can pass. Permeable materials are made up of loosely packed particles; e.g. filter paper and sand are permeable. (say *perm-ee-ible*)

perpendicular (1) *adj.* vertical; exactly upright. (2) *n.* a line at right angles to another line or to a horizontal plane is perpendicular.

perspire (1) *v.* to sweat. In humans, and some other land mammals, to give off droplets of salty water (sweat) through tiny sweat pores onto the surface of the skin. Perspiring helps the body to control its temperature, especially in hot weather and after exercise. As the moisture evaporates, it uses heat energy from the body and cools the skin. (2) **perspiration** *n.* the salty liquid, or sweat produced; the act or process of perspiring.

pesticide *n.* any substance that kills pests. Pests are living animal and plant organisms that can harm humans, other animals or plants. For example, a fungicide is a pesticide that destroys fungi such as the mildew fungus. An insecticide destroys insect pests such as greenfly. Herbicides will destroy unwanted plants and weeds. Most pesticides are poisonous to humans.

pestle *n.* a hard tool with a rounded end, used for crushing or grinding hard substances. A pestle is used with a mortar☐ and is usually made of stone.

pestle

mortar

petal *n.* one of the parts of a flower. Petals are usually brightly colored and of many different shapes. Nectar, a sugary substance, is produced in little pouches at the base of some petals. This helps to attract insects, which pollinate the flowers.

rose petals

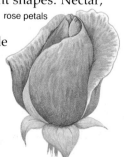

petrified forest a dead forest in which the living, organic, woody tree trunks have been replaced by stone. The trees became petrified when water, containing certain minerals, gradually soaked into the wood. The mineral deposit hardened as the water evaporated, producing a copy in stone of the original wood or tree. There is a petrified pine forest in Arizona.

petrochemical *n.* any chemical substance obtained from petroleum or natural gas. Kerosene, lubricating oils and paraffin are examples of petrochemicals.

petroleum *n.* mineral oil; a yellow, brown or black liquid fossil fuel. Petroleum is a crude mixture of oily substances (hydrocarbons) found beneath the earth. It is trapped in pockets in layers (strata) of porous rock, between layers of nonporous rock. It is brought to the surface through deep wells. Gasoline, kerosene, diesel fuel and many other important substances are obtained from petroleum.

pharmacist *n.* a person who prepares medicines and drugs; a druggist.

phase (1) *n.* a stage in the growth or development of some person or thing over a period of time. For example, adolescence is a phase in the development of human beings. (2) a change of state covering a period of time. For example, a volcano, having been active for two or three years, may enter a dormant phase for hundreds of years. (3) a gradual change throughout one month in the appearance of the illuminated part of the Moon's surface. The phases of the Moon as seen from the Earth include new moon, first quarter, full moon,

The phases of the Moon.

third quarter. (4) *v.* to start or stop some process gradually. A radio transmission can be phased in or out. *The use of robots in our factory will be* **phased** *in over the next five years.*

pheromone *n.* a chemical with a strong smell that is sent out by an animal. It affects the way other animals behave. Pheromones are given out by certain female moths when ready to mate.

phloem *n.* a special tissue, made of tubes and fibers, in the stems and roots of plants. Phloem carries soluble food substances down the stem from the leaves to other parts of the plant. (say *flo-em*)

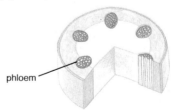

phloem

A section through the stem of a flowering plant.

phosphate *n.* a salt; a substance made from phosphoric acid and a base. Phosphates are used as soil fertilizers.

phosphorescence *n.* a greenish glow of light given out by some substances, without causing heat. For example, calcium sulfide, after exposure to sunlight, will glow in the dark. It is said to be **phosphorescent** *(adj.)*. Fireflies and glowworms produce phosphorescent light in the dark. See **fluorescence**. (say *fossfor-essence*)

photoelectric cell a device in which light controls the flow of current in an electric circuit; e.g. photoelectric cells are used as 'electric eyes' in burglar-alarm systems and to open and close automatic doors. (say *foto-electric*)

photon *n.* a minute amount of light energy that behaves like a wave and a particle, and can be measured.

photosensitive *adj.* being sensitive to, or reacting to, light energy; e.g. the cells in the retina at the back of the eye are photosensitive. The coating on photographic film is photosensitive.

photosynthesis *n.* in green plants, the making (synthesis) of soluble plant foods from carbon dioxide and water, using the energy from sunlight. Light energy is absorbed by chlorophyll⬜. (say *foto-sin-thih-sis*)

pH value *n.* a value on a scale from 0 to 14 that shows how strongly acid or alkaline a chemical solution is. A solution of pH7 is neutral. From 0 to 7 it is acidic, and from 7 to 14 it is alkaline. Pure water has a pH value of 7.

phylum *n.* one of the main units of classification into which the animal kingdom is divided. A phylum is further divided into classes; e.g. a butterfly belongs to the phylum Arthropoda, class Insecta.

physics *n.* the scientific study of space, matter, energy, mechanical forces and the natural laws that control them. Physics deals with heat, light, sound and electrical energy. A physicist is a person who studies and works in a branch of physics.

physiology *n.* the scientific study of the functions of living organisms and the way in which their organs and systems work, e.g. the physiology of digestion, muscle action, or the way impulses are carried along a nerve. A physiologist is a scientist who studies physiology and knows a great deal about how animals and plants function.

pigment (1) *n.* any substance that gives color to the tissues of living plants and animals, e.g. the brilliant colors of flowers, feathers, green leaves and fish scales. (2) any organic or mineral substance such as colored earth that can be ground to a powder and used in paints and dyes, e.g. yellow ochre and rose madder.

pile (1) *n.* in the construction industry, a large beam of concrete or metal, driven into the ground, that forms a support or foundation for a bridge or large building. (2) atomic pile, a nuclear reactor; a device that produces nuclear energy in enormous quantities. (3) a kind of electric cell.

P

pilot (1) *n.* a person who controls an aircraft or spacecraft. (2) a person who steers (navigates) ships into and out of harbours and docks or through dangerous waters. (3) *v.* to control or steer a craft.

The lobster has a large pincer for gripping its prey.

pincer

pincer *n.* a special claw for holding prey, found in certain crustaceans such as crabs and lobsters.

pinion (1) *n.* a small, toothed cogwheel used in gear systems. (2) in birds, a wing; the end joint on a bird's wing; a flight feather. (3) *v.* to remove the end joint of a bird's wing to stop the bird from flying.

pinna (1) *n.* (*pl. pinnae*) in mammals, the visible part of the external ear at the side of the head. The pinna is made of skin and cartilage. It collects sound waves and funnels them down into the ear passage. Some mammals can move the pinna so as to catch sounds from different directions. Elephants have large pinnae. (2) in plants, a leaflet on a pinnate leaf, e.g. a rose leaf. The leaflets are arranged in pairs on each side of the leaf stem, but there is often a single leaflet at the tip.

pip *n.* one of several small, hard seeds found in certain fleshy fruits, such as apples and pears.

pipette *n.* a special glass tube used for measuring and for transferring a small volume of liquid from one container to another. The liquid is sucked up into the pipette. (say *pie-pet*)

piston *n.* a circular disk or a cylindrical piece of metal that moves up and down in a tightly fitting cylinder. The piston may be pushed down by a gas or liquid to produce mechanical energy, or it may act as a pump.

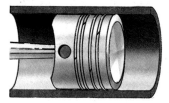

A piston inside a cylinder.

pit (1) *n.* the hard, stony seed in the center of certain fleshy fruits such as cherries. (2) in plants, a thin patch in a cell wall. Substances pass from cell to cell through the pits. (3) a small dent or hollow on the surface of a body or tissue, e.g. chicken pox scars. (4) the shaft of a coal mine; the mine itself.

pitch (1) *n.* a black, sticky liquid made from coal tar. It is sometimes used as a waterproof coating on flat roofs. (2) the highness or lowness of a sound. Pitch depends on the number of complete sound vibrations in a second (frequency). The greater the frequency⬜, the higher the note. A cello produces sounds of a lower frequency than a violin. (3) the angle of incline. *The roofs of mountain chalets have a steep* **pitch** *so that snow slides off.* (4) the angle at which the blades of a propeller are set.

pith (1) *n.* the soft, spongy, central core of certain plant stems and roots. The pith stores food and water. (2) the spongy tissue found beneath the rind in certain fruits, e.g. the pith of oranges and lemons.

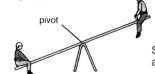

pivot

See-saws turn about a pivot.

pivot (1) *n.* a point or shaft about which a body turns freely. The needle of a compass is mounted on a pivot. (2) *v.* to turn freely on a pivot.

pixel *n.* one of thousands of very small pieces of a picture picked up one at a time in scanning by a television camera.

placenta (1) *n.* the afterbirth; the special organ, full of blood vessels, attached to the wall of the uterus in pregnant mammals. It is joined to the fetus by the umbilical cord⬜. Food substances, oxygen and hormones pass through the placenta from the mother to the fetus, and waste products and carbon dioxide pass from the fetus to the mother. The placenta is passed out from the uterus after the birth of the fetus. (2) in flowering plants, the part of the ovary to which the ovules are joined. (say *pla-senta*)

plain *n.* an expanse of open, level ground with few, if any, trees, e.g. the Canadian prairie. A plain may be low lying, almost level with the sea, e.g. the Plain of Lombardy in Italy.

plane (1) *n.* a large deciduous⬚ tree with broad leaves. The bark peels off in large patches and is replaced by smooth, new bark. (2) a tool for smoothing wood to give a level surface. (3) in mathematics, a flat, level surface. (4) a powered aircraft. (5) *v.* to make smooth or to work with a plane. (6) to soar or glide. (7) to move over the surface of water as a hydrofoil⬚ does. (8) *adj.* flat; level; a plane surface or figure.

planet *n.* any one of the bodies in space, including the Earth, that revolves around the Sun. The major planets are Mercury, Venus, Earth, Mars, Jupiter, Saturn, Uranus, Neptune and Pluto. A planet is not luminous, like a star, but reflects the light of the Sun.

plankton *n.* microscopic organisms that float near the surface of the sea and freshwater lakes. Plankton is a source of food for many water animals, including some whales.

plant (1) *n.* a living organism; a member of the plant kingdom. All plants, except fungi, make their own food by photosynthesis⬚. Like animals, plants respire, grow and reproduce, but, unlike animals, they cannot move from place to place. Because they have no nervous system, they react very slowly to stimuli. Trees, ferns and flowers are all plants. (2) all the machinery and tools in a factory that are used to manufacture goods, e.g. a car assembly plant. (3) *v.* to place a plant, seeds or bulbs in the ground to grow.

plantation *n.* a large area of land where one crop is cultivated, e.g. a sugar, rubber or tea plantation.

plaque *n.* a thin, transparent film of saliva and bacteria which forms on the teeth. Unless removed by brushing the teeth, it hardens into a deposit on the teeth, called tartar.

plasma *n.* the clear, yellowish, watery liquid in which the blood cells are carried in vertebrates. Plasma is mostly water, but it contains soluble salts and food substances, hormones⬚, antibodies⬚ and blood-clotting substances.

plaster (1) *n.* a paste of lime, sand and water that hardens when dry. Plaster is used to coat walls and ceilings to give a smooth surface. (2) **plaster of**

P

Jupiter is the largest planet in our solar system, and Pluto is the smallest.

Paris gypsum: a white powder that forms a paste with water. It dries very quickly and sets hard. Bandages soaked in plaster of Paris are used to make plaster casts to keep fractured bones from moving while they mend. (3) v. to coat with plaster or to apply a plaster cast.

plastic (1) n. any man-made material that can be molded into a shape, film or thread when heated, which sets hard when cooled. Many plastics are formed from petrochemicals□. Polythene, polyurethane and nylon are plastics that have many uses in industry and the home. (2) adj. able to be bent or molded; flexible. (3) made of plastic. *Parachutes are made from nylon, a* **plastic** *fabric.* (4) in physics, describes a material or substance that changes shape under a force but keeps that shape when the force is removed. *Plasticene is a* **plastic** *material used for making models.*

plate (1) n. a thin sheet of metal. Steel plate is used to make things, such as ships and washing machines. (2) a thin coating of one metal on the surface of another metal for protection, e.g. zinc plate, chromium plate. (3) in biology, hard limestone plates in the skin forming an external skeleton (exoskeleton) in certain animals such as starfish; a thin, horny plate or scale on the skin of certain reptiles. (4) photographic plate: a sheet of glass coated with a light-sensitive substance, used in photography. (5) in dentistry, a light plastic frame, shaped to fit the mouth, to which false teeth are fitted. (6) in geology, the plates are the huge sections into which the Earth's crust is broken. They support the continents and oceans and move over a layer of

molten rock in the mantle. (7) v. to coat with a layer of metal. *Cans are* **plated** *with a thin coating against rust.*

plateau (1) n. (pl. plateaus, plateaux) an expanse of fairly level land raised above the surrounding land, e.g. the Deccan Plateau in India and the Table Mountain in South Africa. (2) a flat line on a graph. It indicates a period of no change.

platinum n. a heavy, shiny, silver white metal, more precious than gold; a chemical element. Platinum is easily beaten into shapes and can be drawn out in thin wires. It does not react readily with acids or other substances (inert), and has a very high melting point (1780°C). It is used in industry in chemical apparatus and for making fine jewelry. Platinum is found mainly in the Ural Mountains in the USSR and in North and South America and Africa.

Plimsoll line a line painted on the hull of a merchant ship. It shows the water level to which the ship may be loaded safely. It is illegal to load beyond this line.

plug (1) n. an electrical device that connects a machine to an electrical power supply by means of a cable. (2) a bung made of rubber, wood or

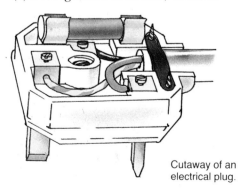

Cutaway of an electrical plug.

plastic, used to close an outlet in a container, e.g. a bath plug. (3) spark plug: a device used in combustion engines to ignite the gases that provide power. (4) *v.* to close a hole or leak by using a plug or bung. (5) to connect with an electrical power supply; to plug in.

plumage *n.* a bird's feathers. The form and color of the plumage is a characteristic of each species, e.g. a bird of paradise and a magpie. *Some species have become extinct because the birds were hunted for their colorful* **plumage**.

plumb line a heavy weight suspended from a line. At rest it hangs vertically (straight down). A plumb line is used to make sure that walls and surfaces are vertical and to test the depth of shallow waters.

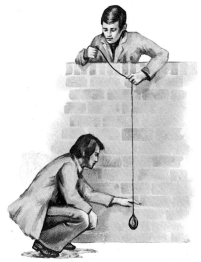

plumule (1) *n.* in plants, the growing tip of an embryo seedling. The plant stem develops from the plumule. (2) a small feather, e.g. a soft down feather from a bird's breast. (say *plume-yule*)

plutonium *n.* a heavy, radioactive metal. A man-made chemical element that exists in several forms (isotopes). Plutonium was developed from uranium. It is used in nuclear reactors and atomic weapons.

pneumatic *adj.* worked by air or gas pressure; filled with air or gas under pressure. *A* **pneumatic** *drill is worked by compressed air, and a* **pneumatic** *tire is filled with air under pressure.* Some robotic actions are controlled by pneumatic devices. (say *new-matic*)

A pea pod; the peas are arranged in a row along the margin of the pod.

pod (1) *n.* in botany, a legume; a dry fruit formed from one carpel that splits down each side to free the seeds. Plants such as beans, peas, clover and vetch produce pods. (2) a small group of whales or seals.

point to point in robotics, a type of movement in which the robot is programmed to move along a path from one place to another. It performs a task, such as welding, at each place.

poison *n.* any substance that harms or kills living organisms if it is taken in. It may be breathed in, swallowed, or injected through the skin in animals. Plants take in poisons through stems, leaves and roots. Pesticides are poisons. Some fungi are poisonous to humans if eaten.

polar (1) *adj.* to do with the North and South Poles, e.g. the polar regions, the polar ice cap, polar bears. (2) polar magnets: describes the way in which the poles of magnets tend to point toward the magnetic poles of the Earth.

P

pole (1) *n.* the north or south end of the Earth's axis. (2) the region around the North and South Poles of the Earth. (3) **magnetic pole**: either of the ends of a magnet where the magnetic force is strongest. If the magnet is allowed to swing freely, one pole will point north and the other south. (4) either of the terminals (electrodes) in an electric cell. (5) in living organisms, the opposite ends of a cell or cell nucleus. *The* **poles** *of dividing cells can be seen clearly through a microscope.*

poliomyelitis *n.* commonly known as polio; infantile paralysis. A virus disease that mainly affects children and young adults. It produces fever, muscle weakness and paralysis and may cause death. The virus damages certain cells in the spinal cord. Nowadays a vaccine prevents poliomyelitis.

pollen (1) *n.* tiny yellow or orange grains produced by the anthers (stamens) of flowering or cone-bearing plants. The pollen grains contain the male reproductive cells of seed-bearing plants. (2) pollen count: a measure of the number of pollen grains in the air at one time.

pollination *n.* the transfer of pollen grains from the male anther to the female stigma in flowering plants. Pollination is usually carried out by the wind, which blows the fine grains from flower to flower, or by insects, which pick up pollen on their bodies as they search for nectar, and then rub it off on the stigma of the same or another flower. Self-pollination takes place when a flower is pollinated by pollen from the same plant. Cross-pollination takes place when the flower receives pollen from another plant.

pollute *v.* to spoil and poison the natural environment and atmosphere, and so harm living organisms. *The smoke from the factory chimney* **polluted** *the air.*

pollution *n.* the act of spoiling and poisoning any part of the environment. Pollution can result from things such as chemical waste, nuclear waste, exhaust fumes, dangerous pesticides and oil.

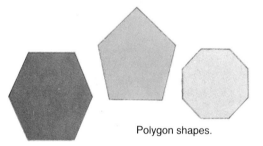

Polygon shapes.

polygon *n.* a closed, many-sided plane figure, e.g. an octogon, a figure with eight sides and eight angles.

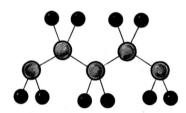

A polymer molecule is formed from a chain of monomer molecules joined together.

polymer *n.* a natural or man-made material made of very large chainlike molecules. Polymers are made from a series of smaller units called monomers which join together. The new material has different chemical properties from the original substance. Many plastics, such as polythene, are polymers.

polystyrene *n.* a polymer; a very light, tough plastic. It is used in packaging. (say *polly-sty-reen*)

polythene *n.* a transparent, plastic substance made from oil. It can be rolled into fine sheets. It has many uses, such as the packaging of food and other goods. (say *polly-theen*)

population *n.* the scientific term for the total number of organisms of a species living in a particular area at any one time. *The ladybird* **population** *of our garden seems much bigger this year.*

pore (1) *n.* in living organisms, a tiny opening onto the surface. Sweat passes through tiny pores on the skin. There are pores (stomata) on the underside of leaves. Water vapor, oxygen and carbon dioxide pass to and fro through them. (2) a tiny opening in rocks and other materials.

porous (1) *adj.* full of pores (2) letting liquids and gases pass through. Sandy soils and unglazed clay pots are porous. Chalk is a porous rock.

positive (1) *adj.* in mathematics, describes a quantity greater than zero. (2) a photographic print taken from a negative. (3) the north-seeking pole of a magnet. (4) having a positive electrical charge. (5) in botany, a plant response (tropism) toward a stimulus; e.g. the growth of a plant toward light is a positive response. The growth of plant roots downward is a positive response to the forces of gravity. (6) in medicine, a response to a chemical or bacteriological test that shows that a suspected condition or disease is present.

potential energy the amount of energy present in a body because of its position or condition. The mass of water held behind a dam wall contains enormous amounts of potential energy. As the water is released, its potential energy is converted into kinetic energy, the energy of movement.

power (1) *n.* force or energy that can be made to do work; the rate of doing work. The power of an engine to drive a machine. (2) force; strength. *The* **power** *of the wind knocked the sign over.* (3) in mathematics, when a quantity is multiplied by itself a given number of times it is said to be raised to a power. Thus 2 raised to the power 4 is equal to $2 \times 2 \times 2 \times 2$, or 16. This is written as 2^4, or stated in words, two to the fourth power. (3) the degree of magnification of a lens in a telescope or microscope or other optical instrument. (4) *v.* to supply power by an electrical current or an engine.

prairie *n.* a large, natural expanse of flat or gently rolling grassland with very few trees, e.g. the Canadian prairies and the prairie in the Mississippi valley.

precipitation (1) *n.* in meteorology, rainfall, snowshowers, hail, sleet, fog and mist; the measured amount of rainfall over a given time; the condensation of water vapor, as the temperature lowers, into droplets of water. When they become heavy enough, the droplets fall as rain. If the temperature falls below freezing (0°C) the water vapor forms ice crystals, which fall as snow or sleet. (2) in chemistry, the production of a precipitate in a solution. In precipitation, a dissolved substance is made insoluble by adding another solution. The insoluble substance separates out as a solid and falls to the bottom of the vessel as a precipitate. (say *presipi-tashun*)

P

predator *n.* any
animal that
hunts and eats
other animals
(prey). Tigers,
eagles and crabs
are predators.

This hawk is a predator; it uses its
curved, sharp beak to tear flesh.

pregnancy (1) *n.* the time that an
embryo mammal (fetus) spends inside
the uterus⬜ of the mother, between
conception and birth. (2) the
condition of being pregnant; carrying
a live fetus within the uterus.

pressure *n.* a pushing, squeezing
force. (1) the force that a body, gas or
liquid exerts on another body or
surface that it touches, e.g. the
pressure of the atmosphere on every
part of the Earth's surface; the
pressure of the sea water on
submarines and deep sea divers.
(2) the measurement of that force over
a given area. It is expressed as units
of force per unit of area.

prevailing wind a wind that blows
from one direction nearly all the time,
e.g. the prevailing westerlies, which
blow from the southwest in the
northern hemisphere and from the
northwest in the southern
hemisphere, between the latitudes
30°–60° north and 30°–60° south.

prey *n.* animals that are hunted and
eaten as food by predators.

primary color one of three colors
which, when mixed, can produce any

The primary
colors of
paint.

other color. The primary colors of
light are red, green and blue. A
mixture of all three produces white
light. The primary colors of paint are
red, yellow and blue. A mixture of all
three pure colors produces black.

A chimpanzee is a
primate; its fingers are
well-developed and can
carry out delicate tasks,
such as peeling fruit.

primate *n.* a group of mammals which
includes monkeys, apes and humans.
Primates have large, well-developed
brains and forward-facing eyes; they
have fingers and large thumbs for
grasping. Man is the only primate
that communicates with speech and
has a written language.

The prism
splits the
ray of
white light
into a
spectrum.

prism (1) *n.* a solid shape with
triangular ends and three sides that
are each parallelograms. (2) optical
prism: usually a triangular prism
made of glass that is used to bend
rays of light and to split white light
into the colors of the spectrum. Such
prisms are used in optical
instruments.

probe (1) *n.* a spacecraft especially designed and equipped for space research and exploration. Many unmanned probes have been sent up to explore the planets. Mariner 2 sent back pictures of Venus and Voyager 1 sent back pictures of the Great Red Spot of Jupiter. (2) a fine, blunt, surgical instrument for exploring a wound. (3) *v.* to search out; to explore thoroughly. *The doctor probed into the possible causes of the outbreak of food poisoning.*

proboscis (1) *n.* a long, flexible tube that projects from the head of certain animals, e.g. an elephant's trunk or  the long snout of insect-eating mammals, such as the tapir. (2) the sucking mouth parts of an insect such as a housefly, a butterfly or a mosquito.
proboscis
(say *pro-bosis*)

process (1) *n.* a sequence of stages that occur in the production or doing of something, e.g. the process of digestion. *A brewer is skilled in the process of making beer.* (2) in biology, a part of a structure or organism that sticks out, e.g. a bird's beak or bill.

product (1) *n.* anything that is produced by humans or nature. Cotton, cocoa, rice, textiles, ores, coal, oil and milk are all products. (2) The quantity obtained by multiplying two quantities together. *The product of 3 and 6 is 18; 3 times 6 is equal to 18.* (3) A substance or material produced by a chemical reaction or process. When an acid reacts with a base, a salt and water are the products of the reaction.

projectile *n.* any object that is thrown or shot into the air by force. Arrows, bullets and rockets are projectiles.

propagate *v.* to reproduce in plants. Plants propagate sexually by producing seeds or asexually by vegetative means. Gardeners propagate some plants by taking cuttings.

propellant *n.* anything that causes a body to be projected forward. A propeller, a ship's screw, the explosive charge in a firearm and the fuel used to launch a rocket are all propellants.

propeller *n.* airscrew; ship's screw; a device that produces thrust to an aircraft or boat. It consists of two or more twisted blades fixed to a central hub. As the propeller revolves, the blades sweep air or water backward and the craft is propelled forward.

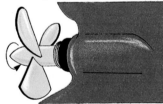

As the propeller of this ship rotates, water is thrust backward.

property *n.* any one of the physical or chemical characteristics of a substance or material that helps scientists to identify it and recognize it as different from another substance. Some of the physical properties of substances are melting points, color and density. The chemical property of a substance is shown by the way it reacts with other substances.

propulsion *n.* a driving force which pushes an object forward. In jet propulsion an aircraft is driven forward as a result of a jet of hot gases being forced backward.

P

protein *n.* a group of complex organic compounds containing nitrogen, important to all living things. Proteins are made of large molecules containing many different amino acids. They are necessary for the life and growth of all living organisms, including humans. Meat and milk are foods rich in proteins. (say *pro-teen*)

proton *n.* a tiny particle in the nucleus of an atom with a positive charge. It has a mass about 1840 times that of an electron.

protoplasm *n.* the living matter, including the nucleus and cell membrane, found in the cells of all living organisms. It is a clear, greyish, jellylike material.

protozoa *n.pl. (sing. protozoan)* one of a group of microscopic animals with one cell. Some live freely in fresh or salt water; others are parasites. Many protozoa can move by using cilia◻ or flagella◻ to drive themselves through the water. Some, such as amoeba, take in solid, microscopic food particles, whereas others absorb food through the cell membrane. Some protozoa cause disease in humans.

pulley (1) *n.* a simple machine; a wheel with a raised rim around its edges, around which a rope or chain is pulled to raise a weight. (2) a system of several such wheels and ropes for lifting heavy weights with a small amount of force.

A system of pulleys for raising loads.

pulsar *n.* a small, very dense star that sends out regular pulses of radio energy. Pulsars are left behind after a supernova explosion.

pulse (1) *v.* to beat rhythmically. (2) *n.* a regular beat or burst of energy in vertebrates and certain invertebrates with a simple heart; the rhythmic beat in the arteries. The pulse is caused by the contractions of the heart forcing blood through the arteries. The pulse can be felt in arteries near the surface, such as the artery in the wrist. The pulse rate is the number of beats per minute. The normal pulse rate for humans is about 72 beats a minute. Many athletes have a slower rate, below 60 beats a minute. (3) a surge in the flow of electricity in a circuit. (4) a short, regular burst of radio waves, such as those given out by pulsars. (5) in botany, the edible seeds of peas, beans and other pod-bearing plants.

A bicycle pump.

pump (1) *v.* to raise or move liquids or gases from one place or container to another by using a pump. *The heart* **pumps** *blood around the body. Oil is* **pumped** *from tankers into storage tanks.* (2) *n.* a device or machine used to raise or move liquids and gases. *The* **pump** *raises water from the well.*

pupa *n.* one of the stages in the development of certain insects, such as butterflies and moths. A pupa does not eat or move. It consists of a hardened case of chitin◻ inside which the insect develops into the adult form. The pupa case splits down the back and the adult insect emerges (comes out).

pupil *n.* the hole in the center of the colored iris⬚ in the eye in vertebrates, including humans. It is usually round but in certain animals, such as lions and tigers, it is a slit, opening wide at night. Light passes from an object through the pupil and lens onto the retina⬚ at the back of the eye.

pure (1) *adj.* not mixed with other substances or materials; made of one thing; without impurities, e.g. pure water, a pure wool jersey, pure chemicals. (2) in breeding plants and animals, pure breeding parents always produce offspring with the same characteristics. *The racehorse was of* **pure** *Arab stock.*

purify *v.* to remove unwanted substances, materials or disease organisms (impurities) from air, water or other substances.

pus *n.* thick, yellowish matter that forms in an infected spot or wound. Pus consists of dead and living bacteria, dead white blood cells and plasma.

putrify (1) *v.* of dead organic material, to rot or decay; to be decayed by microorganisms in the absence of oxygen. (2) **putrefaction** *n.* the breaking down of dead organic material by microorganisms, such as bacteria and fungi in the absence of oxygen. Putrefaction produces a very unpleasant odour.

pylon *n.* a tall structure of metal struts used for carrying overhead electric cables across land.

pyramid *n.* a solid shape consisting of a square base with triangular-shaped sides meeting at a single point at the top.

pyrites *n.* one of the metallic ores⬚ in which the metal is combined with sulphur to form a sulphide. Iron pyrites, or fools' gold, is a yellow shiny ore. When roasted, iron pyrites produce sulphur. (say *pa-ride-ees*)

Q q

quadruped *n.* in most mammals, except primates and certain other vertebrates, an animal that has four feet (paws or hoofs).

This wild boar is a quadruped. Boar still roam wild in the forests of central Europe.

quarantine (1) *n.* the isolation (separation from others) of persons and animals who may be infected with, or carrying, disease organisms or pests. Quarantine prevents the spread of infectious diseases. (2) The length of time such persons or animals may be isolated. Six months is the usual period of quarantine for animals entering one country from another. The quarantine for human diseases depends on the length of time between infection and the onset of illness. It varies with the disease.

quarry (1) *v.* to dig out stone or rock from the Earth's surface. (2) *n.* a place where stone, rock or ores are quarried. *My marble floor came from a* **quarry** *in Italy.* (3) prey; any animal that is being hunted by another animal. *The owl hunted in the dark for its* **quarry**, *a small mouse.*

Q

quartz (1) *n.* a hard, transparent, crystalline mineral containing silicon. Sand is mostly made of quartz. It is used to make glass. The colored forms of quartz, such as amethyst, agate and moonstone are semiprecious stones and are used to make jewelry. (2) a quartz crystal is one that vibrates at a constant frequency under the effect of an alternating electrical current. Quartz crystals are used in watches and other devices.

Quartz is a very common mineral—it is found in sand and rocks.

quasar *n.* one of hundreds of distant, starlike bodies that send out powerful radio waves. Quasars are smaller than known galaxies□ but send out much stronger radio waves. (say *kway-sar*)

quinine *n.* a bitter-tasting drug made from the bark of the tropical cinchona tree. Quinine is used as a medicine to treat malaria.

R r

rabies *n.* an infectious disease in mammals caused by a virus□. A bite from an infected animal can pass the disease to a man or woman. Many countries have very strict laws to control the entrance of animals to try to prevent rabies from spreading.

radar *n.* radio waves are bounced off an object and the return is timed to calculate how far away the object is. Radar is short for '**ra**dio **d**etecting **an**d **r**anging.' (say *ray-dar*)

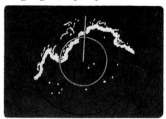

Solid objects appear as bright areas on a radar screen. Ships use radar to scan the ocean.

radiant *adj.* describes energy that is radiated.

radiate *v.* to give out energy in the form of waves such as X-rays, infrared waves and radar waves. *The fire* **radiated** *heat.*

radiation *n.* the energy given out in the form of waves from a source, e.g. heat and light radiation from the Sun, X-ray radiation, ultraviolet radiation. (say *ray-dee-ashun*)

radiator (1) *n.* anything that radiates energy: an electric fire or a radioactive substance such as uranium. (2) a device that gives out heat and is used in heating systems to warm the air in a building. (3) part of the cooling system in some car engines. The radiator consists of thin metal plates and tubes through which water circulates, carrying unwanted heat away from the engine.

The radiator of an automobile prevents it from overheating.

radicle *n.* an embryo root found inside a seed. It is the first part to grow from a germinating seed. The main plant root develops from it.

radio (1) *n.* a device that receives radio wave signals; a radio set. (2) the system of sending out radio waves and receiving them. The radio waves are picked up by an aerial and the electric circuit in the radio sorts out the sound signals from the radio waves.

radioactive *adj.* describes heavy elements, such as radium⬜ or uranium⬜, that give off harmful radiation in the form of waves or particles as the atomic nuclei gradually break up. **radioactivity** *n.* (say *radio-active*)

radio astronomy the study of radio waves sent out by some stars so that astronomical maps can be drawn. These maps are used to identify radio sources and radio galaxies which cannot be observed by using telescopes.

The dish of this radio astronomy station picks up and focuses radio waves.

radio waves some radiation can be used to carry sound and television signals; these are radio waves. The signals are sent through the air or space from a transmitter on a carrier wave. They are then changed into sounds and pictures on radio and television receivers.

radium *n.* a radioactive metal; a chemical element. It occurs naturally in the earth as the ore pitchblende. Radium is used in the treatment of cancer (radiotherapy).

radius (1) *n.* the distance between the center of a circle or sphere and any point on the circumference. (2) one of the two long bones in the lower forelimb of mammals, amphibians, reptiles and birds. In humans the upper end forms the elbow joint with the humerus and the ulna. The lower end forms a joint with the carpal bones at the wrist on the thumb side.

rainbow *n.* an arc in the sky containing the colors of the spectrum. Rainbows are formed when the Sun shines brightly on raindrops. Each raindrop acts like a tiny prism and breaks up the sunlight into the various colors. The rainbows seen in the spray at waterfalls are caused by sunlight falling directly onto the water droplets.

rainfall (1) *n.* the amount of rain, snow or hail falling in a given area in a given time. (2) a shower or heavier fall of rain.

rain forest a thick evergreen forest found in tropical regions near the equator. It has an abundant water supply at all times. The rain forest is made up of three layers: *(i)* an upper layer (canopy) of leaves and branches of the tallest trees; *(ii)* a middle layer of foliage from smaller trees and

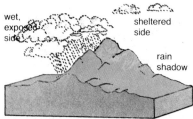

wet, exposed side

sheltered side

rain shadow

Rainfall is far heavier on the exposed side of this mountain than on the rain shadow area.

shrubs and lianas (twining plants); *(iii)* low-growing shrubs, herbs and plant organisms that live off the rotting vegetation on the forest floor. Little sunlight gets through the top canopy. Animals such as birds, insects and monkeys live mainly in the top layer.

rain shadow a characteristic of the leeward (sheltered) side of a mountain in that the rainfall is much less than on the exposed side. The leeward side is said to lie in a rain shadow.

range (1) *n*. the furthest distance that anything can travel. (2) the values between two limits of a measurement. *The **range** of human hearing is between 20 and 20,000 hertz.* (3) the parts of the world in which a plant grows or an animal is found. *The **range** of the coconut palm describes the areas where it grows.* (4) a line, group or chain of mountains. *The Andes is a **range** of mountains in South America.* (5) *v.* to spread over an area. (6) to vary between two limits of measurements. *In my school, the ages **range** from 11 to 16.*

rash *n*. a breaking out (eruption) of red spots or blisters on the skin. It may be caused by an infectious disease, such as measles or chicken pox, or by an allergy.

rate *n*. the relationship between two measurements, usually the change of

a quantity with time; e.g. the rate of climb of a rocket is measured in kilometers per second.

ratio *n*. a comparison of two numbers or two values, usually given as a fraction. *The **ratio** of boys and girls in the class was 3:2 or 3 to 2.* (say *ray-she-o*)

ray (1) *n*. a line representing the direction of a wave motion, e.g. a ray of light. (2) a line representing the direction of a fine beam of particles, such as alpha particles emitted from a radioactive source to form alpha rays. (3) a group of large, flat, saltwater fish. Rays have very long tails and skeletons made of cartilage. Examples include the skate, the sting ray and the electric ray.

The electric ray can give a powerful electric shock.

react (1) *v.* to produce an effect when two different substances are put together. The effect is a reaction. *Most acids **react** with metals.* (2) of living organisms, to respond to a stimulus by movement or a change of behavior. *My dog **reacts** to strangers by barking at them.*

reaction (1) *n*. a process in which two substances have an effect on each other and new substances are produced. There is a reaction between most acids and most metals. Hydrogen and a salt are produced. (2) in living organisms, response to a stimulus. *The migration of birds is a **reaction** to a seasonal change in the weather and the environment.*

reactor *n*. the chamber in a nuclear power plant in which atoms are split to produce great heat. See **nuclear reactor**.

reagent *n.* a substance that produces a reaction, e.g. a reagent used in chemical analysis. (say *ree-agent*)

receiver *n.* a device that picks up electrical signals sent over a distance and changes them to sound or pictures. The electrical signals are received as radio waves or as varying electric currents. Examples of receivers are television, radio and telephone receivers.

receptor *n.* a special cell or organ in the body of an animal that is a part of the nervous system. Receptors receive stimuli (messages) from outside the body or from other nerve cells inside the body. For example, the rods and cones in the eye are receptors for light stimuli. Receptors in the skin respond to touch, pressure, pain and heat. Without these receptors, a body would not be able to see, hear, smell, feel or react to danger. (say *ree-septor*)

recoil *n.* the reaction to a force which causes two bodies to separate. One goes forward (thrust), the other backward (this is a recoil).

record (1) *v.* to write down measurements and observations such as color changes, effects and so on. *She* **recorded** *the number of birds that visited the bird feeder.* (2) to preserve sound and vision, for example, on tape or a record, so that it can be played again when required. (3) *n.* the result of recording measurements and observations.

recording head an electromagnetic device used to change sound or pictures into signals on magnetic tape. As the tape

recording head —
magnetic tape —

moves past the recording head, small crystals on the tape are arranged in a pattern. This pattern of crystals produces sound and vision signals when the tape is played back.

rectangle *n.* a plane (flat) figure with four sides and four right angles.

rectum *n.* a short tube at the end of the large intestine☐ in mammals. It stores the feces until they are expelled from the body through the anus☐.

recycle *v.* to use a product from a chemical or manufacturing process over and over again; e.g. waste paper can be pulped and recycled as new paper.

red blood cell (1) an elastic, disk-shaped cell found in the blood of animals with backbones. It contains a red pigment (hemoglobin) which carries oxygen around the body from the lungs to the tissues. Red blood cells are produced by the red bone marrow.

red giant one of many large, reddish stars, many times the size of the Sun; a star in which the supply of fuel has become low. The star becomes larger and cooler, but the core becomes hotter. In time, the Sun will expand to become a red giant.

reduce *v.* to make a measured quantity or quality smaller, e.g. to reduce the pressure on a gas or to reduce the temperature of a solution to its freezing point.

reef *n.* a ridge of rock, sand or coral at or near the surface of the water.

refine *v.* to remove unwanted materials from a substance in order to get the pure substance. *Sugar is* **refined** *by removing unwanted plant materials.*

R

refinery *n.* a plant or factory where raw materials such as oil or sugar are cleaned and purified. Different ways of refining produce different grades of pure substances.

reflect *v.* to turn back; e.g. when a mirror reflects a beam of light it turns it back. *A bright surface* **reflects** *sunlight more strongly than a dark surface.*

reflection *n.* what happens when a beam of light is turned back by a surface, e.g. the reflection of light in a mirror. Reflection also takes place with sound and other waves. **Reflection** *of sound is called an echo.*

reflector *n.* an object that is used to reflect light, sound or heat. *The bicycle has a red* **reflector** *that shines when the light falls on it.*

reflex action an automatic nervous response by an animal to a stimulus. A reflex action does not have to be learned; it is a type of instinctive behavior. For example, if you touch something very hot, you quickly pull your hand away from the painful stimulus. This is a reflex action. A nerve impulse passes from a pain receptor in the skin of the hand along a nerve fiber to the spinal cord. From there an impulse passes to the muscles in the arm, which jerk the hand away.

refract *v.* to bend a ray of light or a wave of heat or sound and change its direction.

The spoon appears to bend where it enters the water. This is because the light rays are bent or refracted.

refraction (1) *n.* the way a ray of light (or a wave of heat or sound) is bent when it passes at an angle from a less dense to a denser medium, e.g. from air into glass or water. (2) the bending of light from stars when it passes through the Earth's atmosphere.

refractor *n.* a refracting telescope: a simple telescope in which light rays pass through a lens and the image is magnified by a second lens. In an astronomical refractor the image is upside down.

refrigerator *n.* an insulated box or container in which the air and contents are kept very cold by ice or by a refrigeration system. Most systems use a fluid, such as ammonia, which is pumped through pipes in the cold chamber of the refrigerator. Here it absorbs heat from the contents and becomes a vapor. This is compressed and becomes a fluid again. By constant circulation of the substance, heat is taken away from the inside of the refrigerator to the outer air.

region (1) *n.* a large area of land that has particular characteristics, e.g. the hot, dry climate of desert regions and the warm, moist atmosphere of tropical regions. (2) a part of the body. *The abdominal* **region** *contains the stomach, intestines and other organs. The thoracic* **region** *contains the heart and lungs.*

regulate *v.* to control or adjust a mechanism or process at a certain level or according to a set of rules. *The level of water in the canal is* **regulated** *by lock gates.*

relay *n.* an electrical device used as a switch. Current flows through the relay and switches on a second circuit. A mechanical relay has a piece of soft iron that is attracted by an electromagnet (switches on) and returned by a spring (switches off). Electronic relays have largely replaced mechanical relays.

remote control the control of a machine or device at a distance, e.g. the remote control of a toy airplane or a small boat by radio signals.

remote sensing the use of a sensor⊔ at a distance; e.g. all the rooms in a tall building can have devices for the remote sensing of a fire. Remote sensing also describes the process of taking photographs from satellites in space. This relates particularly to infrared photography.

renal *adj.* to do with the kidney. *Blood flows to the kidney through the* **renal** *artery.* (say *ree-nal*)

renewable energy any form of energy which can be used over and over again, e.g. wind power or solar energy.

repel *v.* to cause to move away. *Two north magnetic poles* **repel** *each other.* A force is used to repel an object.

reproduce *v.* to produce offspring. Only living organisms can reproduce.

reproduction *n.* the process by which living organisms produce offspring. In sexual reproduction a new organism is formed by the joining (fertilization) of a male and female sex cell (gamete). In many plants and some lower animals, such as the earthworm, both sex cells are produced by the same organism. Asexual reproduction takes place without the formation of sex cells. It occurs mostly in plants and is rare in animals except in certain microorganisms, such as protozoa⊔. The offspring are identical to the parents and to each other.

A baby crocodile hatching from its egg.

reptile *n.* one of a large group of cold-blooded⊔ animals with backbones and a dry, scaly skin. Most reptiles live on land and lay eggs covered with a tough shell membrane. Some snakes give birth to live young. Apart from snakes, most reptiles have four limbs with five toes on each foot. Some reptiles, such as alligators and crocodiles, live in tropical regions and spend much time in rivers and swamps.

reservoir (1) *n.* a large tank or a natural or artificial lake where water is stored before being used. (2) part of a piece of machinery or apparatus where fluid is stored. *The engine had a* **reservoir** *of oil.*

resin *n.* a gumlike substance which oozes from cracks or cuts in the bark of trees and bushes. It is used to make paints and varnishes.

resistance (1) *n.* something that acts against a force, preventing or slowing down motion. *The* **resistance** *of the water slows the ship down.* (2) a property of substances that reduces the flow of electricity. Resistance is measured in ohms. *Thin copper wire offers more* **resistance** *than thick copper wire.*

resistor *n.* a device used for its known resistance in an electrical circuit. A resistor can be fixed or variable. A variable resistor can have its resistance altered over a range of values.

R

resonance *n.* an effect caused by vibration⬜. A girl strikes a glass and it gives out a note. She sings the same note and the glass vibrates. If it is exactly the same note, resonance occurs. The glass vibrates violently and may break. The violent vibration is resonance.

resource *n.* something that can be made use of; a supply of energy; any raw material that a country possesses, e.g. coal, oil, or timber.

respiration (1) *n.* the breathing process in living organisms. Oxygen is taken in from the air or water and carbon dioxide is passed out. In micro-organisms and the lower types of animals, such as jellyfish, the gases enter and leave over the whole body surface. In fish, respiration takes place through the gills. In land animals with backbones, respiration takes place through the air passages and the lungs as air is breathed in and out. (2) the process that takes place in living cells in which energy is produced from food, using oxygen (aerobic respiration). (3) a similar process in some microorganisms that does not need oxygen (anaerobic respiration).

respiratory system the special tissues and organs found in most animals through which oxygen and carbon dioxide enter and leave the body, e.g. the gills of fish and the lungs of land animals with backbones, such as mammals and frogs.

retina *n.* the light-sensitive layer of cells at the back of the eye in most vertebrates⬜. It is made up of rod cells and cone cells.

revolution (1) *n.* the act of revolving. (2) one complete turn of a revolving or rotating body. *The Earth makes one* **revolution** *per year around the Sun.*

revolve *v.* to move in an orbit or circle about an axis which is outside the turning body. *The Moon* **revolves** *around the Earth.*

rhesus factor (Rh factor) a particular substance found in the red blood cells in humans and the rhesus monkey. In some people this factor is not present; they are Rh negative. It is important to know if a pregnant woman is Rh negative because an Rh positive fetus can be damaged by the antibodies⬜ produced by the mother's blood. It is also important to know if blood is Rh positive or negative when giving blood transfusions.

rhizome *n.* a horizontal underground stem of a plant which acts as a reproductive organ, producing shoots, e.g. an iris. It may be a food-storage organ, such as ginger. A rhizome has buds from which shoots grow. (say *rye-zome*)

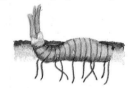

When a rhizome acts as a food store it is large and swollen.

rhythm *n.* a regular action in a process or a series of actions; e.g. the beating of a human heart follows a definite rhythm, and the life cycle of an insect often shows a seasonal rhythm. (say *rith-em*)

rib *n.* a curved bone in the chest region of vertebrates. In humans there are twelve pairs of ribs: true ribs, attached to the backbone⬜ and sternum; false ribs, attached to the backbone and to a true rib; and floating ribs, attached to the backbone only.

rickets *n.* a disease in young children caused by too little vitamin D. The child's bones become soft and bend under the weight of the body.

ridge (1) *n.* a long, narrow strip of high ground joining a line of hills or mountains. (2) the raised edge where two sloping surfaces meet at an angle, as in the roof of a house.

rigid (1) *adj.* describes a body that does not appear to change its size or shape when a force is applied to it. The bones of the sternum are rigid. (2) **rigidity** *n.* the property of bodies that makes them rigid. *Steel girders are used in tall buildings because of their* **rigidity**.

ringworm *n.* a disease of the skin caused by certain fungi. Red, ring-shaped, itchy patches appear on the skin. Ringworm is contagious. It is caught by close contact with an infected person.

ripe *adj.* describes fruit and seeds which are fully developed; e.g. a ripe fruit, such as a nut or rose hip, has seeds ready for dispersal.

river *n.* a natural stream of water that flows in a channel to another river, a lake or an ocean.

rivet (1) *n.* a metal pin or bolt, with a head at one end, used to fasten metal plates together. (2) *v.* to fix together, using rivets.

robot *n.* a machine that can do tasks automatically once it has been programmed. Robots have jointed arms to provide as much freedom of movement as possible. They can do work too hot or too dangerous for humans.

robot assembly putting together a whole piece of machinery from many small pieces, using one robot that does a series of different jobs.

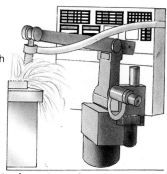
The robot is linked up to the robot control system which controls its movements.

robot control system the computer and other electronic circuits that control a robot.

rocket *n.* a device, usually cylinder-shaped, which is propelled by hot gases. In a chamber inside the rocket, fuel is burned to produce the gases. They escape through a rear vent and drive the rocket forward or upward. Rockets used to launch spacecraft are as tall as multistory buildings and are made up of several sections or stages.

This space craft is thrust forward by a rocket.

rod (1) *n.* a long, thin bar of metal. (2) one of the cells, sensitive to light, found in the retina of most vertebrates (animals with backbones). They are rod-shaped and are used for seeing in dim light.

R

rodent *n.* a small mammal with long, chisel-shaped front teeth (incisors) which it uses for gnawing; it has no canine teeth. The incisors continue to grow throughout the life of the animal but are gradually worn down by the gnawing of hard foods such as nuts. Rodents are herbivores□. *Rabbits, squirrels, beavers and mice are* **rodents**.

root (1) *n.* the part of a plant that anchors it in the ground and takes in water and salts from the soil. Some plants have one swollen main root, such as the carrot or turnip. These are called taproots and are sometimes eaten as food. Other plants have a tuft of roots growing out from the base of the stem; these are fibrous roots. Both types of root may have smaller roots growing out from them. (2) *v.* to dig out, as with a snout or beak. *The wild boar* **roots** *in the ground for fungi.*

rootlet *n.* the smallest branch of a root.

rot *v.* to decay or decompose, because of the action of microorganisms. Dead vegetable matter rots down to form soil compost.

rotary *adj.* describes something which turns around or rotates. *The* **rotary** *blades on a helicopter rotate fast enough to lift the helicopter off the ground.*

The rotary blades of a helicopter.

rotate (1) *v.* to turn about an axis which goes through the turning body; e.g. a car wheel rotates about its axle. (2) **rotation** *n.* the act of rotating.

rotor *n.* the propellor blades and shafts in a turbine□ which rotate when steam is directed on them.

rough (1) *adj.* having an uneven surface; not smooth. *The naturalist clambered over very* **rough** *ground in search of a rare plant.* (2) wild and untamed. *The sea is* **rough**.

roughage *n.* the remains of undigested food that forms the feces. It stimulates the passage of food along the intestines□ and prevents constipation. Bran, cereals, wholemeal bread and green vegetables provide roughage.

rubber *n.* a natural material made from the milky sap (latex) obtained from certain tropical trees. Rubber is an elastic, impermeable material that does not conduct electricity. Rubber is used to make tires.

rudder

rudder (1) *n.* a broad, flat, hinged piece of wood or metal at the stern of a boat or ship. The rudder is used for steering the ship. (2) a similar device at the tail end of an aircraft.

ruminant *adj.* describes a plant-eating animal, with hooves, that chews the cud. A ruminant animal has a stomach with three or four compartments. Food passes directly into the first compartment; it is later returned to the mouth for chewing, during the stages of digestion. This is called chewing the cud. Cattle, sheep, goats, camels and giraffes are ruminant animals. (say *room-inent*)

rust (1) *n.* the reddish-brown coat that forms on iron when it is exposed to moist air. Rust is a form of metal corrosion. The metal combines with oxygen to form an oxide. (2) a fungus disease of certain plants such as wheat. Reddish-brown spots appear on the leaves and stems. (3) the parasitic rust fungus itself. (4) *v.* to form rust on iron.

S s

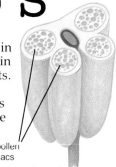

pollen sacs

sac *n.* a small baglike container in the tissue of certain animals and plants. The sacs in the lungs of mammals pass oxygen to the blood and receive carbon dioxide from it.

safety valve an automatic safety device, fitted to a steam boiler, that allows steam to escape when the pressure inside the boiler reaches a certain level. This release prevents the boiler from being damaged by too high a pressure.

saline (1) *adj.* salty or containing a salt, e.g. a saline solution. *Natural* **saline** *springs are found in many parts of the world.* (2) *n.* a salt solution. It is used in medicine for replacing lost body fluids. (say *sa-leen*)

saliva *n.* a clear liquid, without taste or color, secreted by special glands in the mouth. In vertebrates it contains mucus⬜ and a substance that helps to digest starchy foods (bread, potatoes). Saliva makes food slippery and easy to swallow. In blood-sucking insects, such as mosquitoes, the saliva contains a substance that keeps the blood from clotting. (say *sa-lie-va*)

salt (1) *n.* a substance found naturally as a white mineral in the earth and in sea water; it is sodium chloride. Before refrigerators were invented, salt was used for preserving food. (2) a chemical compound formed when the hydrogen in an acid is replaced by a metal. *Calcium sulfate is a* **salt** *formed by replacing the hydrogen in sulfuric acid with the metal calcium.*

sand (1) *n.* tiny, loose grains of rock formed by the wearing down of rocks by heat, ice, water and wind. Some sand is smooth and white; some is gritty. Sand formed from lava rock is grey or black. (2) *v.* to rub or polish with sand or sand-coated paper.

sandstone *n.* a sedimentary⬜ rock, made of small grains of sand compressed in fine clay or other earths. Sandstone is softer than limestone; it is a useful building material.

sap *n.* the solution that circulates in a plant to provide food and water to the living cells. The sap can be seen when the root or stem of a plant is cut.

sapling *n.* a young tree.

satellite *n.* a body in orbit around a larger body in space. The Moon is a satellite of the Earth. Artificial satellites circling around the Earth are used to reflect radio signals and to forecast the weather.

A telecommunications satellite.

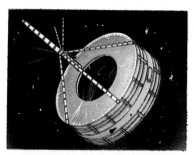

saturate *v.* to fill a gas, liquid or solid so that it cannot absorb any more. Saturated air has all the water vapor it can hold.

scabies *n.* a skin disease caused by mites⬜. The mites burrow under the skin and lay eggs, making the skin itch.

scale (1) *n.* a series of numbered units, from a low value to a high value, marked at regular intervals on a surface. (2) one of the small, thin  plates that cover the body of reptiles and fish. (3) a balance; an instrument used for weighing.

scalp *n.* the soft tissue on the top and back of the human head; it is usually covered with hair.

scalpel *n.* a small knifelike instrument with a very sharp blade.

scan *v.* to examine or search over all parts of something in an orderly way. *Ships use radar in foggy conditions to* **scan** *for approaching vessels.*

scanning *n.* a television picture is broken up point by point by electronic scanning. It is put together again by a receiver to form the picture on the screen.

scar (1) *n.* a mark left on the skin after a wound or burn has healed. (2) the mark on a plant showing where a leaf has been removed.

scarp *n.* a steep slope; an escarpment: a clifflike ridge caused by erosion or faulting⬜.

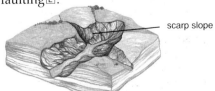
scarp slope

scavenger (1) *n.* an animal or organism that feeds on waste material, especially the remains left by carnivores⬜. (2) scavenge *v.* to look for food. *The vultures are waiting for the lion to leave so that they can* **scavenge** *the remains of the zebra.*

scent (1) *n.* a smell. (2) the sense of smell. (3) *v.* to track or hunt by using the sense of smell.

science (1) *n.* knowledge of the physical or natural world. Science tries to explain how nonliving things work, and how plants and animals carry out their activities. (2) a branch of such knowledge, regarded as a separate object of study. *Biology is the* **science** *that deals with plants and animals.*

scientist *n.* a person involved in scientific study or who specializes in one or more of the sciences.

sclera *n.* the tough, outer coating of the eyeball. It protects the eye and gives it its shape. The muscles that move the eye are joined to it. In the front of the eyeball the sclera forms the transparent cornea⬜. (say *sklir-a*)

scrotum *n.* the pouch of skin that holds the testes in mammals. It hangs outside the abdomen, behind the penis.

scurvy *n.* a disease of humans caused by too little vitamin C in the diet. Vitamin C is found in fresh green vegetables and fruit, especially oranges and lemons. *Sailors used to suffer from* **scurvy** *on long sea voyages because they did not have enough fruit or vegetables.*

sea level the level of the surface of the sea, taken midway between high and low tide. Measurements of height and depth are taken from this level.

season (1) *n.* one of the four divisions of the yearly weather cycle in temperate climates: spring, summer, autumn (fall) and winter. Summer is usually warm and fairly dry; winter can be cold and wet. (2) any period of time noted for particular characteristics, e.g. the very hot, dry season of continental summers; the monsoon (rainy) season; the mating season of certain plants. (3) *v.* to make timber less likely to warp, by aging or drying it. *Cabinet makers only use* **seasoned** *timber for making furniture.*

This seaweed is fixed to rocks by a strong stalk called a stipe.

seaweed *n.* any one of a number of different plants that grow in the sea from high-water level on the shore to a depth of about 200 meters. Many seaweeds are algae⬜. They are usually red, brown or green in color.

second (1) *n.* a unit of measurement of time equal to one-sixtieth of a minute. *There are sixty* **seconds** *in a minute.* (2) a unit of measurement of angles equal to one-sixtieth of a degree. *There are sixty* **seconds** *in a degree of angle.* (3) *adj.* an ordinal number (2nd) that comes after first (1st).

secrete *v.* the making and giving out of a particular material or substance by a cell or gland in an animal or plant. *The liver* **secretes** *bile, and the stomach* **secretes** *gastric juices that digest food.* (say *se-creet*)

secretion *n.* a substance, produced by a gland or cell in animals or plants, that has a special function or effect. Saliva is produced from glands in the mouth; it softens and lubricates the food particles and starts the digestion of starch. (say *se-creeshun*)

section (1) *n.* a part of a whole object or area. *Joyce cut the melon into six* **sections** *and gave one to each of her friends.* (2) cross-section or longitudinal section: a thin slice of tissue, one cell thick, taken across or down a piece of plant or animal tissue. These sections are examined under a microscope. They are used to study how cells are formed and to detect diseases.

sector *n.* in geometry, a part of a circle that lies within two radii and the arc between them.

sediment (1) *n.* particles of solid matter that sink to the bottom of a liquid. (2) in geology, particles of soil or rock that are deposited by moving water or wind. Sediment laid down at the mouth of a river forms a delta.

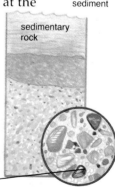

water

mixed sand and water

sediment

sedimentary (1) *adj.* describes rocks, such as sandstone, that were formed from particles of hard rocks laid down by rivers, glaciers and winds. (2) of, or containing, sediment.

sedimentary rock

magnified

S

seed *n.* a ripe, fertilized ovule that will develop into a new plant under suitable conditions. A seed has a tough, protective coat and contains the radicle (seed root), plumule (seed shoot) and one or two seed leaves (cotyledons).

seedling *n.* a young plant, grown from a germinating⬜ seed.

segment (1) *n.* a section; a part of a whole, e.g. a segment of an orange. (2) one of the parts of the body into which certain animals, e.g. earthworms and insects, are divided.

seismic wave a wave of energy or vibration that spreads out in all directions from the center of an earthquake⬚. Seismic waves are felt as a shaking of the Earth's surface at ground level.

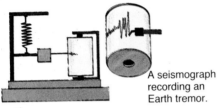

A seismograph recording an Earth tremor.

seismograph *n.* an instrument that detects and measures seismic waves.

semen *n.* the fluid produced by the male sex organs in animals. It contains male reproductive cells. (say *see-men*)

semicircle *n.* a half circle. A semicircle has an angle of 180°.

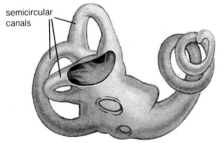

semicircular canals

The semicircular canals tell us whether we are upright, lying down or turning around.

semicircular canal one of the three curved tubes, filled with fluid, in the inner ear of vertebrates. The semicircular canals sense movements of the body in space and help to keep it balanced.

semiconductor *n.* a material, such as silicon, with conducting properties half way between those of a conductor (e.g. metals) and an insulator⬚ (e.g. rubber). Adding an impurity, called doping, increases the conducting properties of a semiconductor. Transistors⬚ are built up from semiconductors.

Thin wafers cut from a rod of silicon are used to make silicon chips.

sense (1) *n.* one of the powers that animals possess that makes them aware of their surroundings. Mammals possess five senses: sight, hearing, taste, smell and touch. (2) *v.* to feel or be aware of surrounding conditions through any of the senses.

sensitive *adj.* able to react to a stimulus. Eyes are sensitive to light. The skin is sensitive to heat and touch. Plants are sensitive to light and grow toward it.

sensor *n.* a device that detects or senses an object or energy such as heat, light or sound. Sensors are used in industry in alarm systems and automatic doors; they are also used in weather satellites.

sensory *adj.* to do with the senses and the receiving of stimuli⬚ from receptor⬚ cells or sense organs. Impulses pass along the sensory nerve fibers from receptors to the central nervous system⬚.

sepal *n.* one of the parts of the calyx of a flower. Sepals are usually green and lie outside the base of the petals. They protect the flower bud.

septic *adj.* describes animal tissues that are infected with pus, formed by bacteria or microorganisms that cause decay.

septum *n. (pl. septa)* a thin wall that divides cavities or separate tissues in animals and plants; e.g. the bony septum that divides the cavity of the nose into two parts.

series (1) *n. (pl. series)* a set of similar objects. (2) a sequence of events or processes, happening one after the other; e.g. the life cycle of a moth consists of a series of changes: from egg to caterpillar to pupa to adult insect. (3) a type of electric circuit in which all the parts are joined, one after the other, so that the electric current flows through all at the same time. (4) in mathematics, a sequence of numbers with a pattern that can be recognized.

serum *n. (pl. sera)* the clear, pale yellow liquid that separates from blood as it clots. (say *seer-um*)

set (1) *n.* a group of things that are similar or connected in some way, e.g. a set of Spanish stamps. (2) in mathematics, a collection of points, values or objects each of which has at least one thing in common. (3) *v.* to place or put in position. *The alarm was* **set** *to go off at 8 o'clock.* (4) to harden or become firm. *Jelly* **sets** *as it cools.*

sewage *n.* waste material and liquid from factories and houses, carried away by drains or sewers.

sex *n.* either of the two divisions, male or female, into which most living organisms are divided. Plants usually have both male and female organs on the same plant or flower. Most animals have only male or female organs.

sextant *n.* an instrument used to measure the angle between the Sun or a star and the horizon. Navigators may use it to plot the position of a ship.

sexual reproduction a type of reproduction in which new offspring are formed by the joining of male and female reproductive cells.

shade (1) *n.* a faint darkness that falls on a patch of ground or a building when a solid object, such as a tree or another building, blocks the Sun's rays. (2) the depth of a color. *The rose was a deep* **shade** *of red.* (3) *v.* to screen or protect from direct sunlight.

shadow *n.* the dark shape that is cast on a surface by an object when it blocks light falling on the surface. *The trees cast long, dark* **shadows** *on the lawn as the Sun set behind them.*

shaft (1) *n.* the main stem of a feather; the fine barbs☐ grow out from it. (2) a metal bar that passes on movement from one part of an engine to another mechanical part, e.g. the propellershaft in a ship.

shale *n.* a soft, sedimentary rock, formed from clay particles. Shale splits into thin layers. It often contains oil.

shell (1) *n.* a hard outer covering that protects the embryos☐ of certain animals and plants, e.g. the shell of a bird's egg, the shell of a nut. (2) a hard, outer, protective cover for animals with soft bodies, such as snails and crabs. Tortoises and turtles also have protective shells.

S

shoal (1) *n.* a large number of fish that swim together in a group. (2) an area of shallow water in a large river or in the sea.

shock (1) *n.* a condition that sometimes occurs in humans after an injury or severe fright. The blood pressure falls below normal, and the person looks pale and sweaty and feels cold and faint. (2) the effect of an electric current passing through the body. An electric shock may cause death.

shock absorber a device, fitted to the springs in a car or aircraft, that reduces the bouncing movement of the springs and gives a smoother ride.

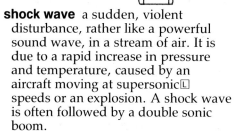

The shock absorber on this wheel has a piston damper which reduces the vibrations.

shock wave a sudden, violent disturbance, rather like a powerful sound wave, in a stream of air. It is due to a rapid increase in pressure and temperature, caused by an aircraft moving at supersonic☐ speeds or an explosion. A shock wave is often followed by a double sonic boom.

shoot (1) *n.* the stem of a young plant that bears leaves and flowers. (2) a new stem that grows out from the base of a leaf. (3) *v.* to produce a new shoot from a seed or from another stem.

shore *n.* a beach: the border of land that slopes down gradually toward the sea or a large freshwater lake. Shores may be sandy, pebbly or rocky.

short circuit an accidental fault in an electric circuit. The current flows along an unwanted path of low resistance between two points in the circuit. This reduces or cuts off the flow to the rest of the circuit and may cause damage or a fire. *The street lights went out because of a* **short circuit** *in the electricity cables.*

short sight myopia: a condition of the eye in humans in which a person cannot see distant objects clearly. It can be corrected by wearing glasses with special lenses.

shortwave (1) *n.* a radio wave up to 60 meters long. (2) a band of radio waves used in transmitting (sending) and receiving shortwave radio. Citizen band radio uses short radio waves.

shrub *n.* a woody perennial plant, smaller than a tree. It does not have a single thick trunk but branches out close to the ground. A shrub produces flowers and seeds. It may be evergreen or deciduous (that is, sheds its leaves in winter).

shutter *n.* in photography, a device that opens the hole (aperture) in the front of a camera for a fraction of a second to let in light.

sial *n.* the upper part of the Earth's crust☐ which is made mainly of silicon and aluminum compounds, hence the name sial.

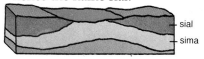

sieve (1) *n.* a utensil with many small holes in its base, used to strain solids from liquids or to separate small particles from larger ones. (2) *v.* to pass materials through a sieve. *The prospector* **sieved** *the fragments of rock in his search for diamonds.* (say *siv*)

sight (1) *n.* the sense of seeing. Sight is one of the senses in humans and other animals. *The eagle has very keen* **sight** *and can see small animals on the ground from a great height.* (2) anything that is seen. (3) a device fitted to telescopes and guns; it helps the observer to line up an object or the target. (4) *v.* to see or notice with the eyes. *The naturalist* **sighted** *an eagle's nest through his binoculars.*

signal (1) *n.* any sign, seen or heard, that is used to send messages between individuals, e.g. the Morse code, semaphore flag signals, the hand signals used by deaf people. (2) an electrical impulse sent out or received as a sound or picture in radio, television or telegraphy. (3) *v.* to send out any type of signal in order to pass on information.

semaphore signals

silica *n.* a hard, crystalline mineral substance found in flint, quartz, sand and semiprecious stones, such as amethyst and opal. Silica is used to make glass. It is the source of the chemical element silicon.

silicon chip a thin wafer of silicon with one or more integrated circuits etched on its surface. Silicon chips are used in computers and other electronic devices.

silt (1) *n.* fine grains of rock, coarser than clay but finer than sand. Silt is a mudlike sediment that falls to the bottom in slow-moving rivers or estuaries. *The deltas of the Amazon, Nile and Ganges Rivers are formed from* **silt**. (2) *v.* to fill up with, or block with, silt.

silver (1) *n.* a precious metal; a soft, greyish-white metal that is easily beaten into shapes and can be highly polished. It is used to make jewelry, tableware and ornaments and to coat other metals (silver plate). Silver is a chemical element. (2) *adj.* being silver in color. *Her grandmother has beautiful* **silver** *hair.* (3) being made of silver. *The baby was given a* **silver** *mug.* (4) *v.* to color something silver. (5) to coat or plate with silver.

sima *n.* the part of the Earth that forms the crust at the bottom of the ocean and the layers beneath the sial. It is called sima because it is made mainly of **si**licon and **ma**gnesium compounds.

simulator *n.* a machine that produces natural effects artificially. Simulators are used to train pilots, astronauts and drivers to cope with conditions and situations that they may meet in real life. Simulators are also used to test vehicles and engines to see how they stand up to tough conditions.

sinew *n.* a tendon; a band of tough, fibrous tissue that fixes one end of a muscle to a bone. Early humans used animal sinews to sew skins together to make clothing.

sink (1) *v.* to go down beneath the surface of a liquid or soft mud. (2) to drill or dig a hole. *Many bore holes were* **sunk** *in the ocean in the search for oil and natural gas.* (3) to descend slowly to a lower level. *The boat slowly* **sank** *after hitting a rock.* (4) to lose strength or weaken. *Mary's voice* **sank** *to a whisper.* (5) a metal, stone or china container that holds water. Waste water is let out through a hole. (6) an opening in limestone rock, called a sinkhole, through which streams disappear underground.

S

sinus (1) *n.* any small cavity or hollow found in certain tissues, e.g. the air cavities in the bony skull of mammals that open into the nose. (2) in botany, the curve between the lobes of a leaf. (say *sign-us*)

siphon (1) *n.* a U-shaped tube with one arm longer than the other. It is used for drawing a liquid out of a vessel. The siphon is filled with water by suction. The pressure of the liquid in the vessel forces the liquid up through the short arm of the siphon, around the bend, and out through the long arm. (2) a tubelike organ found in some molluscs☐ that draws water in over the gills, bringing fresh oxygen to the animal. (3) *v.* to draw off a liquid by using a siphon. (say *sigh-fon*)

skeleton (1) *n.* the hard tissue in certain living animals that supports and protects the soft body tissue. Muscles are fixed to the skeleton at certain points and move the joints. See **exoskeleton** and **endoskeleton**. (2) the dried bones, joined together in the shape of the animal. (3) the tough, woody or fibrous tissue that forms the framework of plants.

A human skeleton.

skin (1) *n.* the soft, flexible outer covering of human and other vertebrate animals (animals with backbones).The skin protects the tissues beneath and is the sense organ for touch, pressure, pain and temperature. In land animals the skin prevents too much water from being lost from the body. In warm-blooded animals it helps to control the body temperature. (2) the skin or pelt taken from a dead animal, e.g. sheepskin, snakeskin. (3) a similar outer protective covering to plants and fruits that helps to keep in moisture. (4) *v.* to remove the outer covering of animals or fruits.

skull *n.* the hard, bony case that holds the brain and sense organs of vertebrates (animals with backbones). In certain fish, such as rays and sharks, the skull is made of cartilage☐.

slag *n.* waste material formed when metal ores are smelted in a blast furnace. Some slags are used to make cement; another slag is a valuable fertilizer.

slate *n.* a hard, fine-grained gray rock formed from clays. It splits easily into thin, smooth plates. Slate is used to make roof tiles.

sleet (1) *n.* a mixture of falling rain with hail or snow. (2) rain that freezes as it falls.

slide rule a simple calculating device, similar to a ruler, with three special scales. The central scale slides between the two outer scales. A slide rule is used to make quick calculations.

sloth *n.* a large, hairy mammal that lives in the branches of trees in tropical forests of South America. It hangs upside down by its strong, curved claws. Its spine is curved to support the weight of the animal when it is upside down. A sloth moves very slowly and feeds on leaves and fruit. Microscopic algae⬜ live on the hairs of its body, giving it a green color that makes it difficult to see among the leaves.

small intestine the first and longest part of the intestine in mammals, birds and reptiles. It begins after the stomach and ends where it joins the large intestine⬜. Glands in its wall secrete enzymes⬜. Food is digested and absorbed in the small intestine.

smell (1) *n.* the sense by which land animals detect a scent or odor through the nose. *Lions use their sense of* **smell** *to seek out prey.* (2) a scent or odor. *Bad eggs have a very unpleasant* **smell**. (3) *v.* to detect a scent or odor with the nose. (4) to give off an odor.

smelting (1) *n.* the process by which metals are obtained from their ores by heating with coke to a high temperature in a blast furnace. (2) **smelt** *v.* Iron is produced by smelting iron ore.

smooth (1) *adj.* having an even surface; a surface that is not rough, wrinkled or hairy. *Calm water has a* **smooth** *surface.* (2) describes an even, flowing movement without bumps. *We had a very* **smooth** *ride in the new car.*

snail *n.* a soft-bodied animal, with a spiral or coiled shell, that lives on land or in fresh water. It has a broad muscular foot on which it moves slowly. A snail has a pair of eyes that stick out on stalks and can be pulled back into the body. It also has a powerful rasping structure, covered with thousands of tiny teeth that it uses to rub off pieces of plants.

snake *n.* a legless reptile with a long, narrow body, a flat head and a tapering tail. The skin is protected by smooth, overlapping scales. Some snakes live on land; others live in saltwater or freshwater. Snakes are carnivores⬜; they kill their prey by crushing or by a poisonous bite. Their jaws are elastic and can stretch to swallow very large whole animals.

snow *n.* soft, white ice crystals, formed from clouds of frozen water vapor, that fall to the ground as snowflakes. Snow crystals form many different shapes, but they all have six sides.

No two snow crystals are exactly alike.

soap (1) *n.* a soluble substance that makes a lather when shaken with water. Soap is made by heating fats or oil, such as olive oil or palm oil, with an alkali⬜. Soap is used for washing. (2) *v.* to lather or rub with soap.

social insect one of a group of insects that live together in organized colonies. Ants, termites and honeybees are examples of social insects. Each insect has a special role in the colony, e.g. the workers, drones and queen in a bee colony.

socket (1) *n.* a natural or artificial hollow part, into which something else fits. (2) in vertebrates (animals with backbones), the bony hollow in which another bone moves to form a

S

joint, e.g. the hip joint: the ball end of the femur⊡ fits into the socket on the hip bone. (3) the bony hollow in the skull that contains the eyeball. (4) an electric socket into which the prongs of an electric plug fit.

soda (1) *n.* washing soda; a general term for sodium carbonate. Impure sodium carbonate is called soda ash.

soft (1) *adj.* giving way easily to pressure; not firm or hard, e.g. a feather cushion, foam rubber. (2) describes certain clays that crumble easily. (3) a soft metal is one that is easily bent or beaten into shape. (4) a soft sound is a quiet, gentle sound. (5) a soft color is one that is not bright or dazzling; a pastel shade.

software *n.* the general term for computer programs, disks and cassettes.

soft water water that does not contain magnesium or calcium salts and easily forms a lather with soap.

softwood *n.* any timber obtained from a cone-bearing tree, e.g. pine, spruce. Softwood is light and easy to work with.

soil (1) *n.* the small, loose particles in the top layer of the Earth's crust⊡. Soil is formed from weathered rocks and contains the mineral salts⊡ needed by plants for healthy growth. The salts are dissolved in a fine film of water around each soil particle. Plants take the salts in through their roots. There are many types of soil, ranging from heavy, sticky clays to light, sandy loams⊡. (2) sewage or waste. (3) *v.* to make dirty. *John's shoes were* **soiled** *with mud.*

soil erosion the gradual removal of topsoil from an area of land by the action of flowing water, rain or wind.

solar *adj.* coming from, or having to do with, the Sun, e.g. solar system, solar energy, solar eclipse.

solar cell a device that changes solar energy into electrical energy. Solar cells were first used in spacecraft, but now they have many uses, e.g. in navigation aids and buoys.

A solar cell.

solar energy energy radiated by the Sun.

solar panel a device that absorbs heat energy from the Sun, which is then used to warm circulating water. Solar panels are fitted into roof slopes that face south and are open to the Sun's rays.

solar system the Sun and the nine planets, including Earth, that orbit around the Sun. The solar system also includes asteroids⊡, meteors⊡ and comets⊡.

solenoid *n.* a coil of wire that behaves like a magnet when an electric current is passed through it. The magnetic effect stops when the current is switched off. Solenoids are used in telephones, doorbells and electric motors.

solid (1) *n.* any material or substance that is not a liquid or gas. A solid has a definite shape and volume. (2) *adj.* having the three dimensions of length, width and depth, e.g. a cube, sphere, or pyramid. (3) not hollow; the same straight through.

solidify *v.* to become hard or solid when cooled. Water becomes solid ice when cooled to 0°C . Oils solidify when cooled below ordinary room temperature. Certain plastics solidify when cooled.

An iceberg is frozen, solidified water.

soluble *adj.* capable of being dissolved in a liquid.

solute *n.* any substance that dissolves in water or other liquid.

solution *n.* a liquid in which one or more solutes are dissolved. The solute molecules☐ are spread evenly throughout the solution.

solvent *n.* the liquid in which a solute will dissolve. In most solutions the solvent is water. Alcohol is a solvent for certain fatty substances that do not dissolve in water.

sonar *n.* (**so**und, **n**avigation and **r**anging) special equipment used by ships to detect mines, wrecks, submarines or shoals of fish and to measure the depth of the ocean. See **echo sounder**. (say *so-nar*)

sound (1) *n.* a type of vibration☐ that travels through air. Sound vibrations also travel through liquids and solids, but they will not travel through empty space. The vibrations are detected by the ear in land mammals. Messages pass from the ear to the brain, which interprets them as sounds. (2) any sound given out or heard. (3) a strait; a channel of water connecting two larger bodies of water

or separating an island from the mainland. (4) the air bladder in certain fishes. (5) *v.* to measure the depth of water, especially by using a lead plumb line. (6) of whales, to dive deeply and suddenly.

source (1) *n.* a thing or place from which something comes; e.g. the Sun is the source of energy needed by plants to make food. (2) the place from which a stream or river starts.

South Pole the point on the Earth's surface at the southern end of the Earth's axis☐.

sow (1) *n.* a female pig. (2) *v.* to plant or scatter seed in the ground in order to grow plants or crops.

space (1) *n.* an empty or blank area that lies between, over or inside objects or boundaries, e.g. a parking space, the space inside an empty box, the space inside a triangle. (2) the part of the universe extending in every direction outside the Earth's atmosphere. Space contains very little matter☐, apart from stars, planets and other objects. (3) *v.* to place with equal spaces in between.

spacecraft *n.* any spaceship or satellite designed to travel in space.

space shuttle a spacecraft that takes off like a rocket, flies like a spacecraft and lands like a glider. It can be used again and again.

span (1) *v.* to stretch across from one point to another, in space or time. (2) past tense of the verb, to spin. *The top* **span** *around and around.* (3) *n.* the length of time that something lasts. (4) a unit of measurement equal to 9 inches; roughly the distance between the tip of the thumb and the tip of the little finger on an adult. (5) an arch of a bridge between two supports, or a complete bridge of one span.

spark (1) *n.* a glowing, burning particle, thrown out by a fire. (2) a flash of light caused by a short, sudden discharge of electricity into the air or across a gap between two wires. (3) an electric spark that fires the fuel mixture in an internal combustion⃞ engine. (4) *v.* to produce or throw out sparks.

spatula (1) *n.* a tool with a handle and a wide, flat blade, used for spreading or scraping materials such as plaster, paints or chemicals. (2) a tool used by doctors to press down the tongue when examining the throat of a patient. (say *spat-tula*)

spawn (1) *n.* fish eggs. (2) the eggs of frogs, toads and other amphibians⃞, laid in water and surrounded by a mass of clear jelly. (3) the tangled mass of underground threads of certain fungi⃞ from which new fungi grow. (4) *v.* of fish and amphibians, to lay eggs in water.

Frogspawn.

species *n.* a unit of classification in animals and plants; a division of a genus⃞. Members of one species can breed among themselves. They cannot usually breed with individuals of another species. (say *spee-seas*)

specimen (1) *n.* one of a group used as an example of the rest of the group. *The botanist collected a* **specimen** *of each different flower.* (2) a small sample of something provided for examination, e.g. a blood specimen for medical examination. (say *spess-imen*)

spectacles *n.* a pair of glasses used to improve sight.

spectrum (1) *n.* the rainbow-colored bands of light seen when white light is split up by water droplets in the

The visible spectrum.

atmosphere or by a prism⃞. The bands are arranged in order of wave length; red is the longest and violet is the shortest visible wave. (2) the whole range of electromagnetic waves, including radio waves, heat and light waves, ultraviolet and X-rays.

speech *n.* the ability to speak, possessed by humans. Any person unable to speak is said to be dumb.

speed (1) *n.* the act of moving fast. (2) the rate at which something moves, measured in miles or kilometers per hour; velocity. (3) *v.* to move or cause to move fast.

sperm *n.* a male reproductive cell. Sperm cells move by means of a whiplike tail (flagellum).

sphere *n.* any solid, round body; a ball; a globe. All points on the surface of a sphere are the same distance from its center. (say *szfere*)

spider *n.* one of a group of small animals with a jointed body divided into two parts, four pairs of legs, simple eyes and no antennae⃞. Most spiders live on land (terrestrial). Spiders are carnivores⃞ and spin fine, sticky webs to catch insects.

spinal column the backbone or vertebral column; a flexible column of small, jointed bones (vertebrae) that stretches from the base of the skull along the back to the tail in vertebrates (animals with backbones). The spinal column is moved by the muscles of the back. It contains and protects the spinal cord.

spinal cord part of the central nervous system◻ in vertebrates (animals with backbones); it lies inside the spinal column. It links the brain to all parts of the body through pairs of nerves that pass out through holes in the spinal column.

spine (1) *n.* the same as spinal column. (2) a sharp, pointed part that grows in place of a leaf from the woody stems of certain plants, e.g. hawthorn and blackthorn. (3) one of the sharp processes that grow out from certain animals, e.g. hedgehog and porcupine spines, the spines in the fins of some fishes such as perch and sticklebacks.

spinneret *n.* an organ, found on the bodies of spiders and caterpillars, used to spin a web or cocoon◻. (say *spin-er-et*)

spinneret

spiral (1) *adj.* coiling around and around a central point, in curves that get larger or smaller, e.g. the thread on a screw. (2) *n.* a curved line that starts at a point and gets gradually farther away from the starting point. Snail shells are often formed in the shape of a spiral.

spleen *n.* a large organ found near the stomach in most vertebrates. The spleen stores red blood cells and breaks down old ones. It also produces antibodies◻.

spoke *n.* one of many strong, steel wires that connect the rim of a wheel to the central hub and keep it rigid.

sponge (1) *n.* a simple, aquatic◻ animal with a hollow body. Water containing food particles is wafted in and out of the body through many tiny holes. Sponges do not move about, but are fixed to rocks, and usually live in groups called colonies. (2) the tough, fibrous skeleton of a sponge can be used for washing. Sponges soak up water and other liquids. (3) any artificial material or mop that acts like a sponge. (4) *v.* to wash or wipe by using a sponge.

A colony of sponges.

spore *n.* a special reproductive cell, produced in large numbers by certain plants. Spores are spread by wind and grow into new organisms when conditions are suitable. Some bacteria◻ and one-celled organisms form spores. Spores can survive for a long time.

spring (1) *n.* a natural flow of water out of the ground; the source of a stream. (2) a season of the year between winter and summer. Plants burst into growth and many animals produce young in the spring. (3) a leap into the air. (4) an elastic metal coil or curved bar. A spring will return to its original shape or position when the pressure or tension acting on it is removed. (5) *v.* to jump into the air from the ground; to leap forward. *The leopard* **sprang** *forward and seized its prey.*

spring tide a very high sea tide that occurs at the time of the new and full moon when the Sun, Moon and Earth are lined up with each other and pull together.

S

spur (1) *n.* a high ridge of land that juts out at an angle from a mountain or mountain range. (2) in biology, a sharp spike on the legs of certain birds. (3) a long, thin, tube-shaped petal found in certain flowers, such as columbine. It usually contains nectar☐.

square (1) *n.* a plane figure with four equal sides and four right angles (90°). (2) the product of a number multiplied by itself ($3 \times 3 = 9 = 3^2$). (3) *adj.* shaped like a square or a cube, e.g. a square brick or box. (4) set at right angles or forming a right angle.

squint (1) *n.* a condition of the eyes in which they do not move together to look at an object. One eye may turn inward or outward. A squint is due to weakness in one of the muscles of the eyeball, which lets the opposite muscle pull too strongly. It can be cured by exercises or an operation. (2) *v.* to peer through half-closed eyelids at a close object or in bright sunlight.

stability *n.* steadiness; being stable or balanced. The lower the center of gravity☐ of an object the greater its stability. If a table or chair returns to its upright position after being tipped, it has stability.

stable (1) *adj.* steady; tending to stay balanced even when tilted or moved. (2) in chemistry and physics, describes a substance that is not easily broken down or changed by heating or by the action of other chemicals. (3) *n.* a shelter where horses and other farm animals are kept.

stagnant *adj.* describes water that is not flowing or moving. Stagnant water often smells of rotting vegetation, and contains a large number of microorganisms.

stainless steel steel that does not easily rust, stain or corrode; an alloy☐ of steel and chromium.

stalactite *n.* a column of lime that hangs down from the roof of a cave. Stalactites are formed by the dripping of water containing lime salts. The water evaporates, leaving the solid lime deposit. (say *sta-lak-tite*)

stalactite

stalagmite

stalagmite *n.* a column of lime, similar to a stalactite, that builds up on the floor of a cave and points upwards. Stalagmites often form beneath stalactites and may in time join to form pillars of lime. (say *sta-lag-mite*)

stalk (1) *n.* in botany, the main stem of a plant; the long, thin structure, similar to a stem but without branches, that supports a leaf or flower. (2) in zoology, a long, thin process that supports an organ or animal body; e.g. snails, crabs and lobsters have eyes fixed to stalks. (3) *v.* to move in a quiet, stealthy way. Predators, such as lions and tigers, stalk their prey before making a kill.

stall (1) *v.* describes when a motor or engine stops because of a lack of speed or power. (2) *n.* a condition affecting an aircraft that causes it to go out of control or drop suddenly. It occurs when air flows over the wings too slowly and not enough lift is produced to keep the aircraft in the air.

stamen *n.* the male reproductive organ in a flower that produces pollen☐. A stamen is a slender stalk with a pollen sac (anther) at its tip. (say *stay-men*)

anther

stalk

star *n.* a luminous body in space made up of very hot gases, mainly hydrogen. A star can be seen from Earth as a bright, fixed point in the night sky. The Sun is a star.

starch *n.* a white, powdery substance with no taste or smell; a complex carbohydrate⬜. Starch is a food substance, found in potatoes; grain, such as rice and corn; and many root crops.

state (1) *n.* a state of matter, either solid, liquid or gas. (2) the condition in which an object or living organism exists. Some animals spend the winter in a state of hibernation.

static (1) *n.* discharges of electrical energy in the atmosphere that interfere with radio signals, causing a crackling sound. (2) an electric charge that builds up on the surface of materials that do not conduct electricity. It is caused by friction⬜. *The cat's fur stands on end and crackles with* **static** *when it is combed.* (3) *adj.* not moving or at rest.

steam *n.* invisible water vapor, produced by boiling water. Steam becomes visible when the molecules of vapor cool and condense to form water droplets.

steam engine a type of engine using steam under pressure to drive a motor that produces mechanical energy.

Power from the steam engine drives a piston which turns the wheel.

steam shovel a large, mechanical digger, powered by a steam engine. Steam shovels are used for digging out channels for pipes, drains and building foundations.

steel (1) *n.* a tough, hard metal, made of iron with traces of carbon. Steel is used to manufacture cars, machinery, tools, girders and pipes; see **stainless steel**. (2) *adj.* made of, or like, steel.

stellar *adj.* to do with the stars or a star.

stem (1) *n.* the main stalk of a plant, branch of a shrub, or trunk of a tree, that bears leaves and buds above ground. (2) a similar part that lives underground, e.g. rhizomes⬜, corm and tuber⬜. Stems carry water and salts up from the roots to all parts of the plants and carry food substances downward from the leaves.

phloem

xylem

step rocket a space rocket, built in several sections. Each section has an engine and fuel supply. When the fuel supply in a section is used up, that section falls away and the next section takes over.

sterile (1) *adj.* completely free from dirt, bacteria⬜ and other microorganisms⬜. Doctors use sterile instruments during operations to prevent infection. (2) in plants, and animals not able to reproduce by means of sex cells. Sterile female mammals are often said to be barren.

sterilization (1) *n.* the complete removal of all micro-organisms by means of heat or chemicals. (2) any means by which a living organism is made sterile (not able to reproduce sexually). (say *ster-eh-lih-zashun*)

stethoscope *n.* an instrument used for listening to sounds in the body. Doctors use stethoscopes to listen to the heartbeat, the lungs and abdominal sounds.

S

stigma *n.* the part of a flower on which the pollen grains are deposited during pollination☐. The stigma is sometimes found on a stalk (style) that leads down to the ovary☐.

(labels: stigma, stamen, style, ovary)

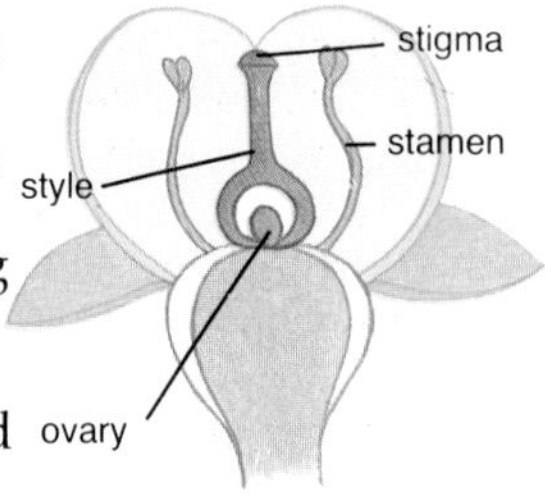

still (1) *n.* an apparatus used in the distillation☐ of certain chemicals, e.g. petroleum. (2) *adj.* not moving.

stimulate (1) *v.* to make a living organism active, or more active, by changing the conditions of its surroundings; e.g. seeds are stimulated into active growth by warmth and moisture. Cold-blooded animals, such as snakes and lizards, are stimulated by the heat of the Sun. (2) to cause a response in an animal or plant through a stimulus to a sense organ or receptor☐; e.g. food in the stomach stimulates the flow of digestive juices.

stimulus *n.* anything that stimulates or causes a living organism or part of an organism to do something.

sting (1) *n.* a sharp, hollow organ, used to prick and inject poison or an irritating substance. Certain insects, such as bees, wasps and hornets, have stings. (2) a fine hair, containing an irritating substance, found on the leaves or stems of certain plants, such as the stinging nettle. (3) the wound caused by a sting. (4) *v.* to prick with a sting.

stir (1) *v.* to rouse from sleep. (2) to mix liquids or other substances by moving them around a container with a spatula, glass rod or spoon.

stirrup *n.* one of the small bones (ossicles) in the middle ear.

stoma *n.* (*pl. stomata*) one of the many minute pores found in the outer cell layer of some plant stems and on the underside of leaves. Plants take in gases from the air through the stomata and give out gases and water vapor. Each stoma is surrounded by two special guard cells that control the size of the pore. When the plant is short of water, the stomata close. (say *sto-ma*)

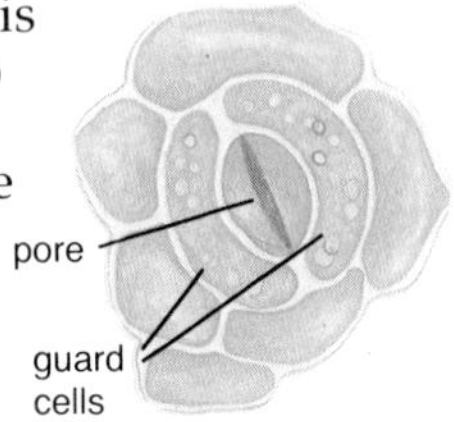

(labels: pore, guard cells)

stomach *n.* part of the digestive system of vertebrates (animals with backbones); a large, hollow organ in the abdomen. Food passes into the stomach from the gullet (esophagus) and is partly digested by the gastric juices. (say *stum-ick*)

stored energy the energy contained in substances such as the fossil fuels☐, which are stored in the Earth's crust☐.

strait *n.* a narrow passage of water that connects two larger bodies of water, e.g. the Strait of Gibraltar.

stratosphere *n.* the layer of the Earth's atmosphere that lies between 11 and 24 kilometers above the Earth's surface.

stratum (1) *n.* (*pl. strata*) in geology, a layer of sedimentary☐ rock. (2) a layer of the Earth's atmosphere. (3) a horizontal layer of material, one of many lying one above the other.

stratus *n.* a low layer of grey cloud that spreads out in all directions, and covers a large area of sky.

stream (1) *n.* a natural flow of water; a river. (2) a current of water in an ocean, e.g. the warm Gulf Stream that flows out from the Gulf of Mexico across the north Atlantic Ocean.

(3) a current of air. (4) a steady flow of energy, as in a beam of light or radio waves. (5) *v.* to flow like a stream.

Dolphins have a streamlined shape.

streamlining *n.* the designing and building of a body, such as an aircraft or ship, so that it moves smoothly through air or water.

stress *n.* in mechanics, the force put on a body that tends to change its shape.

structure (1) *n.* the way in which a number of different parts are joined together to form a whole organism or object, e.g. the cell structure of a plant leaf, the structure of an atom, the structure of a building. (2) in biology, a complete part of an organism that has a function, e.g. a flagellum□, the stalk of a crab's eye, a rose thorn, a deer's antlers.

style *n.* the long slender process that forms part of the carpel□ in some flowering plants. It bears the stigma□.

submarine (1) *n.* any ship or vessel that can travel underwater. Many submarines are armed with torpedoes and sea-to-air missiles used in warfare. (2) *adj.* being or living beneath the surface of the sea.

Submarine.

subside (1) *v.* of soil or rock, to settle or sink to the bottom. *The land* **subsided** *over the old mine workings.* (2) of water, to sink to a lower level. *The flood waters* **subsided** *as soon as the rains stopped.* (say *sub-side*)

subsoil *n.* soil found beneath the fertile topsoil. Subsoil is usually coarse and lacks minerals and humus□. It is not suitable for growing plants.

substance *n.* a chemical element□ or compound□ with a known composition. A substance has characteristic properties by which it can be identified. Salt, calcium and starch are examples of substances.

sucrose *n.* pure sugar obtained from sugar beet or sugar cane. (say *soo-crose*)

suction (1) *n.* the process of drawing air out of a space and making a vacuum□. This causes air or liquid to be sucked in to fill the space. (2) the sucking force; the act of sucking.

suffocate *v.* to kill or die by cutting off the supply of air to the lungs or gills.

sugar *n.* a sweet-tasting, carbohydrate□ substance made of crystals that dissolve in water. Sugar is obtained from sugar cane and sugar beet. There are many different sugars, e.g. sucrose, glucose, fructose and lactose.

Sugar beet.

sulfur *n.* a hard, brittle, yellow substance that burns with a blue flame and forms an unpleasant smelling gas; sulfur is a chemical element□. It occurs in the earth as the element and in the form of ores. Sulfur is an important industrial chemical.

sulfur dioxide *n.* a heavy gas with a sharp choking smell and no color. Sulfur dioxide is used as a bleach□ and to preserve food.

summer *n.* the warmest season of the year; it occurs between spring and autumn. Summer may be very hot and dry, or warm with some rainfall, depending on the geography of the area.

Sun *n.* a large, very hot star, a million times larger than Earth. Earth and the planets revolve around the Sun. Without the Sun, life on Earth could not exist. The Sun gives off radiation in the form of heat, light, ultraviolet light and electromagnetic waves. Ultraviolet light causes sunburn or tanning of the skin.

sunrise (1) *n.* the rising of the Sun. (2) the moment, early in the day, when the Sun is seen to rise above the horizon in the east and darkness gives way to daylight.

sunset (1) *n.* the setting of the Sun. (2) the moment, in the evening, when the Sun is seen to sink below the horizon in the west and darkness falls.

sunspot *n.* a dark patch seen on the surface of the Sun where there is a great disturbance. Sunspots last only a few weeks or months, and tend to appear in bursts of activity every eleven years. They are connected with magnetic storms.

Sunspots may interfere with radio and television signals.

supernova *n.* a very large star that is destroying itself. It explodes and becomes very bright and ends up as an expanding cloud of gas.

supersonic *adj.* moving, in air, faster than sound. *Concord is a* **supersonic** *aircraft that travels at speeds greater than sound.*

surface (1) *n.* the outside or top layer of an object or organism, e.g. the skin of an animal. *The* **surface** *of the sea was smooth and calm.* (2) in geometry, the sides of a solid shape, e.g. the surfaces of a cube; also the space or area inside a plane figure that has length and breadth, but no depth, e.g. the surface of a square. (3) *adj.* of, on or at the surface. (4) *v.* to coat something with a surface. *The road was* **surfaced** *with tarmac and grit.* (5) to come to the surface. *The submarine* **surfaced** *as it entered port.*

surface tension a property of liquids that makes the surface appear to be covered by a thin, curved, elastic film. It makes the liquid take up the smallest possible space.

surge (1) *n.* a sudden increase in the flow of energy, e.g. the sudden increase in the flow of an electrical current, the rush of water in a tidal wave. *When the dam broke a* **surge** *of water flooded the valley.* (2) *v.* of all forms of energy, to increase in strength suddenly.

surgery (1) *n.* a type of medical treatment in which certain diseases, injuries and deformities are treated or repaired. In an operation, the body is cut open in sterile⬜ surroundings, the damaged part is removed or repaired, and the wound is stitched together. A doctor who performs surgery is called a surgeon. (2) the place where a doctor sees patients.

surgical *adj.* to do with surgery. **Surgical** *instruments are used during operations.*

survival *n.* the act or fact of staying alive or existing.

suspension (1) *n.* the act of being held up or dangled from above. (2) any device or mechanism from which a structure, machine or instrument is hung or supported, e.g. the springs on a car, the monorail system. (3) in chemistry, particles of matter spread thoughout a liquid in which they will not dissolve. Particles in a suspension settle to the bottom very slowly and form a sediment.

suspension bridge a bridge that is suspended (hung) from cables fixed at each end and supported by towers.

The Golden Gate Bridge in San Francisco is a suspension bridge.

swallow *v.* to pass food and liquid from the mouth into the throat and down the gullet (esophagus). During swallowing a flap of tissue covers the windpipe and prevents choking.

swamp *n.* a marsh; an area of soft, wet ground. Large swamps are often found near lakes, rivers and deltas⬜.

swarm (1) *n.* a large number of insects flying or moving as a group. (2) a large number of bees, with a new queen, that leaves a hive to form a new colony. (3) *v.* to fly or move off in large numbers, as in a swarm.

sweat (1) *n.* the salty moisture given out through the skin of certain mammals. Evaporation of sweat helps to cool the body. (2) *v.* to give off sweat through the special sweat glands in the skin.

switch (1) *n.* a device used to start or stop the flow of electricity in a circuit, e.g. an electric light switch, a switch on a machine that turns the power on or off. (2) an electronic device used in computers that causes a current to flow through certain circuits and not others. (3) a mechanism connected to two movable sections of railway track. It is used to direct a train from one track to the other. (4) *v.* to turn an electric current on or off. (5) to change course or direction. *The train* **switched** *from a siding onto the main track.*

symbiosis *n.* in biology, a partnership in which two organisms live together for the benefit of each other, e.g. the bacteria⬜ in the root nodules⬜ of plants belonging to the pea and clover family. (say *sim-be-osis*)

symbol *n.* a sign, letter or diagram that represents or stands for something; e.g. in chemistry, each element⬜ is represented by a letter or group of letters: Ca = calcium, S = sulfur. In mathematics, +, −, and = represent add, subtract and equals.

symmetry (1) *n.* the exact matching of shape on opposite sides of something. The two matching sides are separated by an imaginary dividing line known as the axis of symmetry. A butterfly with its wings spread has symmetry. Its axis of symmetry lies along the center of its body. Some objects show symmetry when they are rotated. This is known as rotational symmetry. (2) **symmetrical** *adj.* having symmetry. (say *sim-mih-tree*)

Symmetrical markings.

S

symptom *n.* one of the effects shown or felt by a person, caused by disease, infection or injury, e.g. pain, fever or vomiting.

synthetic *adj.* describes things that are made by humans from chemicals; artificial: not natural, e.g. nylon, plastic, and artificial food flavorings.

syringe (1) *n.* a device used for sucking in liquids and shooting them out again under pressure. Syringes are used to spray plants with pesticides and liquid feeds. (2) a hypodermic syringe: an instrument used to take samples of blood and to inject substances into the body. (3) *v.* to suck liquids into a syringe and force them out under pressure.

A hypodermic syringe.
the plunger forces the liquid out
needle

system (1) *n.* a set or group of things that together form a whole, e.g. the solar system. (2) groups of tissues in a plant or animal that carry out a particular function, e.g. the digestive system in animals. (3) a method of grouping related things in an orderly way, e.g. the system used to classify plants and animals. (4) an orderly way of doing something. *The school had a good* **system** *for teaching chemistry.*

T t

table (1) *n.* a collection of related facts, figures or details arranged in rows and columns, e.g. a multiplication table. (2) **tabulate** *v.* to set out information in the form of a table.

tablet *n.* a small block of solid or compressed material, such as soap or medicine. *The doctor gave her some* **tablets** *for her sore throat.*

tactile (1) *adj.* describes something that can be sensed or felt by touch. (2) of, or related to, the sense of touch, e.g. tactile nerve endings in the skin of the finger tips.

tadpole *n.* the larval stage in the life history of certain amphibians, such as frogs and toads. It lives in water and has a tail and gills. As it grows into an adult, it develops legs; the tail is absorbed into the body, and the gills are replaced by lungs.

tailplane *n.* the surfaces at the rear of an aircraft that form part of the control system of the aircraft.

The tail of an aircraft improves balance.

talon *n.* the sharp, curved nail or claw found in some birds of prey, such as eagles. Talons are used for gripping or wounding prey.

tap (1) *n.* a device for turning the flow of a liquid on or off. (2) a tool for cutting a thread on the inside surface of a nut or pipe. (3) *v.* to hit or strike something lightly. (4) to make a hole for drawing off liquid. *Rubber trees are* **tapped** *to collect latex.* (5) to make a connection to an electrical circuit.

tape (1) *n.* a narrow band or strip of cloth, metal, plastic or other material; adhesive tape. Computers use magnetic tape to store information. (2) *v.* to record sound, video signals, computer data, etc. on magnetic tape.

tapeworm *n.* a flatworm which lives as a parasite. As adults, tapeworms live in the intestines⊡ of humans and other vertebrates. Part of the life cycle of tapeworms is spent in another animal, such as a pig. Humans are infected by eating undercooked meat or fish.

taproot *n.* The main root of a plant that grows straight down. Smaller side roots may branch out from it. Some taproots store food, e.g. carrots.

Swollen primary root that stores food.

tar (1) *n.* a thick, black substance obtained from wood or coal. When hot it is a sticky liquid; when cold it becomes solid. It is used to waterproof and preserve wood. It can be mixed with stones or gravel (tarmac) to make roads. (2) *v.* to cover with tar.

tarsal (1) *n.* in humans, one of a group of several small bones which together form the ankle and heel (tarsus). (2) a similar joint found in the hind limb of amphibians, reptiles, birds and mammals.

taste (1) *n.* in vertebrates, the sense by which substances are detected by the tastebuds. (2) that quality of a substance that is detected by the tastebuds. There are four basic tastes: sweet, sour, bitter and salt. Sugar has a very sweet taste.

tastebud *n.* a group of sensory cells found on the surface of the tongue.

Each tastebud is sensitive to only one of the four tastes. The tip of the tongue is sensitive to sweet tastes.

tear *n.* a drop of salty, sterile⊡ liquid secreted by the tear gland in the eye. Tears keep the eye moist and wash away dust and grit.

tear duct a tiny tube at the inner corner of the eye through which tears drain into the back of the nose.

tear gland a gland found at the outer corner of the eye. In mammals, it is beneath the upper eyelid. It secretes tears all the time.

teat *n.* in mammals, a small swelling on the mammary gland⊡ through which the young suck milk.

technology *n.* the science or study of engineering or industrial skills; the practical use of science in industrial methods. (say *tek-nol-ogee*)

telecommunication *n.* the sending of information by cable, radio, telephone, television, etc. using electromagnetic waves⊡.

telephone (1) *n.* a system for sending speech or sound over long distances. Speech is changed into electrical impulses by means of a microphone. These are carried by radio waves or wires to a receiver or loudspeaker, which changes the impulses back into speech. (2) an instrument consisting of a microphone and loudspeaker for transmitting and receiving speech.

A modern push-button telephone.

teleprinter *n.* a device with a typewriter keyboard for sending and receiving typed messages over a distance.

telescope *n.*
an optical
instrument
with lenses
or mirrors,
that
magnifies
distant
objects.

television (1) *n.* a system for sending
and receiving moving pictures and
sound by means of electrical impulses.
A television camera changes the
pictures and sound into electrical
impulses. These are
sent to a television
receiver, which
changes them back
into pictures and
sound. (2) a device
or set for receiving
pictures and sound.

temper *v.* to harden or strengthen a
material by special treatment; e.g.
steel is tempered by heating and then
suddenly cooling in cold water.

temperate *adj.* neither very hot nor
very cold. Parts of America and most
of Europe have a temperate climate.

temperature (1) *n.* the degree of
hotness or coldness of something.
Temperature is measured by a
thermometer. (2) the degree of heat of
a person's body.

tendon *n.* a
strong cord of
tissue that fixes a
muscle to bone.

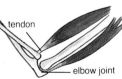
tendon
elbow joint

tension (1) *n.* a pulling force.
(2) the force acting on, or produced
by, a stretched object. (3) the condition
of a cable or spring that is being
stretched. The strings of a guitar are
under tension.

tentacle *n.* one of the long,
thin, muscular organs
found on the head of
some invertebrates,
e.g. octopus or squid.
Tentacles are used for
feeling, gripping prey,
holding on to rocks and
swimming. An octopus
has eight tentacles.

terminal (1) *n.* a point on an electrical
circuit where a connection can be
made. (2) a device connected to a
computer, e.g. a keyboard or
television screen. It may be used to
input or output information (data).
(3) *adj.* of, or at the end, of something;
e.g. toes are the terminal part of the
foot. A terminal illness is one that will
cause death.

termite *n.* a whitish, antlike insect with
a soft body that lives in a large group
or colony. Termites nest mainly
underground but can build huge
mounds aboveground. Termites eat
and destroy wood and can cause great
damage to buildings.

terrestrial (1) *adj.* to do with the planet
Earth, e.g. a terrestrial being.
(2) concerned with, or living on, the
ground or land, as opposed to air,
water, etc. *Cattle are* **terrestrial**
animals. (say *ta-res-tree-ul*)

territory *n.* an area of land in which an
animal or group of animals live, feed
and breed. Other animals entering the
area are attacked, particularly in the
mating season. The limits of the
territory are often marked by scent,
or, in the case of birds, by singing.

test (1) *n.* a simple chemical
experiment to find out if a substance
is present and what its properties are;
e.g. blue litmus paper turns red if an
acid is present. (2) a trial run to see if

a machine or apparatus is working correctly. (3) a medical examination, carried out to see if a particular disease is present. (4) *v.* to perform a test.

testa (1) *n.* the outer covering of a seed. It is usually hard and dry and it protects the seed. (2) the hard, outer covering of some animals without backbones, e.g. the shell of a clam.

A clam shell.   A seed testa.

testicle *n.* the testis; the male gonad☐ that produces sperms. In mammals it is contained in a sac of skin that hangs outside the body behind the penis☐.

test tube a small glass tube, closed at one end, used in chemical tests.

tetanus *n.* lockjaw, a disease caused by a bacterium☐ that usually enters the body through a cut or wound. Tetanus causes painful contractions of the muscles, particularly those of the face. It may result in death, but nowadays most people are protected against it by vaccination☐.

thaw (1) *v.* to raise the temperature of something above freezing point so that it becomes liquid. (2) *n.* a period of weather, warm enough to melt ice and snow.

theodolite *n.* an instrument used by surveyors to measure angles. It has a telescope which can turn horizontally and vertically on two graduated scales. The telescope is aimed at points on buildings and

A theodolite.

land, and the angles are read off the scale. Detailed survey maps are drawn from the information. (say *thie-odd-ilite*)

theory (1) *n.* any idea that appears to explain why something happens and which has been partly proved by experiments or observations. (2) the part of a science that deals only with facts and methods, not the practical experiments.

thermal (1) *adj.* to do with heat or temperature. (2) *n.* a column of warm air rising above the ground. Glider pilots use thermals to gain height when flying.

thermal energy heat energy.

thermal imaging a method of producing pictures that uses the infrared (IR)☐ heat radiation from an object or body to produce an image on an IR sensitive film. Special electronic equipment picks up IR waves from objects and changes them into picture signals on a television screen. This equipment is used to detect people and objects in the dark. Doctors use thermal imaging to detect disease in the body, because the diseased cells give off more heat.

thermometer *n.* an instrument for measuring temperature. Most thermometers are made of a thin glass tube containing mercury or alcohol. As the temperature rises, the liquid expands and rises up the tube. The temperature can be read off the graduated scale.

temperature reading

thermostat *n.* a device for controlling the temperature of something, e.g. as in an oven, central heating system or refrigerator. When the set temperature is reached, the heating (or cooling) unit is switched off.

T

thorax (1) *n.* in animals with backbones (except fish), the part of the body between the head and abdomen⬚. In mammals it is separated from the abdomen by the diaphragm muscle, and contains the heart and lungs. (2) in insects, the part of the body between the head and abdomen. It has three segments that bear three pairs of legs and one or two pairs of wings.

threadworm *n.* a whitish, threadlike, parasitic worm about 1 cm long. Threadworms are found in human intestines⬚. where they lay their eggs. After passing to the outside, the eggs are carried to the mouth by the fingers or on food. They pass into the intestines and develop into adults, and the life cycle starts again.

throat *n.* the passage leading from the mouth and nose into the esophagus (gullet) and trachea (windpipe). A flap of skin closes off the windpipe when food or liquid is swallowed.

throttle *n.* a valve that controls the amount of fuel entering an internal combustion engine, or the pressure of steam in a steam engine.

thrust *n.* a force which causes forward movement, e.g. the thrust of a propellor or jet engine on an aircraft.

thunder *n.* the loud rumbling or explosive sound that follows a flash of lightning. Thunder is caused by the sudden heating and expansion of air by an electrical spark between two clouds.

thyroid gland an endocrine gland⬚ found in the neck of animals with backbones. The thyroid gland produces a hormone⬚ that controls the growth of the body and the way the body uses energy. Too little

iodine⬚ in the diet causes a large swelling of the thyroid gland, called a goiter. (say *thigh-roid*)

tibia (1) *n.* in humans, the larger of the two bones of the lower leg that lies between the knee and the ankle joint; the shinbone. (2) a similar bone in the leg of other land vertebrates (animals with backbones).

tidal (1) *adj.* to do with the flow of a tide. A river estuary is a tidal waterway. (2) tidal air: the amount of air flowing in and out of the lungs during normal breathing.

tide *n.* the regular rise and fall of the surface of seas and oceans caused by the pull of the Sun and Moon. See **high tide** and **low tide**.

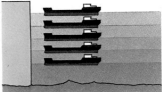

Level at high tide.

Level at low tide.

tilth (1) *n.* finely broken soil prepared for sowing seed. *The gardener prepared a fine* **tilth** *in which to plant his seeds.* (2) preparation of the land for growing crops by plowing and fertilizing.

time (1) *n.* a period during which things happen. *We grow older as* **time** *passes.* (2) an exact moment in that period. *The* **time** *is exactly 11 o clock.* (3) *v.* to measure a period during which something is done. Time is measured in units of seconds, minutes and hours, and periods such as days, years and centuries.

time-lapse *adj.* describing a method of photography for filming very slow activities, such as a flower opening. Single pictures are taken at intervals on film. The film is then projected at normal speed so that the activity is speeded up.

tin *n*. a soft, silver-white, metallic element⬚. Tin is used as a protective covering for other metal objects, such as tin cans.

tissue *n*. any group of plant or animal cells with a similar structure that perform the same functions, e.g. muscle tissue, nervous tissue and leaf tissue.

tone (1) *n*. a musical sound, produced by a vibrating⬚ object. (2) the quality, pitch⬚ or loudness of a particular sound. (3) a shade of color. *The car was painted in two* **tones** *of blue.* (4) the normal, healthy state of an organ or body.

tongue *n*. the muscular organ connected to the floor of the mouth of most vertebrates (animals with backbones). Taste-buds⬚ on its surface are used to taste food. The tongue also helps with chewing and swallowing food. Humans use the tongue for speech. Some amphibians, such as the frog, use their long tongues to catch insects.

tonne *n*. a unit of weight in the metric system, equal to 2204.62 lbs (1000 kilograms).

tooth (1) *n*. (*pl. teeth*) in most animals with backbones, one of a set of hard, bonelike structures found in the mouth and used for biting, tearing and grinding food. A tooth has a root, which lies inside the gum, and a crown covered with enamel. (2) any part shaped like a tooth on the edge of a saw, gearwheel or leaf.

topography (1) *n*. the drawing of accurate detailed maps which show all the surface features of an area, such as marshes, bridges, lakes, mountains, rivers and roads. (2) a similar description or study of parts of the body.

topsoil *n*. the top, fertile, layer of soil above the subsoil⬚. It contains the foods needed by plants for healthy growth.

tornado *n*. a violent, funnel-shaped column of wind spinning at very high speed over a small area. A tornado can destroy nearly everything in its path. Tornadoes often occur over the Gulf of Mexico, the southern part of the United States, and parts of Africa. (say *tor-nay-doe*)

torpid (1) *adj*. not active; dormant⬚; as in an animal that sleeps through the winter. A snake is torpid in cold weather. Animals become torpid during hibernation⬚. (2) *n*. the state of being torpid; inactive or dormant.

torque *n*. a turning force which produces, or tends to produce, rotation. (say *tork*)

touch (1) *v*. to make contact with something. *The wheels of the aircraft* **touched** *the runway.* (2) to place a finger, hand or other part of the body against something in order to feel it. (3) *n*. the sense by which objects are felt. (4) the feeling caused by touching.

toxic *adj*. poisonous. *The rats were killed by* **toxic** *bait*.

trace elements chemical elements needed in very small amounts by plants and animals for healthy growth. Trace elements include copper, iron, manganese and zinc. A lack of trace elements can cause disease or even death.

T

trachea (1) *n.* the windpipe; a hollow tube that joins the throat to the two bronchi⬚, which lead to the lungs. The trachea carries air to and from the lungs. (2) in insects, any of the small, branched tubes that open on to the surface and carry air to all parts of an insect's body. (say *tray-key-ah*)

track (1) *n.* a trail; a series of marks or scents left by an animal that can be followed by another animal or sometimes a human. (2) a pathway formed by the passage of wild animals through the undergrowth. (3) rails on which a train, trolley or monorail carriage run. (4) any parallel recording band on a disk, tape or phonograph record. (5) *v.* to trail or follow an animal's tracks.

traction (1) *n.* the action of pulling or drawing a load along a surface. (2) the friction⬚ force that prevents a wheel from slipping on a track or surface.

trade wind a wind that blows steadily in the same direction over much of the Earth's surface. The trade winds blow from the northeast, north of the equator, and from the southeast, south of the equator. Trade winds were very important to the old sailing ships.

transformer *n.* a device used to increase or decrease force (voltage) of an alternating current⬚. Transformers are used in power stations to increase the voltage to a very high level before it is sent out through the high-voltage cables carried by the pylons.

transfusion *n.* the injection of blood, taken from one person, into the vein of another person. The blood must be of the right group, or it will clot and cause the death of the patient. Blood plasma, serum, saline and glucose solutions are also used in transfusions.

transistor *n.* a small electronic valve through which a current flows at a controlled rate in one direction.

Types of transistor.

Transistors can increase the strength of an electric signal. Very small transistors are used in hearing aids.

translucent *adj.* describes a material that is not transparent⬚ but allows some light to pass through. Objects cannot be seen clearly through a translucent material. Tissue paper is translucent. (say *trans-loo-cent*)

A television antenna transmits and receives television signals.

transmission (1) *n.* the sending out of radio or television signals. (2) the passage of radio and television signals between a transmitter and a receiver. (3) something that is transmitted, e.g. an infectious disease or sound waves. (4) the system in a car that carries power from the engine to the wheels.

transmit (1) *v.* to send out radio and television signals. (2) to carry disease from one person to another.

transmitter (1) *n.* a person or thing that transmits. A mosquito transmits malaria to humans through its bite. (2) the speaking part of a telephone

The mouthpiece of a telephone is a transmitter.

which transmits sound as electrical impulses. (3) any device that sends out radio, television or electric signals.

transparent *adj.* describes any liquid or solid material that lets light pass through it and forms a clear image on the other side. Clear glass and water are transparent materials.

transpiration *n.* the loss of water vapor from the surface of the leaves of plants. The water vapor is lost mainly through the stomata☐ but some passes out through the cuticle☐. If too much water is lost, the plant becomes floppy and wilts. (say *trans-per-ashun*)

Water is taken in through the roots, and water vapor passes out through the leaves in transpiration.

transplant (1) *v.* to dig up a plant and replant it in a new site. (2) to remove an organ from one animal or person by surgery and replace it in another, e.g. to transplant a kidney. (3) *n.* the plant, tissue or organ which is transplanted. Heart, lungs, liver and kidneys have all been used as transplants.

trauma (1) *n.* a medical term; a severe wound or injury to the body. (2) a state of shock caused by a severe emotional upset, fright, or physical injury. (say *traw-ma*)

tree *n.* a tall, woody, perennial☐ plant, with one main stem (trunk), which branches some distance from the ground.

tremor (1) *n.* a shaking or trembling; a vibration, e.g. an earth tremor. (2) a shaking of the muscles of the body caused by nervousness, cold, weakness or disease.

trench (1) *n.* a long, narrow furrow or ditch. (2) a deep underwater furrow or ditch found in the floor of the ocean where the plates of the Earth's crust☐ come together; e.g. the Marianas Trench near the Philippines is 11 km. deep. (3) *v.* to dig a long, narrow furrow or ditch in the earth.

triangle *n.* a plane figure, having three angles and three sides.

The three angles of a triangle always add up to 180°.

triangulation *n.* a method of surveying, used to make very detailed maps. The area is divided up into a series of triangles; each triangle is mapped in detail.

triceps *adj.* a word used to describe muscles, e.g. the triceps muscle at the back of the upper arm in humans.

trilobite *n.* an extinct type of sea arthropod☐; often found as a fossil☐.

A trilobite was similar to the sow bug of today.

triode *n.* an electric valve; a vacuum tube☐ with three electrodes☐. By controlling the current, a triode can be made to amplify (strengthen) a signal.

tropical rain forest see **rain forest**.

tropics (1) *n.* the very hot, damp regions of the Earth, near the equator. They lie between the Tropic of Cancer, north of the equator, and the Tropic of Capricorn, south of the equator. The tropics are rich in plant and animal life. (2) in geography, the two lines of latitude 23.5° N and 23.5° S of the equator.

tropism *n.* the tendency of a plant to grow toward a stimulus (positive tropism) or away from a stimulus (negative tropism). The type of stimulus is shown by the prefix, e.g. **photo**tropism is a response to light; **geo**tropism is a response to gravity. Plant stems show positive phototropism. Plant roots show positive geotropism.

troposphere *n.* the lower part of the Earth's atmosphere reaching to about 15 kilometers above the Earth. The troposphere contains 90 percent of the gases in the atmosphere, water vapor and clouds.

trough (1) *n.* a long, narrow band of low atmospheric pressure between two areas of higher pressure. (2) a U-shaped fold in rock layers (strata). (3) a long, narrow hollow in the Earth's crust, caused by a fault. e.g, a rift valley. (4) the low dip between the crest, or peak, of two waves.

trunk (1) *n.* the main woody stem of a tree that branches at a distance from the ground. (2) the long, flexible proboscis⊑ of an elephant. (3) the body of an animal, not including the head or limbs.

tube (1) *n.* a narrow, hollow pipe with open ends, made of metal, glass, rubber or plastic, in which liquids and gases can flow or be stored and which connects different parts of a system, e.g. the hoses or tubes that carry the water and brake fluids in cars. (2) a tubelike instrument that contains some material or substance, e.g. a mercury barometer or thermometer. (3) a valve, e.g. a triode⊑ or vacuum tube⊑. (4) in anatomy, a hollow tube-shaped organ, e.g. the bronchus and air passages of a lung or the alimentary canal.

tuber (1) *n.* a swollen, underground stem with buds that can grow into new plants. Stem tubers store food for the growing buds, e.g. a potato. Stem tubers are a form of vegetative reproduction⊑. (2) a swollen root that stores food, e.g. a dahlia tuber.

Potato tubers.

tumor *n.* any lump or swelling on or in an animal's body; a growth of tissue that is not normal. Tumors may be harmless or may spread through the body and cause death.

tundra *n.* any treeless plain found in arctic regions that is frozen solid for most of the year, e.g. Siberia in the USSR. Only lichens⊑, mosses, long grasses and a few low bushes grow in tundra regions. Reindeer feed on them. (say *ton-dra*)

tune (1) *v.* to adjust the pitch of a musical instrument. (2) to adjust a radio or television receiver to a particular frequency or wave band. (3) to adjust the parts of an engine or machine so that it performs well. *The racing mechanic* **tuned** *the engine to peak performance before the race.*

tungsten *n.* a heavy, steel-grey, metallic element, with a very high melting point. It can be drawn out into a very fine wire that is used for filaments⃞ in electric light bulbs. Tungsten is also used in steel alloys⃞.

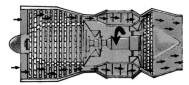

This jet engine uses turbines to suck in air.

turbine *n.* a shaft to which a number of curved blades are fixed. The turbine shaft is made to rotate by steam or water power. Turbines are used to drive ships' propellers and in power stations to produce electricity.

turbulence *n.* the disturbance in a fluid usually caused by a solid body passing through it. A ship's propeller causes turbulence in the water as it turns.

tusk *n.* a long, pointed tooth on the upper jaw that grows outside the mouth of certain mammals. It may be one of a pair as in elephants, or single as in the narwhal (a sea mammal). A narwhal's tusk is spiral in shape and up to 4 metres long.

tusk ——

twin (1) *n.* one of a pair of two similar things, e.g. a twin-engined plane. (2) one of two offspring that have developed from the same fertilized egg cell. Such twins are exactly similar, and are called identical. (3) one of two offspring⃞ born at the same time from one parent but developed from two separate egg cells. Such twins are nonsimilar, and are called nonidentical. They may be of different sexes.

type (1) *n.* a group of things or organisms that have similar characteristics by which they can be recognized. (2) one of such a group, taken to represent the group; e.g. a frog is a type of amphibian⃞. (3) a block of metal or wood with a raised letter or symbol, used in printing. (4) *v.* to arrange similar things, people and organisms into groups. (5) to produce printed information on a screen, or paper, by using a keyboard such as a typewriter or word processor.

typhoon *n.* a tropical cyclone that occurs over the western Pacific ocean. It is caused by warm, moist air rising from the ocean and cooler air being drawn in to take its place. The air currents develop into spiraling winds of over 120 kilometers per hour. Typhoons cause much damage. They destroy property and draw the ocean up into huge waves. (say *tie-foon*)

U u

udder *n.* the baglike, milk-producing organ of certain female mammals such as cows, sheep and goats: it hangs under the abdomen⃞, and has two or more teats for suckling the young.

udder

ulna *n.* one of the two, long, slender bones in the lower arm of humans and the lower front leg of mammals, birds, reptiles and amphibians□. The ulna joins with the humerus and the upper end of the radius to form the elbow joint.

ultrasonic *adj.* describes vibrations or sound waves of very, very high frequency, which cannot be heard by the human ear. Ultrasonic waves are used in medicine to find out about certain conditions.

ultraviolet ray (UVR) an invisible, electromagnetic ray. Ultraviolet rays occur naturally in sunlight and are harmful. Most are filtered out by the Earth's atmosphere.

umbilical cord the soft cord that joins the fetus□ to the placenta□ of the mother. The umbilical cord contains blood vessels that carry oxygen and food substances to the fetus, and waste substances away from it. The umbilical cord is cut at birth. The scar left behind on the abdomen is called the umbilicus or navel.

undiluted *adj.* describes a concentrated solution or substance to which no water or other solvent has been added.

unhygienic *adj.* the opposite of hygienic□; describes unclean habits of behavior, and dirty conditions in the home and surroundings. Unhygienic conditions lead to poor health and the spread of disease. (say *un-hi-jenik*)

unicellular *adj.* describes a living organism made up of only one cell. *Euglena is a* **unicellular** *organism.* (say *yuna-sell-yu-ler*)

A unicellular organism: Euglena.

uniform (1) *adj.* looking the same. *All the petals of the flower were of* **uniform** *size, shape and color.* (2) acting in the same way at the time. *The cars in the procession traveled at a* **uniform** *speed.*

union (1) *n.* a joining together of two or more things to form a whole. (2) the state of being joined together. (3) a junction: a point where two things meet and join.

unit (1) *n.* a single person or thing that is complete in itself. (2) one of many single parts that join together to form a whole, e.g. the sections of track that make up a railroad system. *In a car, the engine, gearbox and clutch are separate* **units** *that work together as one whole to drive the car.* (3) a standard measure; e.g. the centimeter, meter, and kilometer are units of length or distance in the metric system. Degrees Fahrenheit or Celsius are units of measurement of temperature. (4) the quantity represented by the number 1. (5) **units** the group of whole numbers less than the number 10.

universe *n.* everything that exists, including the Sun, Earth, planets, galaxies and everything that is still undiscovered in outer space.

unstable (1) *adj.* unsteady; easily put off balance. (2) in chemistry or physics, it describes a substance that breaks down or changes easily.

uplift (1) *v.* to lift up; to raise up. (2) *n.* the act of lifting up. (3) in geology, the raising up of an area of land above the surrounding land.

upthrust (1) *n.* an upward push or force; e.g. the upthrust of air keeps a balloon afloat; the upthrust of water supports a floating object. (2) a sudden pushing up of parts of the Earth's crust, because of an earthquake or volcanic eruption.

uranium *n.* a heavy, hard, grey, radioactive☐ metal; a chemical element. Uranium is used as a fuel in a nuclear reactor☐ to produce nuclear energy.

urea *n.* a substance found in the urine of mammals. Urea is a waste product of the breakdown of protein.

urine *n.* the yellow, watery liquid, containing urea and other waste substances, produced by the kidneys in mammals. Urine is stored in the bladder and is passed from the body from time to time. (say *yure-in*)

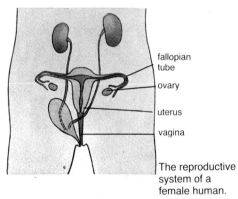

fallopian tube

ovary

uterus

vagina

The reproductive system of a female human.

uterus *n.* the womb; the hollow, muscular organ in most female mammals in which the fetus develops. At the end of the pregnancy the muscular walls contract and push the fetus out of the mother's body.

V v

vaccination *n.* the act of giving a vaccine to protect against a particular disease. Most children have a vaccination against diphtheria.

vaccine *n.* a liquid containing dead or weak disease organisms that is swallowed or injected into the body to protect against that disease. The vaccine does not usually cause the disease, but it helps the body to build up resistance to the disease. Vaccines give protection against many diseases, such as typhoid, German measles, influenza and diphtheria.

vacuum (1) *n.* a space that contains almost no air at all. Heat and sound waves cannot pass through a vacuum, but light waves and other electromagnetic waves, such as radio waves, can. (2) a completely empty space that does not contain any matter, air or gas (absolute vacuum).

vacuum flask a thermos; a container lined by a double glass tube from which nearly all the air has been removed. Heat cannot pass across a vacuum, so any liquid put into a vacuum flask and sealed with an airtight stopper, stays at the same temperature for a long time. It keeps hot things hot and cold things cold.

vacuum tube an electronic tube from which almost all the air has been pumped out. Vacuum tubes are used in television.

vagina *n.* in most female mammals, the tubelike passage that links the uterus☐ with an opening at the lower end of the body. The male penis enters the vagina during copulation. The fetus is pushed out through the vagina at birth. (say *vah-jine-ah*)

valley (1) *n.* a long, narrow strip of land lying between steep hills or mountains. A river or stream may run along the bottom. (2) a large area of land drained or watered by a river system, e.g. the Nile Valley. (3) a canyon, or gorge, is a valley with

V

nearly vertical sides that has been cut by a river or formed by faults in the Earth's crust, e.g. the Grand Canyon in Colorado.

valve (1) *n.* a device that controls the flow of fluids through an opening or along a pipe. A tap is a valve that controls the flow of water in the home. (2) any mechanical device that allows fluids or air to flow in one direction only, e.g. the valve in a bicycle pump. (3) flaps of tissue found in the heart and some blood vessels in certain animals that keep the blood flowing in one direction. (4) one of the hinged parts of the shell of certain molluscs, e.g. oysters, clams and mussels. (5) in plants, one of the parts into which some seed capsules split, e.g. iris.

Section through a tap showing a screw valve. Water flows when the valve is opened.

vapor (1) *n.* the gaseous form of a substance that is usually a liquid or solid at ordinary temperatures. (2) fine particles of matter given off into the air. Smoke fumes, mist, fog and steam are all forms of vapor. Some vapors, such as gases or fumes, may not be seen (invisible) but may be smelled. (3) **vaporize** *v.* to turn a substance into a vapor, usually by heating it.

variegated *adj.* patchy differences in color in some plant parts. Variegation may be an inherited characteristic☐ or caused by disease. (say *vare-eh-gated*)

A variegated holly leaf.

variety (1) *n.* one of the units into which species are divided in the classification of plants and animals. Each variety has a different characteristic that is passed on to the offspring, e.g. the different color forms of flowers in a species. Most varieties occur as a result of special breeding. (2) one of the different types in a species.

vary (1) *v.* to become different or to change in some way. *The apples* **varied** *in size and had to be graded.* (2) to make different or give variety to something. *The gardener* **varied** *the plants to produce a colorful display.*

vascular system (1) tough tissue (mainly phloem☐ and xylem☐) connecting tubes that run through stems, leaves and some roots of certain plants. The vascular system supports the plant and conducts (carries) water and salts up from the roots and soluble food substances down from the leaves. (2) a similar system of tubes in vertebrates and certain other animals that conducts liquids around the body.

vector (1) *n.* a living carrier of disease organisms that carries the disease from one host to another; e.g. mosquitoes spread malaria and yellow fever, dogs transmit rabies. Humans may also act as vectors. (2) a physical carrier of disease organisms, such as air, water or food; e.g. salmonella food poisoning is spread by infected food and by human carriers.

vegetation *n.* all plant life. Forests, grasslands, crops, shrubs, herbs, bulbs and seaweeds are all types of vegetation. (say *vej-eh-tashun*)

vegetative reproduction in plants and simple organisms, a means of producing offspring without the formation of sex cells, e.g. the underground stems of rhizomes⊡, bulbs and tubers⊡; the runners of strawberry plants; fission⊡ in unicellular organisms; the spores of fungi; and the budding of animals such as hydra. Vegetative reproduction produces offspring that are exactly like the parent. (say *vej-eh-tay-tiv*)

vein (1) *n.* in vertebrate animals, a blood vessel that carries blood to the heart. Veins have thinner walls than arteries and valves that keep blood flowing toward the heart. (2) one of the fine tubes or ribs found in leaves. (3) one of the tough, fine tubes that form the framework of an insect wing. (4) a long, thin band of ore or mineral formed inside a mass of rock of a different type. (5) a streak of color in a rock, such as marble, e.g. a grey vein in white marble. (rhymes with **lane**)

velocity *n.* speed; the rate at which a body moves in a straight line in a given time. The velocity of light is greater than the velocity of sound, which is why we see the flash of lightning before we hear the thunder, although both happened together.

venom *n.* a poisonous substance produced by some snakes, spiders, insects or other animals. It is injected into the body of a human or another animal by a bite or sting.

vent (1) *n.* an opening, or hole, through which liquids, steam, air or gases may pass or escape. (2) the long, narrow opening in a volcano through which lava⊡, steam, gases, dust and fragments of rock are thrown out when a volcano erupts. When the volcano is not active the vent is blocked by a plug of basalt⊡ rock. (3) an air shaft sunk into mines

or long tunnels to keep the air fresh. (4) an opening at the rear or underside of vertebrates, except mammals. Urine, feces, sperm or eggs pass out through this vent.

ventilation *n.* the act or process of circulating fresh air through a room or building and removing the stale, used air. It may be done simply by opening windows and doors, causing air currents, or by means of an air-conditioning system that pumps fresh air through a building.

ventricle (1) *n.* one of the chambers of the heart in vertebrates. It has a thick, muscular wall and pumps blood out of the heart into the main arteries. The heart of a mammal or bird has two ventricles. The right ventricle pumps blood into arteries going to the lungs, and the left ventricle pumps blood into the arteries going to the rest of the body. Reptiles⊡, fish and amphibians⊡ have one ventricle, but in some reptiles it is partly divided into two. (2) any one of the four linked chambers in the brain of vertebrates. It contains a liquid that feeds the brain and helps to protect it from injury.

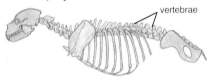
vertebrae

vertebra *n. (pl. vertebrae)* one of the small bones that make up the spinal column or backbone. The vertebral column is the flexible, jointed column of small bones that runs from the skull to the jointed tail down the back of the animal. It forms the main support of the body and protects the spinal cord⊡.

V

vertebrate (1) *n.* any animal that has a skeleton of bone or cartilage with a backbone, a skull and a well-developed brain. Fish, amphibians, reptiles, birds and mammals are all vertebrates. (2) *adj.* to do with animals with backbones.

vertical (1) *adj.* upright; straight up or down, at right angles to the horizon□. *The builder used a plumb line to test if the walls were* **vertical**. (2) *n.* any line or plane at right angles to the horizon.

veterinary surgeon same as veterinarian; an animal doctor, a qualified person who deals with diseases and injuries in animals.

vibrate (1) *v.* to move, or cause to move, to and fro or up and down quickly. (2) to swing from side to side like a pendulum. The strings of a violin vibrate when they are plucked or bowed. This makes the air inside the instrument vibrate and produce musical sounds.

vibration (1) *n.* the action of moving quickly to and fro or up and down (vibrating).

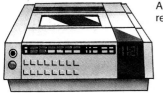

A video cassette recorder.

video cassette recorder (VCR) a machine that records television pictures and sound on magnetic tape□ and winds it inside a cassette. A VCR can also play back recorded television programs.

video head a rotating, drum-shaped electromagnet□ that changes television pictures and sound into signals on magnetic video tape. When the tape is played back, the video head changes the signals back into pictures and sound.

video tape recorder (VTR) a machine that records television pictures and sound on magnetic tape□.

villus *n.* (*pl. villi*) one of a great many tiny, fingerlike processes found in the lining of the small intestine□. Villi increase the surface area of the lining and so help the body to absorb (take in) the digested food substances.

virus *n.* (*pl. viruses*) a form of living matter, smaller than any bacteria□, that lives inside the cells of plants and animals. Viruses cause many infectious diseases, such as measles, mumps, influenza and the common cold. (say *vie-rus*)

viscous *adj.* describes a liquid that does not flow easily. Oil and treacle are viscous liquids. Viscosity is the property of a liquid that stops it from flowing easily. (say *vis-kus/vis-kos-ity*)

visible light (visible spectrum) the range of electromagnetic light waves that can be seen as colored or white light by the human eye.

vision *n.* the ability to see; the power or sense of sight. *Birds of prey have very keen* **vision**.

visual display unit (VDU) an output device of a computer that displays information on a screen.

vitamin *n.* one of a number of substances, found in food, that are needed in small amounts by animals to keep them healthy. Vitamin A helps people to see in the dark. Vitamins can be made artificially and are used by doctors to treat starving and poorly fed people.

vitreous humor (vitreous body) the mass of clear, colorless jelly that fills the space between the lens and the retina☐ and gives shape to the eyeball. (say *vih-tree-us*)

vocal cord one of a pair of muscle bands that stretch across the opening of the larynx (voice box) in amphibians, reptiles and mammals, including humans. The vocal cords vibrate when air is forced past them and produce sounds.

void (1) *adj.* empty; having nothing in it. (2) *n.* an empty space; a vacuum. (3) *v.* to empty out or expel the contents of something.

volatile *adj.* describes a liquid that evaporates☐ quickly when exposed to air. Alcohol and petrol are very volatile liquids.

volcano (1) *n.* an opening in the Earth's crust☐ through which lava (molten rock), hot gases and ash are forced out under pressure from time to time. This is called a volcanic eruption. (2) a cone-shaped mountain with a large hollow or crater at the top, formed from the ash and cooled lava left by a volcanic eruption. A volcano may be active, dormant (inactive) or extinct.

volt *n.* the unit of measurement of the force of an electric current. Named after Count Alessandro Volta (1745–1827), an Italian physicist.

voltage *n.* the strength of the electrical force in an electric current, measured in volts.

voltmeter *n.* an instrument for measuring electrical force in volts.

volume (1) *n.* the space taken up by a solid object, liquid or gas in three dimensions. The volume of a cube equals height × breadth × length and is measured in cubic units. (2) the strength, or loudness, of sound. *Father asked Sarah to lower the* **volume** *on her record player.*

vomit (1) *v.* to bring up the contents of the stomach forcibly through the mouth. (2) *n.* the material brought up by the stomach during vomiting.

vortex *n.* (*pl.* *vortexes* or *vortices*) a whirling mass of water or air which creates a vacuum at its center that sucks in any object in its path; a whirlpool or whirlwind.

vulva *n.* the outer reproductive organ of female humans.

W w

warm-blooded *adj.* describes an animal having a body temperature that stays the same whatever the temperature of its surroundings. The temperature of the animal is usually higher than that of its surroundings, except in very hot desert areas. Birds and mammals are warm-blooded animals.

warp (1) *n.* in textile weaving, the threads that run the length of the fabric or loom. The weft☐ threads weave in and out across the warp. (2) *v.* to twist out of shape. Wood sometimes warps under the action of heat and moisture.

The wood between these blocks has warped.

wart (1) *n.* a verruca; a small, usually hard, lump that grows on the skin. It is caused by a virus☐. (2) any of the small lumps that normally grow on the skin of certain animals, e.g. the warted toad or wart-hog. (3) a wart-like patch on certain plants, such as the potato, due to a fungus disease.

W

washer (1) *n.* a flat ring of metal, rubber or leather put over a bolt or screw. The nut or screw is tightened against it. A washer provides a soft, tight fit. It prevents friction and wear around the hole. (2) a machine or person that washes, e.g. dishwasher or washing machine.

waste (1) *v.* to use resources extravagantly. (2) to lose health, energy and flesh because of disease or starvation. (3) *n.* the unwanted products of digestion, respiration and excretion in living organisms. Urine, feces and carbon dioxide are waste products. (4) the unwanted products of manufacturing and industrial processes. (5) household waste, e.g. bottles, food cans, paper and food scraps. (6) wasteland: land that is not fit for cultivation, e.g. desert waste or land that has been neglected.

water (1) *n.* a clear, colorless liquid with no taste or smell; a chemical compound made of hydrogen and oxygen. It is neither acid nor alkaline (neutral). Water is found naturally in all living organisms and in ponds, rivers, lakes and oceans. Sea water tastes salty because of the chemicals dissolved in it. Water falls to the Earth as rain, sleet, hail and snow. All living organisms need water for life. (2) *v.* to add water to plants or soil.

water-cooled *adj.* describes machinery or industrial processes that are prevented from overheating by having cold water passed around them in pipes.

water cycle the circulation of water in nature. Water evaporates from oceans, lakes, rivers and soil into the atmosphere and forms clouds. Rain and snow fall from the clouds, and water returns to the soil, rivers, and oceans. Plants and animals also take in water and water vapor, use it, and return waste water to the atmosphere or land.

water pollution the presence of sewage and harmful chemicals in ponds, streams, rivers and oceans. These substances can harm or kill plants and animals and upset the balance of nature. Oil from tankers and acid rain may also cause water pollution.

waterproof *adj.* describes any material that will not let water or water vapor pass through it. Rubber and plastic-coated materials are waterproof. *The children wore* **waterproof** *raincoats because it was raining heavily.*

watershed (1) *n.* the area of land drained by a river and its tributaries. (2) a high ridge of land that separates two regions drained by different river systems.

water table the level in the ground below which water collects because it cannot drain away any further. This may be because the rock cannot soak up any more water or because a layer of clay prevents it from draining away.

water vapor the gaseous form of water. Water vapor is always present in air.

watt *n.* a unit of measurement of electric power.

wave (1) *n.* in physics, a vibrating, up-and-down movement of energy or particles traveling in a given direction, e.g. light, heat and sound waves. (2) a raised ridge of water along the surface of an ocean or large lake.

wavelength *n.* the distance between the peak of one wave and the peak of the next wave moving in the same direction.

wax (1) *n.* any of a group of yellow, fatty substances. Wax softens and melts when heated and burns with a sooty yellow flame. It does not dissolve in water and forms a waterproof film when spread on surfaces. (2) a waxy material made by bees (beeswax). (3) a waxy substance made by certain plants. (4) a yellow waxy material found in the ear. (5) paraffin wax, obtained from petroleum. Beeswax and paraffin wax are used to make candles and polishes. (6) *v.* to coat or polish with wax. (7) to increase in size; e.g. the moon waxes from new moon to full moon and then gradually wanes (decreases in size).

weather (1) *n.* the conditions affecting the atmosphere at a particular time and place. Temperature, rainfall, snow, fog, clouds, sunshine and wind are all weather conditions. (2) *v.* to wear away by the action of weather.

weathering *n.* the process in which rocks, exposed to the action of heat, water and ice, gradually flake away. The pieces may be washed away by water or blown away by the wind.

A spider spins its web using the spinneret gland at the end of the abdomen.

web (1) *n.* a network of fine, sticky threads woven by a spider. It traps insects, which the spider eats. (2) a layer of skin or membrane stretched between the fingers of bats and the toes of ducks, geese, frogs, otters and other animals. (3) woven material made of warp☐ and weft☐ threads.

weed (1) *n.* a wild plant growing where it is not wanted in a garden or cultivated area. (2) *v.* to clear the ground of weeds. *John and Mary helped their parents* **weed** *the garden.*

weft *n.* the cross threads that weave in and out of the warp☐ threads in textile weaving.

weigh *v.* to measure how heavy something is by using a scale or balance.

weight (1) *n.* the measured heaviness of something. *Jane's* **weight** *is 100 pounds.* (2) the effect of the force of gravity☐ pulling on something. It is greatest at the poles and least at the equator. (3) a unit of heaviness, e.g. gram, kilogram, that is used to measure this force. (4) an object with a standard heaviness, used to weigh other objects on a scale or balance. (5) a system of units for measuring weight, e.g. the gram and kilogram in the metric system. (6) a heavy object used to hold things in place or to sink a fishing line under water.

weightlessness (1) *n.* the sensation of having no weight. It occurs under conditions of zero gravity☐. Astronauts in space, outside the pull of the Earth's gravity, have no sensation of weight. (2) *adj.* **weightless** having little weight.

This sperm whale lives in the Arctic.

W

whale (1) *n.* one of a group of large sea animals, shaped like a fish, with a flat horizontal tail, no back legs, and flippers in place of front legs. Whales are mammals☐ and breathe air though lungs. (2) *v.* to hunt whales.

wheel (1) *n.* a solid disk or round frame with spokes joined to a central hub that turns on an axle. Wheels are used in machinery and vehicles to carry loads, transmit power and steer. Water-wheels drive mills. (2) *v.* to move or cause to move in a circle; to push or move on wheels.

whirlpool *n.* a powerful current of water that flows rapidly around and around a central point. Water and floating objects are sucked down into the center.

whisker *n.* one of several long, stiff hairs growing from each side of the face near the mouth on some mammals, e.g. cat, lion and rabbit. They are used for feeling and sensing.

whiskers

white blood cell a colorless cell found in the blood of most vertebrates. It has a nucleus⬜ and moves like an amoeba⬜. White blood cells destroy disease organisms and help to fight infection.

white dwarf a very small, heavy star that has used up all its nuclear energy and become cold and dead. White dwarfs do not give out any heat or light.

wilt *v.* said of plants, to become droopy and limp. Plants wilt in hot, dry weather, when they lose too much moisture.

winch (1) *n.* a mechanism for lifting a load by means of a cable that is wound around a drum, which is turned by a handle or motor. (2) *v.* to lift a load by using a winch.

wind (1) *v.* (*past tense, wound*) to turn around and around. (2) to tighten a spring, as in winding up a clock or watch. (3) to coil a rope, cable or thread around a drum or spool. *The sailor* **wound** *the anchor cable around the winch.*

wind *n.* a stream of moving air that blows over the Earth's surface up to a height of 15 kilometers. Sailing ships depend on wind to drive them along. Wind power is used to drive machines. Wind is important in spreading plant seeds. See **tornado** and **hurricane**.

windmill *n.* a simple machine that uses wind power to turn the vanes or arms of the windmill. These are connected to grindstones, which grind or mill the grain and turn it into flour. Windmills also drive water pumps.

A wind turbine uses blades instead of sails.

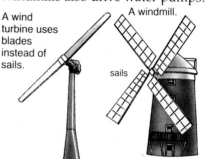

A windmill.

sails

windpipe *n.* the trachea; the general name for the tube that passes from the throat to the lungs. Air is breathed in and out through the windpipe. The voice box, or larynx⬜, is at the top of the windpipe.

wing (1) *n.* any structure forming part of an animal that is used for flying, e.g. the wings of birds, insects and bats and the fins of flying fish. (2) the special structure that supports

an aircraft in flight. (3) a winglike structure on the seeds of certain plants that helps them to be scattered by the wind, e.g. ash and sycamore.

winter *n.* the coldest season of the year. In temperate climates winter comes between autumn (fall) and spring.

wire (1) *n.* metal drawn out into a thin thread of even thickness, used in electric circuits. (2) *v.* to supply a building with wires to carry electric current. (3) to telegraph.

wisdom tooth one of the last four back teeth (molars) to appear in the upper and lower jaws of humans. Wisdom teeth are so called because they do not appear until the age of 18 to 25 years, when a person is thought to be wise and sensible.

woman *n.* an adult, female human being.

womb *n.* the uterus; the female reproductive organ in most mammals in which the fetus⊑ develops before birth.

wood (1) *n.* a forest; an area with many trees growing close together. (2) timber; felled trees cut into logs or planks. (3) the hard, tough fibrous part of tree and shrub stems, between the bark and soft inner pith⊑.

wood pulp broken-down wood fiber, used in the manufacture of paper.

wool (1) *n.* the fine, soft, curly hair of sheep, alpaca, goats, camels and other mammals. Wool is spun into thread and used for knitting or weaving cloth. (2) any fine, man-made fibers such as steel wool or glass wool.

word processor a type of computer⊑, operated by a keyboard. It has a visual display screen and may produce typewritten papers.

X x

X-ray (1) *n.* an invisible form of radiation⊑ of very short wavelength. X-rays pass through many materials that stop ordinary light rays. Some substances, such as bone, absorb more X-rays than softer tissues like

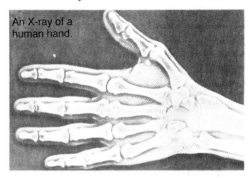
An X-ray of a human hand.

skin and muscle. This fact is used when studying special X-ray pictures of the body. The bones show up clearly as white areas, and soft tissues as grey areas. Doctors use X-ray pictures to detect diseases, broken bones and foreign bodies. (2) an X-ray picture itself.

Section through the stem of a flowering plant. xylem, phloem

xylem *n.* the strong tissue in plant roots and stems, made of tiny tubes, that carries water and salts from the roots up to the stems and leaves. In addition, xylem provides support to a plant. (say *zy-lem*)

X

Y y

yard *n.* a unit of measurement of length or distance, equal to 3 feet or 36 inches. One yard equals 0.9144 meters.

yaw *v.* in ships and airplanes, to move unsteadily from side to side. *The high seas caused the boat to* **yaw**.

year (1) *n.* a period of time equal to 12 calendar months, or 52 weeks or 365 days (366 in a leap year). The year runs from January 1st to December 31st. (2) the time taken for the Earth to make one complete orbit around the Sun.

yeast *n.* a type of single-celled fungus□ that feeds on sugary solutions. Yeasts break down the sugar into carbon dioxide and alcohol (fermentation). Yeasts are used in the brewing, wine-making and baking industries. Yeasts reproduce asexually (see **reproduction**) by budding off new cells.

yield (1) *v.* to give out or produce; to give up or to give way. *The land* **yielded** *a record crop of potatoes.* (2) *n.* anything that is given out or produced. *The farmer increased the* **yield** *of corn by using a fertilizer on the land.*

yolk *n.* the substance that surrounds the ovum (egg cell). It is rich in fat and protein□ and provides food for the developing embryo□. (say *yoke*)

A bird's egg.

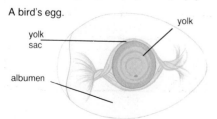

yolk
yolk sac
albumen

Z z

zero (1) *n.* nought; a number, written as 0, which has no value. It does not alter the value of another number if added to or subtracted from it; e.g. $5 + 0 = 5$. $10 - 0 = 10$. $8 - 8 = 0 = $ zero. 2) a point 0 on a scale of measurement; e.g. water freezes at 0°C. Any point below 0 on the scale is a negative (minus) quantity; any point above 0 is a positive (plus) quantity. (3) absolute zero: a state in which there is no movement in the molecules of a substance, and therefore no heat. (4) zero gravity is a condition of weightlessness, when the pull of gravity is zero.

zinc *n.* a bluish-white metal; a chemical element. Zinc does not readily react with water or air, and is used to coat iron to protect it from rusting (corrosion). Zinc is also used in alloys□, in batteries and in medicines.

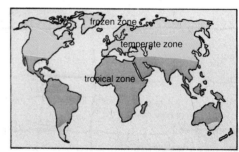

The climatic zones of the world.

zone (1) *n.* one of the broad bands around the Earth's surface which has a particular type of climate, e.g. the tropical (hot) zone around the equator, the temperate zones and the frozen zones at the North and South Poles. (2) a part of a large region of the Earth with special types of vegetation or geology, e.g. the earthquake zones in southeast Europe, and the cotton zones in the southern states of the United States.

zoo *n.* a special area of land or buildings where wild animals are kept so that people can see them.

zoology *n.* the scientific study of all forms of animal life, from microorganisms to elephants and whales. It deals with the form, functions, reproduction, behavior and growth of animals. A zoologist is a person who studies animal life. (say *zoe-oligee*/*zoe-olijist*)

zygote *n.* a cell formed in plants and animals by the joining of a male and female sex cell (gamete); a fertilized egg cell that will develop into an embryo plant or animal.

The planets

Planet	Mean distance from Sun (millions km)	Diameter (km)	Length of day (earth days)	Length of year (earth days)	Approximate surface temperature	Number of satellites
Mercury	57.91	4850	176 days	88 days	noon 350°C night −200°C	0
Venus	108.21	12,104	2760 days	225 days	light side 500°C	0
Earth	149.60	12,756	23 hrs 56 min	365.25 days	average 22°C	1
Mars	227.94	6790	24 hrs 37 min	687 days	noon −20°C night −80°C	2
Jupiter	778.34	142,800	9 hrs 50 min	11.9 years	at cloud surface −150°C	about 14
Saturn	1427.01	120,000	10 hrs 14 min	29.5 years	at cloud surface −180°C	about 17
Uranus	2869.6	about 52,000	about 24 hrs	84 years	at cloud surface −21°C	5
Neptune	4496.7	about 48,000	about 22 hrs	165 years	at cloud surface −220°C	2
Pluto	5900	about 3000	6 days 9 hrs	248 years	about −230°C	1

The history of life on Earth

Fascinating evidence about early life on Earth can be discovered by studying rocks which contain the fossilized remains of plants and animals. The table below shows the eras into which the history of life on Earth can be divided. Some of the early animals that inhabited the Earth are shown opposite.

Era	Geological divisions	Time span	Forms of life
CENOZOIC or CAINOZOIC	Holocene Pleistocene Pliocene Miocene Oligocene Eocene Palaeocene	The era ranging from 65 million years ago to the present day.	Plant and animal life is much as it is today. The ancestors of many mammals, such as the cat and horse, appear. Primitive apes exist, as do all the groups of insects that we know now.
MESOZOIC	Cretaceous Jurassic Triassic	Lasted 165 million years from 230 to 65 million years ago.	Dinosaurs appear and come to dominate the Earth, but are extinct by the end of the period. The first mammals and birds evolve from reptiles.
UPPER PALAEOZOIC	Permian Carboniferous Devonian	Lasted 170 million years from 400 to 230 million years ago.	There is a large increase in the variety of plants and animals on land and sea. Land begins to look green as plants with roots, stems and leaves develop. The first amphibians appear.
LOWER PALAEOZOIC	Silurian Ordovician Cambrian	Lasted 170 million years from 570 to 400 million years ago.	The first plants appear on land, and in the sea some vertebrates develop. Life exists only in the sea in the form of simple invertebrates, such as worms, sponges and trilobites.
PROTEROZOIC	Pre-Cambrian	Lasted almost 2000 million years.	Very primitive life begins in the warm seas of the new Earth.

Triceratops had a head shield and three horns to protect itself against attack.

Pterodactylus was able to keep airborne by gliding, using wind and air currents.

Iguanodon ate only plants. It stood on two legs using its heavy tail for balance.

Tyrannosaurus was a huge flesh-eating dinosaur.

Brontosaurus despite its size, ate only plants. It spent much of its time in water to avoid attack, and to support its heavy body.

Diplodocus was one of the largest animals ever to live on land. It weighed as much as ten elephants.

Stegosaurus was very slow moving. It had two rows of bony plates along its back, and large spikes on its tail, to deter attack.

Ichthyosaurus was a sea-living reptile. It caught fish using its long beak.

Forty important scientists, inventors and discoverers

Archimedes (287?–212 BC) found that submerged solids displace their own weight of water, and worked out the laws of levers and pulleys.
John Logie Baird (1888–1946) Scottish scientist, transmitted the first television pictures in 1926.
Sir Frederick Banting (1891–1941) Canadian physician, discovered insulin for treating diabetes.
Antoine Becquerel (1852–1908) French physicist, discovered radioactivity in uranium.
Alexander Graham Bell (1847–1922) invented the first telephone.
Wernher von Braun (1912–77) was largely responsible for America's first space rockets.
Henry Cavendish (1731–1810) discovered hydrogen and the composition of water.
Christopher Cockerell (1910–) developed the first working hovercraft.

Francis Crick (1916–) and **James Watson** (1928–) discovered the structure of deoxyribo-nucleic acid (DNA), the molecule, found in every living cell, that contains genetic information.
Marie Curie (1867–1934) and **Pierre Curie** (1859–1906) French husband and wife team, discovered radium, a radioactive element.
Charles Darwin (1809–82) English naturalist, developed a theory on how life has evolved.
Thomas Edison (1847–1931) discovered a system of telegraphy and the first phonograph.
Albert Einstein (1879–1955) developed the theory of relativity and the theory of the laser beam.
Michael Faraday (1791–1867) made discoveries that led to the large-scale generation of electricity.
Enrico Fermi (1901–54) His research led to the building of the first nuclear reactor.

The Periodic Table

In 1869 a Russian scientist, Dmitri Mendeleev, proposed a method of classifying the elements. He relied heavily on earlier scientific work which had demonstrated that different elements have different weights, and that some elements have similar properties.

Mendeleev arranged all the known elements according to their atomic weight, and left gaps for elements yet to be discovered.

The modern form of Mendeleev's table arranges the elements according to their atomic number. The elements arranged across the table are called 'periods'. Those arranged vertically are known as 'groups'. There is a scientific connection either way.

HYDROGEN **H** 1								
LITHIUM **Li** 7	BERYLLIUM **Be** 9							
SODIUM **Na** 23	MAGNESIUM **Mg** 24							
POTASSIUM **K** 39	CALCIUM **Ca** 40	SCANDIUM **Sc** 45	TITANIUM **Ti** 48	VANADIUM **V** 51	CHROMIUM **Cr** 52	MANGANESE **Mn** 55	IRON **Fe** 56	COBALT **Co** 59
RUBIDIUM **Rb** 85	STRONTIUM **Sr** 88	YTTRIUM **Y** 89	ZIRCONIUM **Zr** 91	NIOBIUM **Nb** 93	MOLYBDENUM **Mo** 96	TECHNETIUM **Tc** 98	RUTHENIUM **Ru** 101	RHODIUM **Rh** 103
CAESIUM **Cs** 133	BARIUM **Ba** 137	LANTHANUM **La** 139	HAFNIUM **Hf** 178	TANTALUM **Ta** 181	TUNGSTEN **W** 184	RHENIUM **Re** 186	OSMIUM **Os** 190	IRIDIUM **Ir** 192
FRANCIUM **Fr** 223	RADIUM **Ra** 226	ACTINIUM **Ac** 227						

A simplified version of the Periodic Table.

Sir Alexander Fleming (1849–1945) discovered penicillin, a bacterium that destroys many germs.
Galileo Galilei (1564–1642) proved that the Earth and planets revolve around the Sun.
William Harvey (1578–1657) discovered the circulation of blood in the body.
Heinrich Hertz (1857–95) discovered radio waves, and their length and frequency.
Sir Frederick Gowland Hopkins (1861–1947) discovered substances later called vitamins.
Edward Jenner (1749–1823) discovered a vaccination against the disease smallpox.
Joseph Lister (1827–1912) founded the practice of antiseptic surgery, reducing hospital deaths.
Guglielmo Marconi (1874–1937) developed the wireless telegraph, and performed the first transatlantic wireless transmission.
Gregor Mendel (1822–84) discovered the laws of heredity after conducting experiments with peas.
Sir Isaac Newton (1642–1727) discovered the laws of gravity and motion.
Nikolaus Otto (1832–91) developed the first successful 'four stroke' internal combustion engine.

Louis Pasteur (1822–95) developed an inoculation that protected people from rabies, and he worked on destroying bacteria.
Max Planck (1857–1947) studied the radiation of energy, and developed the quantum theory.
Joseph Priestley (1733–1804) discovered oxygen.
Wilhelm Roentgen (1845–1923) discovered short electromagnetic waves which he called X-rays.
Ernest Rutherford (1871–1937) developed the nuclear theory of the atom, and split the atom.
Sir Clive Sinclair (1940–) developed the first pocket calculator.
George Stephenson (1781–1848) designed and built the first successful steam locomotive.
Alessandro Volta (1745–1827) developed the first instrument to produce an electric current.
James Watt (1736–1819) developed the first efficient steam engine.
Sir Frank Whittle (1907–) designed a turbo jet engine, from which modern engines developed.
Wilbur Wright (1867–1912) and **Orville Wright** (1871–1948) made the first controlled flight in a powered machine.

						HELIUM
						He 4

		BORON **B** 11	CARBON **C** 12	NITROGEN **N** 14	OXYGEN **O** 16	FLUORINE **F** 19	NEON **Ne** 20
		ALUMINUM **Al** 27	SILICON **Si** 28	PHOSPHORUS **P** 31	SULFUR **S** 32	CHLORINE **Cl** 35.5	ARGON **Ar** 40

NICKEL **Ni** 59	COPPER **Cu** 64	ZINC **Zn** 65	GALLIUM **Ga** 70	GERMANIUM **Ge** 73	ARSENIC **As** 75	SELENIUM **Se** 79	BROMINE **Br** 80	KRYPTON **Kr** 84
PALLADIUM **Pd** 106	SILVER **Ag** 108	CADMIUM **Cd** 112	INDIUM **In** 115	TIN **Sn** 119	ANTIMONY **Sb** 122	TELLURIUM **Te** 128	IODINE **I** 127	XENON **Xe** 131
PLATINUM **Pt** 195	GOLD **Au** 197	MERCURY **Hg** 201	THALLIUM **Tl** 204	LEAD **Pb** 207	BISMUTH **Bi** 209	POLONIUM **Po** 209	ASTATINE **At** 210	RADON **Rn** 222

KEY

	HYDROGEN		ALKALI AND ALKALINE EARTH METALS		METALS		NON METALS INCLUDING HALOGENS		NOBLE GASES

The SI system of units

The SI system of units (Système International d'Unités) was set up in 1960. It is used as the standard system of measurements in most countries today. The basic unit is the meter. The meter is measured very accurately by measuring the wavelength of radiation from the chemical element Krypton-86. A meter is exactly equal to 1,650,763.73 wavelengths.

The capacity of a cube with sides measuring one tenth (1/10) of a meter is said to equal 1 liter. The weight of 1 liter of water is said to equal 1 kilogram.

SOME PREFIXES COMMONLY USED IN SI MEASUREMENTS

Prefix	Factors less than 1	Sign
deci	$\times 10^{-1} = 0.1$	d
centi	$\times 10^{-2} = 0.01$	c
milli	$\times 10^{-3} = 0.001$	m
micro	$\times 10^{-6} = 0.000001$	μ
nano	$\times 10^{-9} = 0.000000001$	n
pico	$\times 10^{-12} = 0.000000000001$	p

Prefix	Factors more than 1	
tera	$\times 10^{12} = 1,000,000,000,000$	T
giga	$\times 10^{9} = 1,000,000,000$	G
mega	$\times 10^{6} = 1,000,000$	M
kilo	$\times 10^{3} = 1,000$	k
hecto	$\times 10^{2} = 100$	h
deca	$\times 10^{1} = 10$	da